Iran, Islam and Democracy

Iran, Islam and Democracy

The Politics of Managing Change

Ali M. Ansari

THE ROYAL INSTITUTE OF
INTERNATIONAL AFFAIRS
Middle East Programme

© Royal Institute of International Affairs, 2000

Published in Great Britain in 2000 by
Royal Institute of International Affairs, 10 St James's Square,
London SW1Y 4LE
(Charity Registration No. 208 223)

Distributed worldwide by
The Brookings Institution, 1775 Massachusetts Avenue NW,
Washington DC 20036-2188, USA

British Library Cataloguing in Publication Data
A CIP catalogue record for this book is available from the British Library.

ISBN 1 86203 117 7

Index by Indexing Specialists, Hove, UK
Typeset in Times by Koinonia
Printed and bound in Great Britain by the Chameleon Press Limited

Cover design by Matthew Link
Cover photograph reproduced by kind permission of Agence France Presse.
The photograph shows a student at a rally in Tehran in summer 2000; one
placard reads 'Thought cannot be imprisoned'; the other shows Akbar Ganji.

Contents

For my brother Ahmad

Foreword

One often hears that Iran is a difficult country to understand, let alone follow. I have no argument with this, but why might this be the case? The Iranian state today is a product of some very complex and long-term social relations, deep-rooted political interactions and socio-economic processes. To understand modern Iran, one must know how to measure its depth. For this reason, history has a certain resonance not found even in the Arab world's deeply historical attitudes towards the contemporary world. In modern Iran such shared concepts as *douleh* and *hokoumeh* (*doulat* and *houkomat* in Farsi) have come to typify specifically Iranian realities and do not tend to conform easily to the universal understanding of the differences between 'state' and 'government'. One of the reasons for such epistemological confusions and distortions is to be found in the unique nature and history of the Iranian state itself. It is partly for this reason that in Iranian discourse, Middle Eastern political science concepts tend to get caught up in other Iranian currents designed more accurately to reflect the other political realities of the country. Thus, such concepts as *nezam*, commonly meant to depict the prevailing system of governance in post-Pahlavi Iran, emerge to convey the all-pervading nature of the Islamic Republic, and in fact supersede the more traditional and precise notions of state and government. Such ephemeral and deliberately imprecise concepts as *nezam* come to mean, symbolize, portray different realities to different, and often competing, political and social forces in twenty-first-century Iran. The onus of clarification and meaning is then left very much to the exponent to deliver. For instance, there is still serious debate over the question of whether reform means democracy or merely improvement of the current system of administration. It is all, it seems, in the language. Reformers say what they mean, but others do not understand what they say! Indeed, it could be suggested that in Iran today, for all the talk of the entrenchment of traditional concepts and values, a post-modern surrealism has been prevailing for some time. The introduction of such terminology as *nezam* (depicting the ruling elite and their social allies and beneficiaries, but also the state and the government) within Iranian intellectual discourse is sufficient evidence for the thesis that the Iranians entered the post-modern realm well ahead of their Western counterparts!

Any serious piece of research and writing on the politics of post-Pahlavi

Iran, therefore, must first grapple with the conceptual content of the Islamic Republic and then be alert to the impact of the analysis on the historical context of change in the country, where in recent times the legacy of *bargasht be din* (a return to Islam), as exemplified by the popular founding of an Islamic republic, has been presented as the ultimate solution to the chasm between religion and government/state (*din va doulat*).

Ali Ansari's book is sensitive to both these intellectual problems. He begins the lucid and readable introduction to his pioneering study of the management of socio-political change in a revolutionary and politico-religious setting with the observation that the process of democratization in Iran was 'ignited by the political revolution of 1979 ... whose roots stretch back to Iran's first revolution of 1906'. The rest of Ali's thoughtful book develops this theme by offering a deeper understanding of the forces of change in post-Khomeini Iran, where everything seems to be rapidly changing while apparently also staying the same. But is it?

As Ali himself notes, while it is not too difficult to provide a comprehensive critique of the republic's mistakes and excesses in the first ten years of its existence, one must look with some wonderment at its second decade. After eight years of war, it is remarkable to witness the rapidity and intensity of change under Khomeini's successors and the test of reforms and transformations that Iranian society has willingly put itself through.

These changes need analysis and, perhaps more importantly, interpretation. Before the election victory of Hojjatoleslam Khatami in May 1997, much had been written on the coming of age of the Islamic Republic in the post-Khomeini period. While some saw this as the end of the revolution, others interpreted the post-Khomeini era as a new beginning. Few, however, could have predicted the impact of Khatami's candidacy on the political map of Iran, let alone the force of his victory on society as a whole. His success opened up the floodgates to open and free debate about the future of a peculiarly Iranian Islamic republic, as well as new interpretations of its origins and past. Both the boundaries of, and barriers to, open debate and free thinking were now being challenged. Virtually nothing was sacred any more, or at least that is how it seemed in 1998 and 1999, and the debates, in the street, in newspapers, in universities and colleges, were being fuelled not only by the intelligentsia or *kolahis* but by the leading members of the new administration, its allies and a wide section of the clerical establishment itself.

That Khatami changed the political dynamics of the Islamic Republic is therefore beyond question, but was it Khatami who led the charge or was he merely articulating the frustrations of the previous 17 years of life in an overtly revolutionary and religious state? It is this which is most interesting, for it is not so much that Khatami has ever been ahead of the people but that, in a manner of speaking, he has been alongside them. All the evidence suggests that it is the majority of Iranian people who are pushing open the doors of debate and reform in the country, egging the reformers on and, by virtue of asking for a better future, demanding change at all levels of society, culture and government. In many ways, it is they and their actions which have given substance to the reforms of the Khatami administration.

Despite the reformers' best efforts, however, the paradox at the core of the Islamic system remains unresolved: how can a political system which values elections and the will of the people, and allows (indeed enables and digests) the rise of such pro-democracy movements as the 2nd Khordad – with all its liberal paraphernalia and aspirations – then use imprisonment, archaic rules, forceful closure of the popular media and vengeful attacks as its legitimate tools for silencing the reformers and curtailing the process? Is the bottle of reform, then, half-full or half-empty? Is the tabling of reforms a new and promising beginning for the Iranian people, or the beginning of another unhappy ending? Ali spends considerable time and effort on this question. His deliberations lead him to conclude that the reform process is perhaps irreversible but that it still has a fair way to go. A sound assessment. I would only add that while President Khatami has championed the path of reform, he has also been trying to end the paradox between the pluralism of society on the one hand and the monopolism of the *nezam* on the other, and to attempt once and for all to tip the scales towards civil society. If he were to be successful in this endeavour, I would suggest that the question of whether Iranian civil society will have an Islamic make-up or not will probably no longer matter.

Durham, September 2000   Anoushiravan Ehteshami

About the author

Dr Ali M. Ansari is Lecturer in the Political History of the Middle East at the Centre for Middle Eastern and Islamic Studies (CMEIS), University of Durham, and an Associate Fellow of the Middle East Programme at the Royal Institute of International Affairs. His recent publications include 'Iranian Foreign Policy under Khatami: Reform and Reintegration', in A. Ehteshami and A. Mohammadi (eds), *Iran and Eurasia* (2000); 'The Iranian Revolution 20 Years On', *Politique Etrangère* (2000); and 'Alternative Futures: Iran' in *World Defence Systems 2000* (RUSI, 2000).

Acknowledgments

Any study of this nature is very much a collective effort, and it remains for me to thank those pivotal individuals who facilitated the conception, articulation and final completion of this work. First and foremost, I wish to thank Rosemary Hollis, head of the Middle East Programme at Chatham House, who not only commissioned the project but had sufficient faith to provide a hitherto untested post-doctoral student with such a fascinating opportunity. Throughout the conduct of the research, and most especially during the writing and final stages of publication, Rosy has proved the quintessential 'pillar of support'. I would also like to thank other members of the Chatham House 'team', in particular Emma Brigham, for so ably mediating my comments; Gillian Bromley and Margaret May, for coping with my queries and transforming a draft text into a publishable manuscript; and Toby Dodge and Mai Yamani, for their intellectual stimulation and moral support. In addition I thank the sponsors not only for providing the necessary financial lubrication for the wheels of research, without which the project would not have got off the ground, but also, in their capacity as members of the steering committee, for patiently reading through and commenting on the draft manuscript. Other members of the steering committee I should particularly like to thank are Edmund Herzig and Chris Rundle, whose comments were both constructive and thought-provoking. Beyond Chatham House there are many people to whom I owe a debt of gratitude for their intellectual and moral support: my many friends and colleagues in Iran whose hospitality, insights and vibrant discussions shed considerable light on the complex processes at work; my good friends Anoush Ehteshami and Emma C Murphy for their enthusiasm and consistent encouragement; Colin Turner, Paul Luft, Nick Hostettler, Ben Fortna and, last but by no means least, Charles Tripp for reading, commenting and generally discussing drafts and ideas, however wayward they occasionally may have been!

December 2000   A.A.

Glossary

Basij: Literally 'mobilization'; in the Islamic Republic the term used to denote the Islamic Militia; a volunteer unit drawn mainly from those not liable for regular military service (i.e. too young or too old). Used extensively in the war against Iraq.

Dowreh: A regular social gathering of friends, normally for a particular purpose, occasionally but not always political discussion. Approximates to the French salon. For further details see W.G. Miller, 'Political Organization in Iran: From Dowreh to Political Party', *Middle East Journal* 23, 2/3, 1969, pp. 159–67 and 343–50.

Ijtehad: The use of independent judgment, usually through analogical reasoning, to derive new legal rulings from the existing body of law.

Majlis: Full title *Majlis-e Shora-ye Islami* – Islamic Consultative Assembly; normally shortened to 'Majlis', and approximates to 'Parliament'. The Constitutional Revolution in 1906 established a 'National Consultative Assembly', and this was replaced in 1979.

Marja-e Taqlid: Source of Emulation; a qualification acquired by only the most senior and respected (Grand) Ayatollahs.

Mujtahids: Shi'a *ulema* (religious scholars) whose education and training in jurisprudence and Islamic legal texts allow them to practise *ijtehad*. Applicable in the main (and certainly in the modern period) to Ayatollahs and Grand Ayatollahs, though not all of the former are acknowledged *mujtahids*.

Pak-Sazi: To clean up; essentially a policy aimed at removing corrupt personnel.

Rahbar: Leader. *Rahbar-e moazam*: Supreme Leader.

Talabeh: Term used to designate the most junior (trainee) *ulema*, essentially student *mullahs*.

Ulema: Literally, 'those with knowledge'; essentially religious scholars, and since the rise of 'secular education' a term which has become synonymous with the Shi'a clergy. An individual *alem* is known as a *mullah*.

Velayat-e Faqih: Guardianship of the Jurisconsult; the term *vali-e faqih* is used to denote the person.

Chronology

	Seizure of US embassy (4 November)
1980	Iraq invades Iran
1988	End of Iran–Iraq war
1989	Ayatollah Khomeini dies
	Ali Akbar Hashemi Rafsanjani elected President
	Seyyid Ali Khamene'i appointed Leader
	Constitution amended
1990	Elections for the Assembly of Experts
1992	Elections for the 4th Majlis
1993	Presidential elections – Rafsanjani elected for second term
1996	Elections for the 5th Majlis
1997	Presidential elections – Seyyid Mohammad Khatami wins landslide victory
	President Khatami presents cabinet (August)
	Islamic Conference Organization meeting in Tehran (December)
1998	Elections for the Assembly of Experts (October)
	President Khatami interviewed on CNN (January)
	Student activism on campus sanctioned by the Ministry of Interior (March)
	Crowds celebrate Iranian victory over US in World Cup competition (June)
	Abdullah Nuri impeached as minister of interior, appointed vice president (June)
	Trial of former mayor of Tehran, Gholamhussein Karbaschi (summer)
	Assassination of former prison chief Asadollah Ladjevardi (August)
	Attempted assassination of Mohsen Rafiqdoust (September)
	President Khatami visits United Nations (September)
	Mohajerani and Nuri attacked by Islamic vigilantes during Friday prayers (September)
	Tensions with ruling party in Afghanistan, the Taleban (summer)
	First moves to close down papers, in particular *Jame'eh* (summer)
	Revelations about the 'chain murders' of leading dissidents (November)
1999	First local council elections
	Trial and imprisonment of Mohsen Kadivar (April)
	Assault on the student dormitories of Tehran University; widespread unrest (July)

Head of judiciary and head of the Foundation of the
Oppressed are replaced (August)
President Khatami visits France (October)
Trial and conviction of Abdullah Nuri (November)
2000   Elections for the 6th Majlis (February)
Assassination attempt on Saeed Hajarian (March)
Widespread clampdown on press (April)
Second round of voting for Majlis (May)
2001   Presidential elections scheduled for June

'Historians who write in aristocratic ages are inclined to refer all occurrences to the particular will and character of certain individuals; and they are apt to attribute the most important revolutions to slight accidents. They trace out the smallest causes with sagacity, and frequently leave the greatest unperceived.

Historians who live in democratic ages exhibit precisely the opposite characteristics. Most of them attribute hardly any influence to the individual over the destiny of the race, or to citizens over the fate of a people; but, on the other hand, they assign great general causes to all petty incidents.'

Alexis de Tocqueville, *Democracy in America* Part II, Chapter XX (1835).

Introduction

Iran's geostrategic situation and possession of extensive hydrocarbon resources have made it a player of far higher significance on the international stage than its political and economic strengths might suggest. It is certainly true that Iran is the one issue on which American presidents have foundered in recent decades.[1] Carter had his hostage crisis, Reagan the Iran-Contra affair, and Bush his October surprise. Clinton probably took more steps to reassess Iran's relationship with the United States and by all accounts became fascinated, like many Western politicians before him, with 'Persia and the Persian question'. Fascination aside, there are sound economic and political reasons for continued interest in Iran. Not only does it possess the fourth largest reserves of oil (with new reserves being discovered), it also has the second largest known reserves of natural gas, exceeded only by Russia, and much of which has yet to be exploited. Beyond its own resources, it straddles the two main energy emporiums of the world, the Persian Gulf and the Caspian Sea littoral; as one Iranian official has pointed out, even if Iran possessed no hydrocarbon resources of its own, it would remain an important player. Indeed, as American politicians have discovered to their cost, Iran's extensive cultural influence in the region (especially in the Caucasus and Central Asia) is difficult to ignore, let alone isolate. Moreover, Iran possesses other extensive mineral and human resources which give it the potential to become the economic powerhouse of the region. It has considerable reserves of copper, coal and iron, while its relatively large population of some 63 million is mostly literate and comparatively well educated. For all its ethnic diversity, it remains, as visitors have noticed, a culturally cohesive nation with a strong sense of national identity – a unity cemented by the growth in telecommunications and national broadcasting. Furthermore, with the exception of the prolonged war with Iraq (1980–88), Iran has enjoyed relative peace with its neighbours for nearly 150 years, does not harbour irredentist claims on territory,[2] and, in spite of Iraq's 1980 invasion, enjoys stable, relatively well defined borders. Indeed, Iran's western border has remained essentially unchanged since 1501 – a stability others might envy.

---

[1] Some Iranian writers have taken this international significance to heart; see, for example, Y. Mazandi, *Iran: Abar ghodrat-e Gharn?* (Iran: Superpower of the Century?) (Tehran: Alborz, 1373/1994).
[2] Though the UAE would disagree on this, given its dispute with Iran over Abu Musa and the Tunbs islands.

Since 1979, however, such geopolitical and economic advantages have been overshadowed by the onset of the Islamic Revolution and Iran's assumption, not entirely by design, of the 'fundamentalist Islamic mantle'. A bitter divorce with the United States turned Iran overnight from an object of positive interest in Washington into one of negative concern. Rhetorical mutual recrimination was compounded by a US policy of containment, and had repercussions in the sphere of intellectual debate. For many analysts, Iran simply became an irritating anomaly whose stubborn determination to remain distinctive put it beyond the pale. Others have sought to challenge this increasingly dogmatic US-inspired assumption, and it is to that trend that this study belongs.

One of the central arguments of this book is that while Iran retains many distinctive characteristics inherited from a very long and complex history, it is absurd to quarantine it in a category all its own. Moreover it challenges broader assumptions about the incongruity of Islam and democracy by arguing that a mutually constructive relationship between these two concepts is indeed possible, and that Iran is leading the way in demonstrating this through an admixture of elite and mass politics. In addition it seeks to show the mechanics of this process, situating it firmly within the historical development of the country, but also drawing on social and political concepts to further illuminate and illustrate the central thesis that Iran is forging a path for Islam and democracy. This is in essence a book about ideas, as espoused and traded by different political factions. Not only does it suggest a method by which to understand political developments in contemporary Iran, but it also seeks to explain how ideas operate to motivate and initiate political change in Iran. The work both reflects and is informed by debates current in contemporary Iran, many of which draw extensively on Western thinkers. The inclusive, occasionally ambiguous mixture of ideas dealt with here may assist in bridging the cultural divide in understanding and in mitigating the problems inherent in inter-cultural interpretation.[3] The central motif of the study is the existence of a powerful *myth of political emancipation in Iran* which has driven political activists since its inception during the Constitutional Revolution of 1906.[4]

[3] I.e.the perennial problem of students of the Middle East, 'Orientalism'.
[4] The term 'myth' is used as an aspect of ideology, and is not intended to imply falsehood. See H. Tudor, *Political Myth* (London: Pall Mall Press, 1972).

Structure of the book

The book is divided into two unequal parts. It begins with a brief assessment of the conceptual problems confronting such a study and how they may be overcome. It looks at issues of 'orientalism' and the assumptions which determine many Western perceptions of the Middle East and its potential for development. The intention here is to challenge many of these assumptions and to show how the debates taking place in Iran are in fact more fluid and open than may at first be apparent. This is especially true of debates over the meaning of secularization in Iran. The aim here is not to refute a given argument but to provide the intellectual context for the discussion which will follow. Chapters 2–4 deal in increasing depth with the historical inheritance of contemporary Iran, putting developments in perspective but also highlighting how the myth of political emancipation has evolved and is subject to interpretation and re-interpretation. The purpose is to show how ideas have driven political change. This culminates in Chapter 4 in a discussion of the structure of the state under Hashemi Rafsanjani's presidency. The chapter argues that the reconstruction of the state after the Iran–Iraq war witnessed the development of an alliance between the 'patrimonial' Rafsanjani and the increasingly powerful 'mercantile bourgeoisie'. It was the fractures in this otherwise powerful alliance, encouraged in large part by the social and intellectual changes that had taken place, which facilitated the election of Seyyid Mohammad Khatami to the presidency in May 1997.

The second, larger part of the book – Chapters 5–9 – deals with the developments since Khatami's election, drawing on the analysis of the previous section and extending it, with the intention of also reflecting the complex dynamic of Iranian political development. It aims to show both the depth of the reform movement and the inherent strengths of the mercantile bourgeoisie determined to retain their political and economic interests. This section *can* be read in isolation, with periodic reference to the historical and theoretical chapters, although I would encourage the reader to study Chapter 4 to dispel any misconceptions about the nature of the 'mercantile bourgeoisie' and to better appreciate the depth of Soroush's ideas. Certainly, the arguments put forward will be better understood, and hopefully appreciated, if the preparatory conceptual and historical chapters are read in conjunction with the rest of the text. These chapters outline the recurrent themes, but my view is also that only by standing back and taking the long-term view can one better appreciate the *processes* of change and their consequences for the present and avoid the frustrations of pernicious detail. However, with accessibility in mind, the chapters have been organized to accommodate the needs of different readers and levels of interest. A chronology and glossary of terms and names has also been included to assist the lay reader. This study has attempted throughout to maintain a balance between accessibility and a faithful reflection of the exciting, albeit sometmes frustrating, complexity and richness of Iranian political development.

Sources

This study is based on materials gathered and interviews conducted over several years during which I had the opportunity to travel to Iran on numerous field-trips and to explore the country, including most of the major urban centres and many rural areas, from villages in the Alborz Mountains to farms in the vicinity of Arak. These trips were augmented by specific research trips conducted for this project in the summer and winter of 1999. As such the interpretation of Iranian political history and development reflects the summation and synthesis of a wide range of views from Iranians in different professions and in different socio-economic groups. The integrated nature of Iranian society facilitated this process, particularly as individuals approached often enjoyed a wide network of acquaintances from a variety of social and economic backgrounds. Moreover, people were on the whole extremely open about their views. It was clear from the start that Iran was not a 'totalitarian' society, whatever the tendencies and aspirations of some sectors of the state. The more cautious and moderated comments of those in senior government positions often offset the more exaggerated speculations of some members of the public. Indeed in Iran shortage of information is not a problem; rather, one has to digest and select from a surfeit of information. Iran's is a highly communicative social structure. While an assessment of public perceptions is essential, it is also important to be able to judge and verify comments against the broader context of historical and social developments. It is certainly true that on occasion, comments I felt were very wide of the mark turned out not only to possess a kernel of truth but actually to be largely reflective of reality. Indeed by and large I discovered a high level of social sophistication and knowledge about the pervading political reality, reflecting perhaps the growth in literacy, education and means of communication. Nevertheless, where possible I sought to confirm more contentious statements through other, often conflicting sources, who could at the very least provide the alternative explanation. The following list is by no means exhaustive but illustrates the range of people and backgrounds I had the good fortune to encounter:

- *Ulema*
  - Senior and junior clerics
  - Governmental and non-political
- University students and staff
- Senior government officials, including ministers and civil servants
- Junior civil servants
- Members of the bazaar, including members of the younger generation
- Landlords and farmers
- Rural labourers
- Rural professionals
- Lower and lower middle class professionals
- Commercial sector
- Members of the religious foundations
- Upper middle and middle class professionals
- Journalists
- Local councillors
- Members of the armed forces

These interviews were complemented by a wide range of printed material, again reflecting the growth in the availability of books, newspapers and magazines, and the expanding literate market to consume them. Since 1997, the newspaper market has grown exponentially – a trend that, despite the closure of various titles in 2000, is unlikely to be reversed in the long run. Newspapers in Iran tend to be overtly political in their orientation, and their respective sales are a good indication of the public mood. But the sheer quantity and quality (in terms of relevant content) of the print media mean that once again, some form of selection has to be made. It would be well-nigh impossible for a single individual to read and digest the entire corpus of material which, including magazines and journals, runs to some 800 separate publications. Furthermore, in the continuing contest with the judiciary it is often difficult to keep pace with the change in titles, as newspapers are closed and replaced with new titles employing the same staff.

One important point to recognize is that the whole pace of change has so accelerated in recent years that it is no longer a realistic possibility to study contemporary Iran exclusively from beyond its borders. Even though the Internet provides relatively immediate news, there is no substitute for periodic visits in which one can assess the environment without additional mediation. At the same time, those in the middle of the maelstrom rarely see the broader picture and are often overtaken by the immediacy of events. This book attempts to provide a balanced combination between local access to primary sources and socio-historical awareness, all within a coherent theoretical framework. The exciting story of Iran is still unfolding; this work is intended to convey a 'moving picture' of the contemporary scene, both forward-looking and grounded in Iran's historical and intellectual heritage.

1 Iran, Islam and Democracy: The Theoretical Context

> No great historical event is better calculated than the French Revolution
> to teach political writers and statesmen to be cautious in their speculations.
> Alexis de Tocqueville, *The Ancien Régime and the French Revolution*

Few societies are more difficult to analyse and understand than those in the throes of revolutionary upheaval and transformation. Indeed, by definition, revolutions challenge the normative and often unconscious assumptions of analysts and social scientists, with the consequence that they tend to frustrate understanding and confuse analysis. Alexis de Tocqueville recognized this phenomenon when he noted how bewildered contemporary observers of the French Revolution became in seeking to understand and chart the development of this particular political and social upheaval. Even the English, he noted, who should have had some empathy with the developments in France, 'watched the gradual advance of this epoch-making revolution as if through a thick veil'.[1] The metaphor is apt. While the Islamic Revolution which unfolded in Iran in 1978 and 1979 initially enjoyed the support of many left-leaning politicians and commentators in the West, the apparent usurpation of power by 'reactionary theocrats' resulted in an almost universal rejection of the movement which had overthrown the Pahlavi monarchy. Many commentators who had initially drawn analogies with the French Revolution were now quick to point out the distinctions; others, such as Michel Foucault, who had described the movement as an almost unique manifestation of the 'collective will',[2] were later derided for their errors of judgment.

The reasons for this collective change in sentiment among most well-wishers are not hard to discern. Like all revolutions, the Islamic Revolution in Iran rapidly descended into bitter retribution and a brutal civil war

[1] Alexis de Tocqueville, *The Ancien Régime and the French Revolution* (Manchester: Fontana, 1966, first published 1856) p. 34.
[2] M. Foucault, 'Iran: The Spirit of a World Without Spirit', in *Politics, Philosophy and Culture: Interviews and Other Writings 1977–1984* (London: Routledge, 1988), p. 215. In this interview, Foucault acknowledged the 'epidermic reaction' to the Iranian revolution.

between the contending factions which had initially cooperated to overthrow the monarchy. Unlike in previous eras, the brutality of this process was recorded for posterity on television and broadcast around the world. This might have been tolerable had the victors in the ensuing struggle not apparently been turbaned clerics, figures seemingly not only of a different age, but of a profession long since banished from politics in the West. Televisual images confirmed the worst prejudices and fears of those in the West who began to construct a compound image around the picture of the turbaned mullah straight out of an orientalist textbook. All other facets of the revolution gradually became subsumed within this overtly 'Islamic' construction borne of a quintessentially orientalist imagination. It was a powerful myth, founded in reality, but pandering to Western prejudice, indeed confirming and extending it. It was, of course, encouraged by the revolutionaries themselves, whose very rebelliousness and rejection of what had come before was held as a virtue to be cherished. Yet already the language of political discourse was different and differentiating. Within Iran, while the concept of 'Islam' was undoubtedly contested, for most Iranians it remained essentially a positive force, while in the West, Islam as a religion was deemed both anachronistic and reactionary. Thus two intellectual schools of thought emerged which used the same words but to mean different things.

It was all too easy for Western commentators – and in this category must be included the Western-trained elite which so dominated the Pahlavi state (and, indeed, administered it) – to characterize the Islamic Revolution as 'irrational' and anachronistic. Far from being a 'progressive' revolution, as some on the left had hoped, it was soon being presented as reactionary and intended to 'restore' the traditional status quo.[3] As one commentator noted, 'The reaction I've heard most often about Iran is that people don't understand. When a movement is called revolutionary, people in the West, including ourselves, always have the notion of progress, of something that is about to be transformed in the direction of progress. All this is put into question by the religious question.'[4] This contention led to the Islamic Revolution being effectively quarantined into a category all its own, viewed not only as a geographically contained, local event but as equally

---

[3] Some historians pointed out that this was indeed the original meaning of the term – hence the 'Glorious Revolution' of 1688. See G. Watson, 'How Radical is Revolution?', *History Today*, November 1988, pp. 42–9.

[4] Claire Briere, conversing with Michel Foucault; see Foucault 'Iran: The Spirit of a World Without Spirit', p. 213. See also S. A. Arjomand, *The Turban for the Crown* (Oxford: Oxford University Press, 1988), p. 3: 'The unfolding of the Islamic Revolution ran completely counter to the conventional wisdom about revolutions, and more generally, about the philosophy of history.'

sharply bounded intellectually, isolated as an anomalous aberration in an otherwise rational world. Concern over its possible implications for regional security were soon countered by the contention that what was being witnessed was – to use the words of de Tocqueville – nothing 'more than a local, transient phenomenon'.[5] Indeed, it is remarkable how what was initially perceived as a universalist threat was in time contained and particularized, the Islamic Revolution being endowed with distinctively Shi'a and then Iranian characteristics which ensured its essential irrelevance for the rest of the Islamic world.

In fact, the Islamic Revolution was neither exclusively universalist nor entirely particular in character. Like all revolutions, and certainly those it aspired to emulate, the Islamic Revolution harboured certain universalistic pretensions, seeking to justify its relevance and importance not only to the world's Muslims but to the 'oppressed', wherever they might be found. At the same time it was and remained a product of a peculiarly Iranian historical and intellectual experience. This core was never dismissed in Iran itself, nor, although some revolutionaries exploited the universalism and internationalism of the movement (usually expressed in the familiar terms of Islamic discourse), was there ever a systematic attempt to eliminate it.

What had changed was the emphasis, from a 'secular' to a 'religious' nationalism. This arguably distinguishes Iran's experience from the great revolutions which preceded it, but it is worth remembering that de Tocqueville considered the French Revolution more akin to religious revolutions than to national ones.

Whereas all social and political revolutions had so far been confined to countries in which they took their rise, the French Revolution aspired to be world-wide and its effect was to erase all the national frontiers from the map. We find it uniting or dividing men throughout the world without regard to national traditions, temperaments, laws, and mother tongues, sometimes leading them to regard compatriots as foes and foreigners as their kinsmen. Or perhaps, it would be truer to say that it created a common intellectual fatherland whose citizenship was open to men of every nationality and in which racial distinctions were obliterated. In all the annals of recorded history we find no mention of any *political* revolution that took this form; its only parallel is to be found in certain *religious* revolutions. Thus when we seek to study the French Revolution in the light of similar movements in other countries and at other periods, it is to the great religious revolutions we should turn.[6]

[5]De Tocqueville, *The Ancien Régime*, p. 34
[6]Ibid., p. 41. Emphasis in original.

Just as the 'Great' revolution in France gradually became 'French', so too the 'Islamic' revolution in Iran became 'Iranian'. This reflected not only the general tendency to contain the movement but also a recognition that such phenomena cannot be studied in isolation from their historical and cultural contexts. Paradoxically, in redefining its particularism the commentators restored the comparative significance of the Islamic Revolution. It was re-universalized into a familiar discourse. Thus, as Halliday argues:

> For all its apparent exceptionalism, the Iranian revolution of 1979 followed, in many respects, the pattern of other modern revolutions ... the Iranian revolutionaries saw themselves in an international context of two kinds – a historically constituted *Islamic* tradition ... and the contemporaneously constituted *anti-imperialist* context, in which they appealed to Muslims and other 'oppressed' to rise up against their oppressors. Consequently, in the years after coming to power, they did what other modern revolutionaries did: issued internationalist proclamations, organised meetings and training for radicals from other states, and provided, within the constraints of resources and inter-state relations, assistance to 'strugglers' in other states.[7]

But familiarity does not preclude distinction, and the important point here is simply to recognize the complex traditions and values which were incorporated into the revolutionary movement. These underlie the pattern of development by which an authoritarian revolutionary regime has ostensibly given birth to a vibrant civil society and a process of democratization more dynamic and promising than in any other overtly Islamic society. Indeed, it is only by locating Iran within its own historical and cultural context that the roots of present developments become apparent and trends distinguishable. This process of democratization, it will be argued, is the consequence of a social and intellectual revolution, ignited by the political revolution of 1979, but whose roots stretch back to Iran's first revolution in 1906. It is a process characterized by a remarkable degree of ideological cohesiveness centred upon a myth of political emancipation which has been gradually and effectively disseminated throughout the population. In short, it has facilitated and encouraged the growth of political consciousness, which in turn has transformed the political landscape of Iran and thrust an otherwise traditional society headlong into the modern age.

[7]F. Halliday, *Revolution and World Politics* (London: Macmillan, 1999), pp. 124–5.

Iran, Islam and the 'secularization thesis'

In order to begin to understand the mechanics of this change it is necessary to challenge a number of assumptions, born of the Western intellectual tradition, which have shaped and occasionally prejudiced the Western conception of the 'East'. The first of these, and arguably the most damaging, in part because it forms an implicit rather than explicit component of many arguments, is the conception of the East as unchanging, and indeed unable to generate change without impetus from the outside world. The problem has been compounded by the unthinking application of 'modernization theory' and its corollary concept, 'secularization', to analysis of Third World development, with prejudicial consequences for the role of Islam.

The philosophical distinction between the historical identities of East and West can be traced, like so much else in the modern Western philosophical tradition, to Hegel. The dialectical process which he depicted driving historical development in the Western world was absent from his depiction of the East, which, by contrast, he represented as static.[8] This idea was developed further by Marx, who argued forcefully that Western imperialism at least had the benefit of initiating the process of historical development – in contrast to the lethargic East. The influence of Hegel and Marx on Western characterizations of historical progress facilitated what is now seen as the 'orientalist' view of the 'East'.[9] Unfortunately, as Said has argued, the 'Orient' became in a very real sense the *object* of study.[10]

Thus Islam, and likewise 'Iran' – or 'Persia', to use a more appropriate term – was regarded as an unchanging, rather exotic (if not quixotic) environment. In many ways, the image proved the ideal foil to the frenetic and dynamic pace of change galvanizing Western societies in the nineteenth and early twentieth centuries, and it was perpetuated as such by Western orientalist scholars and traditional elites alike. Indeed, one of the reasons why the government of Reza Shah in 1935 insisted on the use of the name 'Iran' as opposed to 'Persia' was the fact that the term 'Persia' had become laden with negative connotations of exotic backwardness. Now, of course, the Iranian government has discovered that the reverse is probably true!

---

[8] G. W. F. Hegel, *The Philosophy of History* (New York: Dover, 1956), p. 173: 'With the Persian Empire we first enter on continuous History. The Persians are the first Historical People; Persia was the first Empire that passed away. While China and India remain stationary, and perpetuate a natural vegetative existence even to the present time, this land has been subject to those developments and revolutions, which alone manifest a historical condition.'

[9] As we shall see, the Hegelian notion of the 'cunning of reason' and the unfolding of freedom is enthusiastically encouraged by contemporary Iranian thinkers.

[10] E. Said, *Orientalism* (London: Penguin, 1991), pp. 1–4.

However, while the pace of change in Persia in the nineteenth century was undeniably slower, and in many cases resisted, it is erroneous to suggest that no change occurred at all. Limited though its reach may have been, a process of change, initially slow but accelerating, was set in motion by the stimulus from Europe. Whether or not in keeping with the Hegelian-Marxist historical paradigm, the impact of the West upon the East in this period engendered a local reaction and initiated at the very least an imitative process of development. Even so, the prevailing view on the limits of indigenous change persisted in intellectual terms.

Alexis de Tocqueville did grant a place for religion in social development, but compared Islam unfavourably with Christianity:

> Mohammad professed to derive from Heaven, and has inserted in the Koran, not only religious doctrines, but political maxims, civil and criminal laws, and theories of science. The Gospel, on the contrary, speaks only of the general relations of men to God and to each other, beyond which it inculcates and imposes no point of faith. This alone, besides a thousand other reasons, would suffice to prove that the former of these religions will never long predominate in a cultivated and democratic age, while the latter is destined to retain its sway at these as at all other periods.[11]

De Tocqueville was of course arguing for the centrality of religion, specifically Christianity, to the success of American democracy – an argument which has since been taken up and adapted by the democratic tendency in Iran. This aspect of his argument, however, has been largely ignored by modern social scientists anxious to emphasize the secular dimension of democratic development, and it is the inherent incompatibility with democracy of an unchanging dogmatic Islam which continues to predominate in modern arguments. Indeed, while some see its merits as a transitional force, few if any are willing to view it as other than a necessary hurdle to overcome. Thus John Waterbury, some 150 years after de Tocqueville, can argue that, 'Whether or not Islam and Middle Eastern "culture" are separable phenomena, the two work in ways that do not augur well for democracy. I believe that basic tendencies in regional culture and in religious practice must be overcome rather than utilised in any efforts to promote pluralism and democracy.'[12] In a contemporary critique Sadowski argues:

---

[11] Alexis de Tocqueville, *Democracy in America*, vol. 2 (London: Everyman's Library, 1994), p. 23.
[12] J. Waterbury, 'Democracy without Democrats? The Potential for Political Liberalisation in the Middle East', in G. Salame, ed., *Democracy without Democrats? The Renewal of Politics in the Muslim World* (London: I. B. Tauris, 1994), p. 33.

The thesis that Middle Eastern societies are resistant to democratisation had been a standard tenet of Orientalist thought for decades, but in the 1980s a new generation of Orientalists inverted some of the old assumptions and employed a new vocabulary which allowed them to link their work to a wider international debate about the relationship between 'civil society' and democratisation. These updated arguments sought to prove not only – as neo-Orientalist Daniel Pipes put it – 'that Muslim countries have the most terrorists and the fewest democracies in the world', but that they always would.[13]

Olivier Roy writes that 'Islamism is above all a socio-cultural movement embodying the protest and frustration of a generation of youth that has not been integrated socially or politically.'[14] He adds, 'The defensive *rigidity* [italics added] of neofundamentalism ... demonstrates its inability to incorporate modernity.'[15] Roy cites the Taleban as an exceptionally cogent example of this – which might be an unintended cause for comfort to Tehran, given the mutual antagonism with which the Islamic Republic of Iran and Afghanistan view each other. In a later article written specifically on Iran, Roy concedes the possibility of transition, saying, 'The crisis of the religious legitimacy is leading to the supremacy of politics, and subsequently to a *de facto* secularisation.'[16] In short, Islam is the hurdle which has to be cleared before Middle Eastern states can join the progressive march of history. As Piscatori and Eickelman point out, 'The idea that Islam is a hindrance to the process of development ... owes its currency to the persistence of modernisation theory.'[17]

One of the dominant themes of modernization theory is that 'secularism' was a key, if not *the* key, to peaceful, sustainable political and economic development. This argument was predicated on a view of the Western experience of church–state relations, according to which religious thought

[13] Y. Sadowski, 'The New Orientalism and Democracy', in J. Beinin and J. Stork, eds, *Political Islam* (Berkeley and Los Angeles, CA: University of California Press, 1997), p. 34.

[14] O. Roy, *The Failure of Political Islam* (Cambridge, MA: Harvard University Press, 1994), p. 194. This echoes a similar argument made earlier by Edward Mortimer in his *Faith and Power: The Politics of Islam* (London: Faber, 1982).

[15] Roy, *The Failure of Political Islam*, p. 203. Other writers are more direct on their assault on the compatibility of Islam and democracy. See M. Kramer, 'Islam vs Democracy', in *Commentary*, Jan. 1993, pp. 35–42. Kramer seems intent on extending the arguments first presented by Elie Kedourie when he criticized 'The Chatham House version' as espoused by Arnold Toynbee. See E. Kedourie, *The Chatham House Version and Other Studies* (Hanover, NH: Brandeis University Press/University Press of New England, 1984), pp. 351–95. For Toynbee's response see 'Was Britain's Abdication Folly?', *Round Table*, July 1970, pp. 219–27.

[16] O. Roy, 'The Crisis of Religious Legitimacy in Iran', *Middle East Journal*, vol. 53, no. 2, Spring 1999, p. 202.

[17] D. Eickelman and J. Piscatori, *Muslim Politics* (Princeton: Princeton University Press, 1996), p. 22.

was dogmatic, authoritarian and essentially monopolistic. There was, intrinsically, no room for discussion – certainly not outside the narrow circles of those permitted to engage in debate – critique, or doubt. Faith precluded doubt and essentially facilitated the very real power of the church, to the extent that, eventually, it was argued, 'faith' became simply a vehicle for the support and perpetuation of the material power of the church and its allies. The transition from the early modern state to the modern state in Europe essentially witnesses the retreat of the church following a rigorous assault from the forces of secularism. This 'secularization thesis' thus correlates secularism with modernism. As Keddie points out,

> While there have been modifications of the thesis over time, one recent definition shows that it still retains its essential characteristics: the secularisation thesis is a 'research programme with, at its core, an explanatory model' which 'asserts that the social significance of religion diminishes in response to the operation of three salient features of modernisation, namely, 1) social differentiation, 2) societalisation, and 3) rationalisation'.

In addition, she says, 'Advocates of the secularisation thesis have also tended to see it as a progressive one-way process; societies and their constituent members become more secular as they become more modernised.'[18] The proponents of this narrow view have not always been consistent:

> When the consensus of social scientists held that democracy and development depended upon the actions of strong, assertive social groups, Orientalists held that such associations were absent in Islam. When the consensus evolved and social scientists thought a quiescent, undemanding society was essential to progress, the neo-Orientalists portrayed Islam as beaming with pushy, anarchic solidarities. Middle Eastern Muslims, it seems, were doomed to be eternally out of step with intellectual fashion.[19]

Overall, it is clear that the secularization thesis posits a definition of 'secular' which takes little account of its genesis as a Western conceptual construction or of its inherent ambiguity. As Ruedy succinctly argues:

[18] N. Keddie, 'Secularism and the State: Towards Clarity and Global Comparison', *New Left Review*, no. 226, 1997, pp. 21–2, 41. For a particularly cogent critique of American political science approaches to the Middle East and modernization, see L. Anderson, 'Policy Making and Theory Building: American Political Science and the Islamic Middle East', in H. Sharabi, ed., *Theory, Politics and the Arab World: Critical Responses* (London: Routledge, 1990).

[19] Sadowski, 'The New Orientalism and Democracy', p. 41.

Secular is a term used to distinguish the temporal or worldly from the spiritual, while secularism has come to denote a philosophy that privileges the domain of the temporal and diminishes that of the spiritual. The former grows to cover civil affairs and education, while the latter is increasingly restricted to the areas of private belief, worship and conduct. While secularism as a philosophy is central to the Western experience, it should be borne in mind that the concept has evolved historically and it is still doing so. What was considered the proper province of human rational decision was different in the 15th century than in the 19th century and is even more different in the late 20th. Secondly, it should be stressed that the struggle over the frontier between the secular and the religious is one characterised by continuous tension and that, up to now the exact line of the frontier between the two has never been agreed upon. One must also recognise that in the West there has seldom been agreement among secularists as a group, nor among the religious as a group, as to where exactly that frontier should be.[20]

As Keddie points out, 'No state today is entirely secular or entirely non-secular.'[21] Just as the Western intellectual tradition, subjected to close scrutiny, loses definition and exposes its multiple characteristics, so it becomes apparent that the Middle Eastern and Islamic traditions are likewise composed of a multiplicity of competing paradigms. Some are clearly more dominant than others, but nevertheless the monolith begins to look much more fractured and pluralistic in construction. Indeed, as Eickelman and Piscatori correctly point out:

In the specific context of Muslim politics, de-emphasising paradigms and re-imagining the challenges policy-makers will face in the years ahead entail listening to the many Muslim voices, not merely those of a Westernised elite. The first step is to learn to elicit their cultural notions of legitimate authority and justice and to recognise that ideas of just rule, religious or otherwise, are not fixed, even if some claim they are.[22]

A good example of the complexity of the Islamic world-view is the case of Jamal al Din al Afghani. Afghani has gained a reputation as a pan-Islamist and a leading proponent of an Islamic revival, yet his contribution was not as straightforward as many of his principally Arab disciples would

---

[20] J. Ruedy, ed., *Islamism and Secularism in North Africa* (New York: St Martin's Press, 1994), p. xiv, quoted in Keddie, 'Secularism and the State', p. 24, n. 8.
[21] Keddie, 'Secularism and the State', p. 24.
[22] Eickelman and Piscatori, *Muslim Politics*, p. 164.

claim. Afghani did indeed argue that an Islamic revival was necessary if Middle Eastern states were to shake off the yoke of European colonialism, but he reserved considerable criticism for the reactionary *ulema* (religious scholars) and the dogmatic, irrational and unscientific Islam they propounded. His response to the French philosopher Ernest Renan, who had criticized Islam in much the same way as de Tocqueville, is revealing:

> If it is true that the Muslim religion is an obstacle to the development of sciences, can one affirm that this obstacle will not disappear someday? How does the Muslim religion differ on this point from other religions? All religions are intolerant, each one in its way. The Christian religion, I mean the society that follows its inspirations and teachings and is formed in its image, has emerged from the first period to which I have just alluded; thenceforth free and independent, it seems to advance rapidly on the road of progress and science, whereas Muslim society has not yet freed itself from the tutelage of religion. Realizing, however, that the Christian religion preceded the Muslim religion in the world by many centuries, I cannot keep from hoping that Muhammedan [*sic*] society will succeed someday in breaking its bonds and marching resolutely in the path of civilisation after the manner of Western society, for which the Christian faith, despite its rigours and intolerance, was not at all an invincible obstacle ...
>
> Religions, by whatever names they are called, all resemble each other. No agreement and no reconciliation are possible between these religions and philosophy . . . It will always be thus. Whenever religion will have the upper hand, it will eliminate philosophy; and the contrary happens when it is philosophy that reigns as sovereign mistress. So long as humanity exists, the struggle will not cease between dogma and free investigation, between religion and philosophy; a desperate struggle in which, I fear, the triumph will not be for free thought, because the masses dislike reason, and its teachings are only understood by some intelligences of the elite, and because, also, science, however beautiful it is, does not completely satisfy humanity, which thirsts for the ideal and which likes to exist in dark and distant regions that the philosophers and scholars can neither perceive nor explore.[23]

What this passage immediately reveals is that, far from being a homogeneous tradition, Islamic intellectualism was becoming re-energized under the impact of the Western challenge. While it may be overstating the

---

[23] Jamal al Din al Afghani, 'Answer to Renan', in N. Keddie, ed., *An Islamic Reponse to Imperialism* (Berkeley and Los Angeles, CA: University of California Press, 1983), pp. 181–7.

case to posit an intellectual renaissance, there is little doubt in retrospect that Afghani had a profound influence on a series of subsequent thinkers anxious to accommodate Islamic thought to the challenge of the modern age – or, more specifically, to reason and rationality. In other words, the goal was to free it from the dogma of its self-appointed interpreters. In order to achieve this, Afghani sought to draw on the philosophical tradition in Islam, much dismissed by orthodox *ulema*, and to restore the centrality of reason, which, he argued, had once made Islam the most scientifically advanced civilization of its day. In short, Afghani reinvigorated the debate between the philosophical and theological traditions in Islam, arguing that the former had much more to offer.

This was, to be sure, a radical departure for many members of the *ulema*, and Afghani's views were by no means prevalent; but his subsequent influence has been immense, and for our purposes his importance lies in the revitalization of an alternative tradition that was not necessarily antagonistic to or suspicious of Western intellectual achievements. For Afghani, Islam was a dynamic, politically relevant belief-system which could not necessarily be simply juxtaposed against a concept of 'secularism'. Indeed, Afghani's conceptualization of 'Islam' was potentially fully compatible with 'secularism', in so far as his 'Islam' dealt with the temporal world. What Afghani began, through his deconstruction of the traditional orthodox Islam so prevalent in orientalist discourse, is still being reconstructed in a more inclusive framework by his intellectual successors in Iran today.

The aim here has not been to replace one definition of 'Islam' or 'secularism' with another (though it will be necessary to return to the question of definition later). Rather, the intention has been to show how contested and ambiguous these terms remain, and to indicate that this reality remains salient for both the Western and oriental intellectual traditions. Indeed, it may be argued that the challenge posed by political Islam, in particular in its Iranian form, has forced a reassessment of certain assumptions, though this process is by no means ubiquitous. In seeking to deconstruct and redefine accepted paradigms it is clear that nothing is static and everything is renegotiable. Furthermore, it is the continuing existence of this intellectual ferment which allows for the possibility of a synthesis between Islam and democracy, the dialectical nature of the process facilitating such a synthesis. As Mannheim argues persuasively, 'In a realm in which everything is in the process of becoming, the only adequate synthesis would be a dynamic one, which is reformulated from time to time.'[24] What

---

[24] K. Mannheim, *Ideology and Utopia* (London: Routledge & Kegan Paul, 1960), p. 135.

is happening in Iran today, it will be shown, is a reformulation and synthesis, which, it is argued, constitutes a profound 'paradigm shift'.[25]

Civil society and democratic development

Current debates on democratization are dominated by competing views of the concept of 'civil society' – conducted, as Sadowski points out wryly, 'with an enthusiasm that has not made its meaning any clearer'.[26] This fascination with civil society, variously defined, reflects an intellectual response to developments in eastern Europe and Latin America during the 1990s following the collapse of Soviet communism and the apparent peaceful transition of many authoritarian states to democratic practices. While more recent developments, particularly in Russia, have taken some of the shine off the initial euphoria, and revealed that such transitions are rarely smooth, the study of 'civil society' as an essential component of the process of democratization is increasingly prevalent in political science discourse. This alone would suggest its eventual application to the great 'exception' from global trends, the Middle East. However, the immediate reason why scholars went in search of civil society and the green shoots of democracy was the onset of the Persian Gulf War of 1990–91 and the popular scepticism surrounding its motivation.

The war to liberate Kuwait exposed the Middle East to the glare of Western publicity and public scrutiny on a hitherto unprecedented scale; and Western governments, needing to convince and mobilize public opinion, had to provide a moral argument more convincing than oil. Arab states demanded a solution to the Palestinian problem, while the Western public queried the morality and utility of fighting on behalf of semi-feudal auto-cratic states. The solution was to argue that (once again) the 'impact of the West' would facilitate and encourage the process of democratic develop-ment. Despite considerable scepticism, attempts were made to justify the existence of such a process through a mixture of semantic somersaults and emphasis on genuine advances, such as the opening or reopening of legislative assemblies. Kuwait itself provides a good example of this latter development, and a number of other states have recognized the important

---

[25] The term not only encapsulates the significance of the process taking place, but also echoes one of the major intellectual debates in postrevolutionary Iran about the nature of change. Furthermore, it should be noted that Thomas Kuhn (with whom the term is associated) was an important early influence on Abdolkarim Soroush, the highly influential contemporary lay religious scholar and philosopher.

[26] Sadowski, 'The New Orientalism', p. 34.

legitimizing qualities of consultative assemblies, both domestically and for the purpose of persuading foreign sceptics. Nevertheless, progress could be said to be at best erratic and at worst superficial. This has encouraged the 'rejectionists' in the view that the Middle East is the exception; but at the same time, the assertion of an antagonistic determinism in Huntington's thesis on the 'clash of civilizations' has encouraged further efforts to overcome this exceptionalism. This quest has yielded some interesting results, since it would appear that Iran, the very state considered anathema by the United States, possesses the prerequisites for democratization. More frustrating is the realization that the growth in popular participation is likely to yield governments unsympathetic to Western interests. The acquiescence of Western governments in the suppression of the outcome of Algerian elections at the beginning of 1992 is a good example of the contradictions in Western policy. Indeed, a cynic might be forgiven for believing that the problem in the Middle East is not so much a lack of democracy as the governments democracy might engender. Thus Jeane Kirkpatrick could say, somewhat astonishingly, that: 'The Arab world is the only part of the world where I've been shaken in my conviction that if you let the people decide, they will make fundamentally rational decisions.'[27]

In Iran, the situation was doubly frustrating: not only were democratic tendencies emerging within a country many in the West considered quintessentially 'fundamentalist', but these tendencies were also developing in a country which for twenty years had been positioned in opposition to all that the West stood for. In other words, positive democratic developments could not easily be attributed to Western influence. Yet all the indicators were present: a growing, vibrant press; the constitutional division of powers between judiciary, executive and legislature; and, most impressively, the regular conduct of elections, which despite their limitations appeared to endorse political participation on a scale unimagined in neighbouring states. In the same way that the apparent populism of the Islamic Revolution had forced a reassessment of social forces within Iran, so too the emergence of the accepted characteristics of a 'civil society' was encouraging a tacit, somewhat cautious reassessment of the consequences of the unleashing of those social forces.[28]

Nevertheless, whatever the extent of democratic development, certain limitations were also apparent, most explicitly exemplified by the existence of a 'Supreme Leader', *Rahbar*, whose religious authority augmented constitutional powers far exceeding those of the president. Consequently, some have accompanied reflections on the emergence of civil society with words of caution about the limited nature and possibilities of the process,

---

[27] Quoted in Kramer, 'Islam vs Democracy', p. 37.
[28] Sadowski, 'The New Orientalism', p. 36.

while others have simply dismissed the whole exercise as one of superficial legitimation.[29] More adventurous and enthusiastic commentators tend to emphasize the 'state versus society' model, which does not capture the highly integrated nature of state–society relations in Iran. Indeed, acceptance that change is occurring in Iran has in large part been gradual and grudging, and it should therefore come as no surprise that observers are unwilling to signpost it without attaching pointed caveats. Another way of seeking to circumvent criticism (and possibly ridicule) has been to view the Iranian experience within a comparative framework modelled on the French Revolution. This approach – which would gratify most Iranian revolutionaries – does have value, albeit limited.

One characteristic often attributed to Iran is the patrimonial nature of its political structure, which, as Kazemi points out, would appear to be the 'dominant force in Iranian politics'.[30] In this connection, Max Weber's ideal types, of which 'patrimonialism' is one, may usefully be employed to assess the nature of political development in Iran, as long as they are not applied too rigidly. Certainly, when considering *traditional* forms of legitimacy, Weber's notions of patrimonialism and charismatic leadership capture facets of Iran's political and social structures, for example the *ulema*, while also allowing for an explanation of the rise of Ayatollah Khomeini as the quintessential 'charismatic' ruler. As Weber says, 'In traditional periods, charisma is the great revolutionary force.'[31] Weber's sociological categorization remains popular in Western social science discourse, in part because he sought to explain the differences between the Occident and the Orient and therefore, unlike other theorists, dealt explicitly with the latter; but his conception of 'patrimonialism' conformed with notions of 'oriental despotism' and other orientalist preconceptions. It also encouraged an elite-centred approach to politics and enjoyed the huge advantage, for American political science (especially in the Cold War), of not being Marxist and not being embroiled with 'social forces'. Thus Weber somewhat unfortunately became the theoretical justification for a new orientalist discourse which viewed the Middle East political cycle as one of a succession of patrimonial rulers punctuated by periodic bouts of charismatic leadership.[32] This is one of the more sophisticated interpretations of the 'unchanging East' thesis, although few commentators seem to

---

[29] For example, J. L. Esposito and J. O. Voll, *Islam and Democracy* (Oxford: Oxford University Press, 1996), p. 74: 'Many might dispute majority support for the regime. However its *quasi-democractic* nature is clear' (emphasis added).

[30] F. Kazemi, 'Civil Society and Iranian Politics', in A. R. Norton, ed., *Civil Society in the Middle East*, vol. 2 (Leiden: E. J. Brill, 1996), p. 119. See also Arjomand, *The Turban for the Crown* (Oxford, OUP, 1988).

[31] M. Weber, *Economy and Society*, vol. 1 (Berkeley, CA: University of California Press, 1978), p. 245.

[32] Ibn Khaldun has of course been pressed into service in support of this cyclical theory.

have noticed that Weber argues that the routinization of charisma can lead to *either* a restoration of patrimonialism *or* the emergence of rational/legal structures.[33] This is a crucial caveat which would seem to indicate that Weber acknowledged the possibility of the cycle being broken. It is this possibility which will be explored here, but not exclusively in Weberian terms. Some aspects of Marxist analysis have relevance too.

As Turner shows, there is a good deal of complementarity in the views of Marx and Weber on 'oriental' society: 'although Marx stressed the importance of the monopoly of economic power and Weber emphasised the monopoly of political power, the outline, assumptions and implications of their perspectives on Asian-European contrasts are very similar.'[34] For the purposes of this study, the intention is not to approach Iranian political development from either an exclusively Weberian or an exclusively Marxist framework, but to draw on the approaches of both to indicate developments in both the political centre and the social periphery.[35]

Studies focusing on the social forces, or 'crowd', in Iranian politics are of course nothing new; but the acceptance recently apparent for this approach, previously associated with Marxist historians, reflects the reinvigorated enthusiasm for 'civil society'. Indeed, the notion of civil society carries with it many of the definitional problems associated with the concept of social forces, and yet the concept provides an essential component of most theories of democratization. It is used to characterize those organizations and associations, however loosely defined, which mediate between the power of the state and the liberty of society and which for our purposes can be said to reflect the integrated nature of state and society.

The origins of civil society in Iran can be identified in the various groups and associations which formed to mediate and administer political processes within the periphery of the Qajar kingdom – a development which was indeed vital to the functioning of the Qajar state, given the limitation of Qajar 'despotism'.[36] In fact, during much of this period the greatest single manifestation of an organized civil society mediating the power of the state was the *ulema*, whose independent financial means, social penetration and religious authority made them a force to be reckoned with. Viewed in this light, the growth of the Iranian state, particularly under the

---

[33] Weber, *Economy and Society*, vol. 1, p. 246; this argument is in fact explicitly expressed by Akbar Ganji, in an article for the newspaper *Khordad* of 3 Dec. 1998/1377, which appears in Ganji, *Tarik-khaneh-ye ashbah* (*The Cellar of Phantoms*) (Tehran: Tar-e No, 1999/1378), p. 68.

[34] B. Turner, *Weber and Islam* (London: Routledge & Kegan Paul, 1974), p. 3.

[35] The emphasis here is on developments in Western Marxism. For another 'dual' approach to democratization see Ruth B. Collier, *Paths to Democracy* (Cambridge: Cambridge University Press, 2000).

[36] E. Abrahamian, 'Oriental Despotism: The Case of Qajar Iran', *International Journal of Middle East Studies*, vol. 5, 1974, pp. 3–31.

Pahlavi regime, in which political centralization loomed large and the *ulema* were constrained, limited and ultimately marginalized this 'civil society'. Against this background, the Islamic Revolution, in a very real sense, represented the triumph of civil society over the authoritarian state, certain elements of which then took on the trappings of the state. The point, however, is that the roots of a functioning civil society had existed and were later augmented by a secular civil society epitomized by the development of the *dowreh* (regular gathering of friends or salon), the growth of the press and a vibrant student body.

The Pahlavi attempt to suppress such elements and create a bourgeois public sphere did not succeed definitively. Indeed, much like the Brazilian model, 'civil society or its residues survive authoritarian rule in forms of interest associations, autonomous agencies, local government, and church life,' in great part assisted by 'memories of earlier mass mobilisation'.[37] This civil society survived as a much more fluid and dynamic entity throughout the period of Khomeini's 'charismatic' rule, to re-emerge across society following his death in 1989. Indeed, it was in the decade following the Iran–Iraq War that Iranian civil society witnessed its most dramatic period of accelerated growth; slow at first, but gathering momentum. This was in part a consequence of the transformation of Iranian social attitudes engendered by the traumatic experience of a near-total war, but it also crucially reflected the structural changes in the state orchestrated and encouraged by Ali Akbar Hashemi Rafsanjani during his eight-year tenure as president. Central to the thesis of this study is the argument that Rafsanjani constructed what will be described as a *bourgeois republic* dominated by a bureaucratic–authoritarian structure (with patrimonial tendencies) which sought to compensate for the loss of charismatic authority by establishing a political network founded on mercantile interests. To complement this structure, civil society was to be manipulated to provide additional sources of legitimacy:

> While this effort from above is always expected to stay within careful limits, it cannot amount to a complete farce if the goal of legitimacy is to be attained, and the elements of actual democratisation that are established in this way are by definition unpredictable and cannot be kept within any given predefined limits.[38]

At the same time, the process of the 'enlargement' of civil society was facilitated by internal splits in the authoritarian regime, as reflected in the

---

[37] J. L. Cohen and A. Arato, *Civil Society and Political Theory* (Cambridge, MA: MIT Press, 1992), p. 49.
[38] Ibid., p. 50.

events and political disputes which surrounded the Iranian presidential elections of 1997 and the emergence of Seyyid Mohammad Khatami. The acquiescence of the Iranian political establishment in developments which may result in their political disenfranchisement has been counterbalanced by a determination to secure legitimacy and a measure of control over the process of change:

> these elites expect to channel politics 'away from the ebullience of civil society' and perhaps even to win elections by dividing the opposition and being rewarded by the electorate. When elections are only gradually decontrolled, as in Brazil, the hope is to slow down the rate of change while still achieving procedural legitimacy. The hopes of victory and legitimacy are generally frustrated, but not those of demobilisation and where pertinent, gradualism.[39]

Contemporary Iran bears witness to such a development, where a political establishment has forfeited its popular legitimacy in return for controlled, gradual change. The process involves both elites and civil society. Nevertheless, the pace and scope of this change are proving increasingly difficult for the elites to restrain, and while the process may have been initiated and to some extent cultivated by divisions among the political elite, Iran may yet prove the exception to the model of coexistence and provide an example of a democratization process emphatically (though not exclusively) determined by society.

> Equally important is the issue of whether or not the pressure of civil society, once mobilised, is capable of pushing to the end a process of transition to democratic politics. It seems obvious that an evolutionary strategy involves important negotiating and bargaining processes with those authoritarian rulers who are able and willing to moderate their rule, while at a later stage any transition to democracy must involve organisation for elections. It is not obvious in either of these contexts, however, how civic associations, social movements, grass roots organ-isations, or even media of communication can substitute for the differentiation of a political element capable of strategic considerations. In fact, a strategy from below on its own has nowhere succeeded.[40]

---

[39] Ibid., pp. 54–5.
[40] Ibid., p. 51.

2 The Politics of Managing Change

A contested inheritance

'History' in Iran is contested. Indeed, it might be better to talk of many conflicting and competing 'histories' reflecting different political perspectives. The purpose of this chapter is not to detail the various histories on offer in contemporary Iran but to provide an overview or context for the contemporary debates in Iran and to introduce the various historical themes which serve to illuminate and explain contemporary developments.

While the past may be the subject of discussion and debate within Western societies, and there is a recognition and acknowledgment of the political relevance of historical interpretation, few societies are as intense in this respect as Iran. In Iran, the past enjoys an immediate political relevance which is almost ahistorical. This can be best seen in contrast with the United States, where fifty years ago is the distant past, while in Iran the coup against the nationalist premier Dr Mohammad Mosaddeq in 1953 is of immense contemporary importance.

One of the explanations for the Iranian preoccupation with history may be the traditional basis of society and the tendency to relive historical events as if they occurred yesterday – the Shi'a passions (passion plays) perform such a function explicitly. It also, however, reflects the medium of historical communication, which remains personal and anecdotal, and the dominance of myths within Iranian society. What is meant here by 'myth' is *not* the perpetuation of falsehoods, but the transfer of information and knowledge through the medium of familiar and personalized morality tales. Such myths carry within them implicit (and sometimes explicit) social values which resonate in society. Thus, while few Iranians are aware of the details of Dr Mosaddeq's premiership, they are acutely aware that he was a 'nationalist', a 'patriot', possibly a 'democrat' and most definitely a 'martyr' to his cause. Mosaddeq therefore personifies many of the moral attributes which appeal to ordinary Iranians, and as such, whatever their veracity, he becomes less important as a historical figure than as a mythic one. Mosaddeq is almost unique, however, in the way he has come to dominate the Iranian historical landscape, for most other events and personalities remain contested – in part because of the political instability and revolutionary character of modern Iran. Indeed, as one historian has pointed out, 'No Muslim country besides Iran has such a string of modern revolts and revolutions.'[1] Continued tension, and the fluidity of political establishments seeking to impose their version of history, have also encouraged the multiplication of histories and myths.[2]

The roots of democratic development

Iranian political development can conveniently be subdivided into five distinct phases:

- the constitutional period, 1906–21;
- the rise and rule of Reza Shah, 1921–41;
- the Pahlavi interregnum, 1941–53;
- the rule of Mohammad Reza Shah, 1953–79;
- the Islamic Revolution and Republic, 1979 to the present.

The constitutional period, 1906–21

It is a common perception that the nineteenth century was a period of stagnation and decay in Iranian political and social life. Certainly this was a thesis encouraged by the Pahlavis and their supporters in an effort to distinguish their own modernizing monarchy from the comparative inactivity of the Qajars they had deposed. This view was in many ways justified, given that the Qajars oversaw the decline of Iran from a 'great power' into a pawn of the imperial powers and an aspect of the European 'Eastern Question'. While Iran's economy had in fact grown for much of the nineteenth century, in comparison with the accelerated industrial development of the West it had fallen behind substantially. The state was neither centralized nor organized on rational grounds, and the shahs required consensus in the provinces if their remit was to run much further than the environs of the capital, Tehran.

[1] N. Keddie, *Iran and the Muslim World: Resistance and Revolution* (London: Macmillan, 1995), p. 60.
[2] The definitive statement on myth and revolution must be that of Marx. See K. Marx, *The Eighteenth Brumaire of Louis Bonaparte* (Peking: Foreign Language Press, 1978), p. 1.

Despite the appearance of slumber, however, there were some serious attempts to address the country's political and economic woes. Members of the royal court, as well as lay intellectuals and bureaucrats, sought to find ways in which to strengthen the Qajar state and to modernize it along the lines of the major monarchies of Europe. This was, it should be noted, an exercise in bureaucratic authoritarianism, not political emancipation; and Europe in the middle of the nineteenth century was in any case a better example of the former than the latter. The most interesting attempt to revitalize and re-energize the Qajar monarchy was administered by the prime minister Amir Kabir (1848–51), whose attempts were ambitious but ultimately doomed to failure under a monarch too easily swayed by the machinations of his rivals. Amir Kabir was encouraged to commit suicide, and with him, in the eyes of many Iranians, died Iran's last serious attempt to avoid the humiliations that were to follow. Amir Kabir was the first significant personality of modern Iranian history to be romanticized into myth. A patriot, fighting against the odds, ultimately martyred to his cause, he possessed all the major requisite traits; and his posthumous fame was enhanced by Iran's seemingly accelerated decline following his death and the very public remorse of the Qajar shah who had him removed.

In the fifty years to 1906, the political, military and, in particular, economic domination of Iran by the European imperial powers – above all, Great Britain and Russia – appeared almost complete. A number of economic concessions provided to governments and private entrepreneurs confirmed the humiliation of a state that a mere half-century earlier had been the dominant regional power. The Reuter's concession of 1872, for instance, while not ultimately honoured, would have effectively handed over the entire economy of the country in a single commercial transaction described by Lord Curzon as 'the most complete and extraordinary surrender of the entire industrial resources of a kingdom into foreign hands that has probably ever been dreamed of, much less accomplished, in history.'[3] Iranian merchants were unhappy about the concessions offered to foreigners at the expense of local interests. The combination of their restiveness, increasing disenchantment among members of the *ulema* and frustration among a select band of lay intellectuals led to a major countrywide protest against the concession covering tobacco, resulting in its annulment in 1892. This resistance, while limited in popular terms, was not only effective in attaining its immediate goal but also signalled the emergence of a political consciousness throughout key sectors of society, which themselves were

---

[3] G. Jones, *Banking and Empire in Iran*, vol. 1 (Cambridge: Cambridge University Press, 1986), p. 10.

influential on account of their wider social contacts. Reaction to the apparent incompetence of the state helped generate the foundations of a civil society. The 'secularists' – those who most strongly espoused the secular nationalism, as they understood it, of the West – were the radicals of their age, whose trajectory was in the ascendant.[4]

Some thinkers, such as the nineteenth-century intellectual and proto-nationalist Kermani, argued in favour of a vigorous Iranian nationalism, stripped of the deviations of Arabism and, to some extent, Islamism, although many lay 'secular' intellectuals, while antagonistic to the organized faith, were not irreligious. Indeed, many arguably viewed the state of Islam in much the same way as the proponent of Islamic revival Jamal al Din al Afghani – namely, as in need of fundamental reform which would free it from reactionary dogma.[5] To confuse matters further, it should also be remembered that some key members of the *ulema* also thought in this way. What these various groups shared in common was a growing disillusionment with the Qajar monarchy.[6] For instance, although the tobacco concession had been successfully baulked, the state still saw fit to offer other concessions, two of which were of particular importance for later political developments. One was in effect an act of compensation to Baron Julius de Reuter for the failure to implement the original 1872 concession, and it enabled the establishment of the British Imperial Bank of Persia in 1889.[7] This institution came to dominate Iranian fiscal policy until the 1930s and the establishment of the Bank Melli. The other concession which proved portentous, that made in 1901 to William Knox D'Arcy, led to the foundation of the Anglo-Persian Oil Company (APOC), which was to dominate the Iranian oil industry until 1951.[8]

The activities of the Qajar state led to the one response it could not cope with, namely the gradual unification of the various disparate elite groups with the sole purpose of bringing the monarchy to account. The events which were ultimately to lead to what became known as the Constitutional

---

[4] It was during this time that Jamal al Din al Afghani was active in the Muslim world, and while his attentions were not entirely focused on Iran, one of his disciples took the fateful step of assassinating the reigning monarch Nasir al Din Shah (1896). While many people were critical of the political lethargy of the monarchy, regicide was regarded as a step too far, and this event, combined with the unorthodoxy of Afghani's thinking, ensured that his ideas stayed out of the mainstream of political thought.

[5] See for instance E. G. Browne's contention that there was little difference between the labels 'Shi'a' and 'Persian'.

[6] According to Curzon, 'The Shah is about as likely to undertake a genuinely great public work as he is to turn protestant.' Quoted in Jones, *Banking and Empire in Iran*, vol. 1, p. 8.

[7] See ibid., p. 29.

[8] The bank is the ancestor of HSBC, while the oil company ultimately became known as British Petroleum, later still BP.

Revolution of 1906 resulted from a new-found ideological cohesiveness among the elites, assisted in some measure by the emergence of newspapers sponsored by proponents of reform. The key event was the alliance of convenience engineered by the two leading Shi'a *mujtahids*[9] of Tehran, Behbahani and Tabatabai, who between them could draw on a considerable popular following within Tehran. Their agreement, arranged for different reasons on each side and reflecting the different traditions within the *ulema*, ensured the entrance of the crowd into Iranian politics. The catalyst for the Constitutional Revolution was a trivial affair involving the punishment of a number of Tehran merchants, later compounded by the death of a lowly Shi'a cleric following street demonstrations, which further enraged the Tehran populace. Initial demands for a 'House of Justice' were transformed into calls for a fully-fledged 'National Consultative Assembly' – a parliament, which would pass legislation and hold the shah and his ministers to account. The Constitutionalists, as they came to be known, were supported in their quest by the British, who afforded many of them sanctuary in the British embassy, while the authoritarian tendency was supported by tsarist Russia, which by 1906 was in no position to act, because of its own revolution. The new constitution was thus adopted in 1906, complete with a parliament, limited franchise and elections.[10]

Very soon, however, the allies began to splinter into rival groups, as some members of the *ulema* criticized and indeed condemned the notion of a legislative assembly or the blasphemous idea, propounded by secular nationalists, that sovereignty resided with the people. So contentious did these ideas become that the country drifted into a limited civil war which ultimately witnessed the triumph of the secular nationalists and the execution in 1909 of the most ferocious critic of the new constitution, Sheikh Fazlollah Nuri. Subsequently, Russian interference, along with internecine factional strife and a realization that positive support for the movement was in fact much more limited than had previously been believed, combined to immobilize the government, for all its good intentions, and the state failed. The details of this process need not concern us here, though many of the elements of later political contests were established at this stage, including the persistence, and to some extent destructiveness, of factions; the emergence of a vibrant and combative

[9] *Shi'a ulema* (religious scholars) whose education and training in jurisprudence and Islamic legal texts allow them to practice *ijtehad* or interpretation. The definition is applicable in the main (and certainly in the modern period) to Ayatollahs and Grand Ayatollahs, though not all of the former are acknowledged *mujtahids*.

[10] For details see E. G. Browne, *The Persian Revolution 1906–1909* (Washington, DC: Mage Publishers, 1995).

press; and the use of the crowd. The Constitutional Revolution also revealed the multiplicity of traditions which combined only to challenge the monarchy, and the cleavages between secular nationalists, monarchists and the religious classes, all of whom faced further divisions among themselves.

Notwithstanding the material failure of the Constitutional Revolution, it was and has remained a pivotal moment in the formation of the modern Iranian identity. It established the parameters of political discourse and provided a reference point for all subsequent political movements. Most important, it unleashed the potent myth of political emancipation as writers and intellectuals recorded events for posterity, highlighting those mythic motifs of patriotism against the odds and martyrdom. The movement may have failed to achieve its goals, but the flame, so to speak, had been lit; and, its supporters contended, it continued to burn. More practically, the Constitutionalists did have to acknowledge that for all its apparent populism, their movement had not been popular. For all their enthusiasm, the elites had not succeeded in awakening political consciousness among the broad masses of the people, who remained for the most part rural and apathetic. The solution, for many intellectuals steeped in the history of the French Revolution, was obvious, as will be seen.

Reza Shah and the Pahlavi autocracy

The rise to prominence and power of Reza Khan, a hitherto unknown officer in the Cossack Brigade, reflected the urgent need among intellectuals and the political establishment to restore order within the state and rescue Iran from the dire consequences of the First World War, which, despite the country's neutrality, had seen it become a battleground for the belligerents. It also reflected both Britain's dominance in Iran following the Russian Revolution, and the British desire to limit the costs of empire in the aftermath of a costly world war. Lord Curzon, the Foreign Secretary, had developed something of an affection for the 'Persians', and despite his own better judgment was convinced that they would be grateful for all the assistance Britain could offer. He therefore expended considerable time developing the Anglo-Persian Agreement of 1919, which many Iranian nationalists considered would reduce the country to the status of a protectorate. That Curzon misread the relatively widespread reaction to his programme reflects perhaps his over-reliance on a particularly narrow section of the political elite. Nationalism could still not be considered a popular force in the country, but it had so embedded itself among a broad swathe of the political elites that the leading political cleric of his age,

Seyed Hassan Mudarres, proved to be one of the most nationalistic critics of the agreement. The failure of the 1919 agreement signalled that the era of the backroom deal, signed and sealed irrespective of the consequences, had run its course. But the 'coup' of 1921, in which some two thousand men under the command of Reza Khan supported the seizure of power by a journalist called Seyyid Zia Tabatabai, also served notice that the era of mass politics was as yet some way off.

Reza Khan was quick to dispose of his civilian colleagues, becoming minister of war, prime minister and ultimately the first shah of the Pahlavi dynasty, in 1925. His rise was predicated on the tacit approval of the British minister in Tehran and the overwhelming desire of Iranian intellectuals to discover – or, more pertinently, invent – a saviour. He was applauded in his efforts to restore order and government to the country, and though suspicions were raised by his predisposition towards the army and his tendency towards authoritarianism, these were considered tolerable up to a point, especially as many intellectuals considered him a means to an end – a transitional monarch who might lead the country to republicanism. Republicanism indeed was pervasive among many intellectuals, and even Reza Khan himself toyed with the idea in 1924; but fears that it would only encourage his worst dictatorial instincts and lead to an overt secularization of the country on the Turkish model encouraged many, not only within the *ulema*, to oppose this development. Reza Khan became king or shah under the assumption that it would temper his worst characteristics. He was theoretically a constitutional monarch, governing with a parliament, and in actual fact appointed by parliamentary decree. Reza Shah was therefore both traditional and modern; more accurately, he was a traditional patrimonial king with the trappings and tools of bureaucratic authoritarianism. He and his key lieutenants provided the myth of the Constitutional Revolution with its material dimension: a modern, bureaucratic, centralized state – secular, industrial and fervently national. There is little doubt that Reza Shah in twenty-one years succeeded in transforming the political landscape of the country; but this was achieved in an erratic manner and at substantial cost.

Reza Shah alienated not only the *ulema*, who still enjoyed considerable support among the mass of the people, but (arguably more importantly) the intellectual pillars of his support. His tendency towards autocracy resulted in a decreasing tolerance, which led to the deaths of three key allies, one of whom had shaped and directed a considerable amount of state policy. His accumulation of land and disrespect for the traditional aristocracy, as well as the unwelcome extension of the state into a periphery hitherto untouched by the central government, all won him more enemies. There was popular resistance in particular to imposition of the Western dress code and the forced unveiling of women.[11] As a consequence, Reza Shah came to rely more and more on the army – his own 'tribe' – and a small clique of Pahlavi courtiers. Appreciation of his significant economic and social achievements was tempered by the knowledge that they were either poorly planned and administered or incomplete. One of his most durable achievements was the foundation of Tehran University in 1934; yet, like all autocrats, he remained suspicious of any free debate. Education to serve the state really meant serving the dynastic state, and he warned students being dispatched abroad not to come back with curious ideas about 'democracy'. For his supporters, Reza Shah's overthrow and abdication in 1941 in the face of the Allied invasion was a catastrophe which confirmed his patriotic martyr status and has since spawned the contention that the Allies bear responsibility for the incompleteness of the task he had begun. Yet his suppression of political development had by 1941 won him few friends, and outside his core supporters there were few regrets at his departure.

The Interregnum, 1941–53

While the autocracy had restored order and encouraged some measure of social and political development, it was the volatile years to 1953 which saw mass politics come of age in Iran. Under Allied tutelage and reflecting the social and educational changes wrought by Reza Shah, the years 1941–53 were a second period of political pluralism, marked by a rising tide of political consciousness. Politics remained intensely personal, but the spread of education and industry, and new methods of communication, in particular the wireless radio, along with the protection and encouragement of the occupying Allied powers, all facilitated the growth of political consciousness. Nationalism was confirmed as the paramount ideology throughout Iran, and the reference point from which legitimacy could be gauged. Indeed, it was at this time more thoroughly divested of its religious aspects than before, although by the end of the period a new, more vigorous 'religious nationalism' would re-emerge under the leadership of Ayatollah Kashani.

The level of political activity in the interregnum is quite astonishing and reflects perhaps the repression of the previous two decades and the durability of non-state political activity despite those conditions. One scholar has noted that between 1941 and 1946 alone there were at least twenty-two separate political parties, largely centred on personalities, but all boasting

---

[11] See e.g. FO 371 18992 E4628/608/34, 12 July 1935. There is of course a striking if unstated parallel with today's enforced dress codes.

distinct party manifestos.[12] These numbers mushroomed when elections loomed as branch associations also emerged to channel activity. Most parties adopted nationalist and socialist agendas and argued for a constitutional monarchy stripped of direct powers. The most influential mass party was the communist Tudeh party, which took as its model European communist parties and was most similar to Western parties in structure. Other party organizations, despite being centred on individual leaders, tended to have to learn quickly from Tudeh organization and strategy, which were seen to be successful. However, the Tudeh party was largely limited to urban centres, in particular those with industrial development.

Press activity was if anything more frenetic than ever, both surprising and impressing foreign observers. The British ambassador in Tehran, Reader Bullard, noted in 1943 that 'There are 47 newspapers in Tehran, a city of only 750,000 inhabitants, the large majority of whom are illiterate.'[13] By 1951, in the heightened activity leading up to the nationalization of the oil industry, this figure had mushroomed to 700 papers in Tehran alone![14] An astute observation of the influence of the burgeoning press was made by Cuyler-Young:

> In few countries of the literacy percentage of Iran are journalists more numerous, facile, superficial and irresponsible. Yet for all the spawning and specious nature of the Iranian press, it can be said that a considerable section of it is substantial and serious, and influential beyond what literacy statistics might lead one to expect, since papers are read in groups and news and opinions passed on by readers to illiterate friends and acquaintances.[15]

Political consciousness was also extending beyond the boundaries of the urban centres, as a British diplomat noticed:

> A member of the Qajar family who owns a good deal of land near Arak told me the other day that there are many wireless sets in the villages in that area to which all the peasants listen. The effect of this and of the bundles of Tehran newspapers which periodically reach the village is to give people an interest in politics which they never had before and a critical attitude towards their landlords.[16]

---

[12] F. Machalski, 'Political Parties in Iran in the years 1941-46,' *Folia Orientalia* III, 1961, p. 169
[13] FO 248 1427, 24 April 1943.
[14] FO 248 1514, file 10101/4/51, 5 Jan. 1951.
[15] T. Cuyler-Young, 'The Problem of Westernization in Modern Iran', *Middle East Journal*, vol. 2, 1948, p. 130.
[16] FO 248 1531 10105/50, memorandum by Pyman, 28 Jan. 1950.

The myth of political emancipation was being disseminated, and while the British were to remain dismissive of the power of Iranian nationalism, the appointment of Dr Mohammad Mosaddeq as prime minister was to prove a rude awakening. Mosaddeq was a scion of the Qajar family, a French-educated lawyer and a passionate nationalist, and while very much part of the political establishment was a proponent of constitutional democratic government. He was a theatrical political performer who knew how to mobilize not only his fellow parliamentary deputies but also the general populace, and in targeting the assets of the Anglo-Iranian Oil Company he had achieved 'something which is always dear to Persian hearts: he has flouted the authority of a great power and a great foreign interest and he has gone a long way towards damaging the prestige of the first and the prosperity of the second'. In so doing, Mosaddeq had 'succeeded in making himself a symbol of the Persian conception of nationalism'.[17] Mosaddeq himself, in echoes of later developments, sought to characterize the movement as one of enormous, almost universal, historical significance: 'No nation has succeeded in shaking off the foreign yoke without struggle, as can be testified by ancient and modern histories of nations and freedom movements ... Our movement served as inspiration to national risings of other peoples, and today peoples of north and south Africa anxiously await our success.'[18]

Mosaddeq managed to collect beneath this anti-imperialist banner two groups of allies who were to bring with them the 'masses' he needed behind him if he was to push through his agenda. One, represented by the vehemently anti-British Ayatollah Kashani, consisted of the religious nationalists and traditional groups including members of the bazaar;[19] the other was represented by the Tudeh communists. These two groups between them had the organization and social penetration needed to transform an elite movement into a mass movement. Indeed, it is often forgotten that without Kashani, the National Front, as Dr Mosaddeq's movement was known, would have been politically handicapped, and that there was a strong religious flavour to the movement despite the leadership being dominated by secular nationalists and socialists.[20]

---

[17] FO 248 1514, internal situation, file 10101, situation report, file no. 10101/277/51, 4 Sept. 1951.

[18] FO 371 104561, file 1015, text of Mosaddeq's speech, file no. 1015/26, 23 Jan. 1953.

[19] The term 'bazaar' implies the traditional mercantile community but is not necessarily limited to those who physically operate within the bazaar (in Tehran or elsewhere); essentially, it includes anybody whose chief source of capital accumulation is trade.

[20] See in particular Y. Richard, 'Ayatollah Kashani: Precursor of the Islamic Republic?', in N. Keddie, ed., *Religion and Politics in Iran: Shi'ism from Quietism to Revolution* (New Haven: Yale University Press, 1983), pp. 101–24.

Mosaddeq's political failure – which paradoxically confirmed his status as the supreme icon of Iranian nationalism, and by extension embellished the myth of political emancipation – was caused by a number of interrelated reasons and was not, as nationalists have contended ever since, the simple consequence of a foreign-inspired coup. Indeed, the precise nature of Mosaddeq's fall is important, given his contemporary relevance and the strategy apparently being espoused by conservatives at the turn of the twentieth century in order to undermine President Khatami. Put simply, for all his political ability and ideological coherence, Mosaddeq failed to address the decline in the economy, which had been severely hit by the British-led oil boycott. This added to tensions in the country which encouraged or forced (depending on one's viewpoint) Mosaddeq to accumulate further powers and to appear, to all intents and purposes, dictatorial – a perception fostered by his increasingly melodramatic performances. Many members of the political establishment found these, and his leanings towards the communist Tudeh, disconcerting. Faced with the uncompromising reality of economic austerity and potential dictatorship, the establishment began to look for alternatives; and they found one in the impotent young shah, Mohammad Reza, and the institution, though not the person, of the monarchy (a distinction most royalists were unable to make). The withdrawal of support by Ayatollah Kashani proved in many ways the turning point for the Mosaddeq movement – and an act few nationalists have been willing to forgive, although it shows the centrality of Kashani's role. It is within this ferment that the British-inspired and American-administered coup was mounted; and it proved ultimately successful, though it is often forgotten that in the initial stages the coup failed and the shah fled, leading to calls for the deposition of the dynasty.[21]

Mosaddeq's fall was to have widespread consequences for Iranian political development in the rest of the twentieth century and arguably led directly to the revolution of 1979. He himself was effectively sanctified as the great nationalist hero cut down by foreign forces and the treachery of domestic elements. The shah was marked with the stigma of having been restored to power by a foreign government; and this proved impossible to shake off. Indeed, far from being a secret, foreign involvement in the change of regime was widely rumoured and generally recognized. This would in turn prove extremely damaging for the Americans, who had previously been considered potential allies. While Iranians had arguably come to expect this sort of behaviour from the British, that the Americans should have become involved was regarded as profoundly disappointing.

---

[21] FO 371 104569, file no. 1015/205, 16 Aug. 1953.

Although mass politics had been contained, and some continued to choose to ignore it, others were aware that traditional 'Persia' was changing.

> In Reza Shah's Iran life was governed by tradition and custom. Poverty prevailed but ignorance and traditionalism formed a strong shield against discontent. Today, however, poverty remains but the shield has been pushed aside by changing conditions. The political ideas and new hopes which were disseminated up and down Iran by the outlawed Tudeh Party will now be carried, either unwittingly or consciously, further afield by new literates. Poverty and education, when allowed to meet, are an explosive mixture.[22]

The restoration of autocracy, 1953–79

Supporters of the Islamic Revolution often argue that their movement began in 1963, with Ayatollah Khomeini's protests against the White Revolution. In many ways, they were curiously correct in this assessment. Many of the hallmarks of the revolutionary movement which was to galvanize the country and the world in 1978 were in fact established by Mohammad Reza Shah – the king who aspired to be a revolutionary and to lead a 'White Revolution'. This is important, because it confirms the view that the Islamic Revolution was less anomalous in relation to historical trends than its opponents would have us believe. Like his father, Mohammad Reza Shah oversaw a period of dramatic economic growth, fuelled by substantial oil revenues, indeed one which arguably outstripped his father's achievements. Yet, unlike his father, the new shah was unwilling, or unable, to be satisfied with the trappings of traditional Persian kingship; he was intent instead to transform his monarchy into something approaching a revolutionary dictatorship. Indeed, during the fifteen years preceding the Islamic Revolution, Iranians became inured to the idea of 'revolution', and in many ways it is not surprising that they were ultimately so willing to go for the 'real thing'. Mohammad Reza Shah was a man with both a vision and a mission but, as with his father, his weaknesses – a penchant for *folie de grandeur*, a tendency to prevaricate and an enthusiasm for flattery – were to undermine his achievements. Like his father, he tended to antagonize the very social groups that were natural supporters of the monarchy, while his apparent dependency on the United States robbed him of legitimacy even in nationalist eyes, and his pivotal role in securing the oil price hike of 1973 lost him public support in the West as well.

[22] FO 371 127138 EP 1743/1, 30 May 1957.

The White Revolution which the shah launched with much fanfare in 1963 was intended to initiate and complete a social and political transformation of the country. Though it was ostensibly a programme of economic reform, the underlying agenda was political, with the aim of disenfranchising what were regarded as reactionary landlords, and empowering the holders of small farms, who were expected to feel undying gratitude towards their liberator. The scheme was almost Bonapartist in its pretensions, and while commentators continue to debate its efficacy, it is clear that it inaugurated a period of vast socio-economic dislocation, if nothing else. Economic growth was sustained at a steady pace by the gradual increase in oil revenues until the early 1970s, when a dramatic explosion in these revenues (a tenfold increase between the fourth and fifth economic plans) destabilized the development programme. By then, the country was changing, with growth in education, literacy and political awareness. More people were travelling abroad, and more foreigners were residing in Iran. In 1961 there were an estimated 10,000 foreigners in Tehran; a decade later the number was over five times that. The same could be said for student numbers, which stood at 17,000 in 1961 and had grown fivefold by 1976. At the beginning of this period some 15,000 students were studying abroad; at the end, the figure had risen to around 75,000. It was inevitable that political awareness, particularly among this ideological vanguard, would grow. A technological revolution had also had its impact upon the country – the number of radios had increased tenfold from the 1940s to some one million sets, while the advent of the television provided a whole new medium through which Iranians could connect to each other and the outside world. More importantly perhaps was the idealism of a new generation of radicals, a development the White Revolution was clearly intended to tame. As one British diplomat noted:

> Throughout the upper and middle classes, there are professional people, politicians, economists, planners, bankers, architects, journalists and writers who have been highly educated abroad; the elder, or pre-war, generation for the most part in France, the younger in the US, Germany, Switzerland and the United Kingdom. Although most of these people belong to privileged or prosperous families, whether of the upper or upper middle classes, they comprise a number of the real Iranian reformers and even revolutionaries. Many indeed would readily connive at revolution, if they judged that it would serve to amputate the 'dead hand' of social and bureaucratic tradition and would offer a hope of more efficient administration and fulfilment of their own ideas whether political and economic aspirations or personal ambitions. These people

have seen what is going on in more highly developed societies. They are well read, they have been members of students' unions and debating clubs; and above all they have escaped for a few years from the autocratic system of domestic relations of Iranian family convention. They are acutely conscious, not so much of the absence of political freedoms in their own country, as of social injustice, nepotism, corruption and incompetence ... The bulk of them are not more than 45 years old, and some of them together constitute virtually a corporate intellectual elite.[23]

This corporate intellectual elite was to find itself in an increasingly antagonistic relationship with the shah, as well as with the institution of the monarchy itself. Monarchists resorted to describing this intellectual elite as woolly liberals who at best were seeking to impose political reforms too quickly, and at worst simply did not understand the genius of the shah. Indeed, while some argued that the shah's reforms were an essential transition to a more liberal political environment, others saw no need for any such political development. By the 1970s the shah himself, who had once appeared to support 'democracy', had managed to redefine 'Iranian democracy' to incorporate and extend his own autocratic position. The arguments used are in fact curiously similar to those which dominate the conservative–reformist divide today. The shah's vulnerability on this issue and on the question of political legitimacy in general was accentuated by his alienation of the landlords, intellectuals and important sections of the *ulema*. Indeed, the seeds of the revolution of 1979 were sown almost immediately after the White Revolution when the shah, to the horror and indignation of the nationalists, offered extra-territorial rights to all American 'government' personnel working in Iran, by which they were not subject to the Iranian judicial process and could be tried in American courts for crimes committed in Iran. The restitution of 'capitulations', followed injudiciously by the grant of a $200 million US loan, was regarded as a betrayal of everything even his father had stood for. It was the monumental mistake of his reign, for it led to a haemorrhaging of the nationalist constituency he so badly needed. His mistake proved an absolute gift for a hitherto relatively unknown ayatollah.

Ayatollah Khomeini had come to political prominence after the launch of the White Revolution, by condemning among other things the seizure of private property in the land reform and the granting of votes to women, and articulating the general perception that the shah was operating less in concert with his own people than with the United States. Khomeini was an

[23] FO 371 157610 EP 1015/229, 1 Aug. 1961.

unorthodox cleric who felt it was his duty to be politically relevant. His knowledge of political texts, both those written by Iranian intellectuals and those of Western political philosophers, was unusual and drew extensive criticism from his colleagues; but their disapproval was more than counterbalanced by his attraction for many disillusioned young Iranian Muslims. Indeed, the failure of the National Front and the ideology of secular nationalism to bring about serious political change pushed more people towards a more religiously defined nationalism characteristic of writers such as Ali Shariati. It also provided opportunities for members of the *ulema*, who were interested in seizing the political initiative. Khomeini's outspokenness against the granting of extra-territorial rights to US nationals captured the imagination not only of his traditional supporters, but also of many secular nationalists who were impressed by his courage.

The shah, of course, was less impressed and in 1964 the ayatollah was sent off into exile. This was a grave mistake, for Khomeini was probably one of the most politically astute and modernizing of all *mullahs*.[24] While some have commented on his admiration for the reactionary Fazlollah Nuri (a vehement opponent of the Constitution), his intellectual roots were certainly more complex, and his views much more in line with those of Jamal al Din Al Afghani, Tabatabai, Mudarris and, more recently, Ayatollah Kashani. His unique political strength lay in transcending the divide between those religious modernizers and the traditional constituencies that had largely been ignored by the White Revolution and whose members felt increasingly alienated by the antics of a north Tehran political elite more in tune with Western mores than with those of traditional Iran. It is important to recognize that the Islamic Revolution was to a great extent the reaction of a neglected traditional society composed of a wide range of groups and that many senior clerics had in fact been suspicious of it. The following passage, written by a British diplomat in 1957, reveals more about the character of the Islamic Revolution than any discussion of its theological foundations, and amply sets the scene for what was to come.

> Here the mullahs preach every evening to packed audiences. Most of the sermons are revivalist stuff of a high emotional and low intellectual standard. But certain well known preachers attract the intelligentsia of the town with reasoned historical exposés of considerable merit ... The Tehran that we saw on the tenth of Moharram is a different world, centuries and civilisations apart from the gawdy superficial botch of

---

[24] A recent document released by the United States shows that as early as 1965 the US State Department had recognized Khomeini's potential in this respect.

cadillacs, hotels, antique shops, villas, tourists and diplomats, where we run our daily round ... But it is not only poverty, ignorance and dirt that distinguish the old south of the city from the parvenu north. The slums have a compact self-conscious unity and communal sense that is totally lacking in the smart districts of chlorinated water, macadamed roads and (fitful) street lighting. The bourgeois does not know his neighbour: the slum-dweller is intensely conscious of his. And in the slums the spurious blessings of Pepsi Cola civilisation have not yet destroyed the old way of life, where every man's comfort and security depend on the spontaneous, un-policed observation of a traditional code. Down in the southern part of the city manners and morals are better and stricter that in the villas of Tajrish: an injury to a neighbour, a pass at another man's wife, a brutality to a child evoke spontaneous retribution without benefit of bar or bench.[25]

---

[25] FO 371 127139 EP 1781/3,7 Sept. 1957.

3 Revolution, Republic and War

The Islamic Revolution was undoubtedly a defining moment in the late twentieth century. It introduced the world, in full televisual technicolour, to the reality of revolution and political Islam, with all its passion and brutality; and, along with the Iran–Iraq War, it transformed Iranian society. Yet despite its momentous impact, it remains both highly contested and contentious. This, of course, as noted in Chapter 1, is characteristic of contemporaneous interpretations of revolutions, particularly in the absence of accessible documentation. The intense dynamic of events tends to bewilder observers, and the Islamic Revolution was no exception; indeed, if anything, the general assumption of the durability and stability of the Pahlavi state made its collapse all the more astonishing, to both supporters and opponents. Ironically, both concluded that higher powers must have been involved. For the revolutionaries, the apparent miraculous collapse of the Pahlavi state apparatus confirmed the righteousness of their cause, success bringing its own justification, while monarchists, including the shah himself, lapsed into a destructive fatalism which hastened their demise. Faced with the shah's procrastination and Khomeini's stubborn decisiveness, by the end of 1978 few Iranians, whatever their political views, had any doubts where their future lay, and the social momentum gradually became truly revolutionary.[1]

The dialectics of the 'collective will'

Not only was there a growing air of inevitability about the impending collapse in 1978, characterized by the shah's abrupt decision to 'recognize' the revolution,[2] but the actual dynamic could best be described as dialectical.

[1] See H. Arendt, *On Revolution* (London: Penguin, 1990), pp. 21–58.
[2] BBC SWB ME/5962/A/9, 7 Nov. 1978, shah's speech to the nation, 6 Nov. 1978. Some commentators observed that this was the first time they realized they might indeed be in a revolutionary situation. It was by all accounts a remarkably imprudent speech.

The initial protests, which had occurred in the holy city of Qom following the publication of an article attacking Khomeini for (among other things) licentious behaviour,[3] led to further protests which seemed positively trivial and entirely containable. Yet by the end of the year these had accumulated in a dialectic of protest and suppression, until society eventually overcame the state, and an estimated two million people rallied against the shah in Tehran – a city, it should be borne in mind, whose population at the time probably did not exceed four million. Michel Foucault, observing developments in Tehran, was so impressed by this multitude that he considered it a rare actual manifestation of the 'collective will':

> Among the things that characterise this revolutionary event, there is the fact that it has brought out – and few peoples in history have had this – an absolutely collective will. The collective will is a political myth with which jurists and political philosophers try to analyse or to justify institutions, etc. It's a theoretical tool: nobody has ever seen the 'collective will' and, personally, I thought that the collective will was like God, like the soul, something one would never encounter. I don't know whether you agree with me, but we met in Tehran and throughout Iran, the collective will of a people. Well, you have to salute it, it doesn't happen every day.[4]

Arguably what Foucault was witnessing was the social manifestation of the myth of political emancipation, which had finally come of age.[5] Indeed, it is worth emphasizing that the Islamic Revolution cannot be understood outside the popular movements which had preceded it in 1906 and 1951–3. That some (particularly supporters of the monarchy) resisted this conclusion reflected the tendency, still current in many circles, to neglect the social dimension in Iranian politics and to focus on the mechanics of elite politics. While particular elites dominated the Constitutional Revolution and sought (more or less unsuccessfully) to manage the National Front movement of the 1950s, the social forces unleashed in 1978 were of a different scale and passion altogether. That is not to say that rival political elites did not play or come to play important functions. But the transfer of power which occurred and rendered the Pahlavi elite ineffective and irrelevant was a social initiative. However, it was a social initiative united only in its determination to rid society of the shah. As Foucault points out, 'this collective

[3] *Ettela'at*, 8 Jan. 1978.
[4] M. Foucault, 'Iran: The Spirit of the World without Spirit', in *Politics, Philosophy, Culture: Interviews and other Writings 1977–1984* (London: Routledge, 1988), p. 215.
[5] See also in relation to this point C. Mouffe, 'Hegemony and Ideology in Gramsci', in C. Mouffe, ed., *Gramsci and Marxist Theory* (London: Routledge & Kegan Paul, 1979), pp. 182–3.

will has been given one object, one target and one only, namely the departure of the shah.'[6] Once the shah had departed, the complexity of the underlying dynamic became increasingly apparent, as did the limits of Khomeini's charisma.

The limits of 'charisma'

The characterization of Ayatollah Khomeini's rule as 'charismatic' has tended to disguise the very real fluidity of the situation. As Weber has explained, 'charismatic authority' is simply one of the ideal types devised by him to assist analysis; these are not expected to be accurate depictions in themselves, and to think otherwise would be to oversimplify reality.[7] There is little doubt that Khomeini was an extraordinary and charismatic leader; but his authority can best be described as 'traditional charismatic', in so far as he manifested many of the characteristics of patrimonial rule. This assessment would seem to be confirmed by his acknowledged ability to manipulate the various factions which operated in the Islamic Republic, which is a characteristic of patrimonial domination, and also, it may be argued, by his populism. Indeed, for all his emphasis on the rule of law and genuine aspirations to a particular conception of legal/rational authority, Khomeini operated within a traditional framework which imposed its own limitations.

Whether Khomeini is considered to be patrimonial or charismatic, or, as is the contention here, a combination of both, the corollary or implication is that Iranian society remained in essence traditional, and yet not as easily led as might be supposed. For the all the transitional characteristics of Pahlavi Iran, society at large remained wedded to its traditional patron–client networks of political relations; and Khomeini was accordingly often less master of all he surveyed and more subject to circumstance than is generally acknowledged. His was in many ways a case study of Weber's 'paradox of sultanism'.[8] As Abrahamian has correctly observed, Khomeini was reacting to events as much as he was dictating them.[9]

---

[6] Foucault, 'Iran', p. 215.

[7] M. Weber, *Economy and Society,* vol. 1 (Berkeley, CA: University of California Press, 1978), p. 215.

[8] Ibid., vol. 2, p. 1020; see also Turner, *Weber and Islam* (London: Routledge & Kegan Paul, 1974), p. 80.

[9] See the excellent essay by E. Abrahamian, 'Fundamentalism or Populism?', in his *Khomeinism* (London: I. B. Tauris, 1993), pp. 13–38; also R. Stephen Humphreys, *Between Memory and Desire: The Middle East in a Troubled Age* (London: University of California Press, 1999), p. 35.

It is a reflection of the commonplace tendency to personalize and anthropomorphize states that commentators have inclined to identify the complexity of Iran with the more easily grouped attributes of the individual. Khomeini himself nurtured no such illusions, and while he successfully established his authority in the absence of the shah, he had a good deal more trouble securing his power. Far from issuing lofty decrees which were instantly obeyed, Ayatollah Khomeini appears to have been constantly frustrated by social forces which simply refused to settle or submit to any order. The following comment, issued soon after his arrival in Iran, when his 'charisma' should have been at its most potent, is revealing:

> I have often said, and I repeat again, that no one has the right to attack or enter peoples' homes. If an offender is known to be in a house he should be watched lest he escape and the matter should be reported to the authorities so that he may be arrested in accordance with norms. Those interested in the movement should refrain from such acts. The people must act on the basis of religious norms.[10]

Anarchy is sometimes considered a stepping-stone to absolute power, but Iranian society was proving extremely unaccommodating and difficult. Theorists preoccupied with the state may lament this 'anarchy'; others may see in the ferment the germinating shoots of civil society. After twenty-five years of systematic if gradual suppression, it would have been surprising if the social reaction had not been vigorous; and in 1978 political consciousness was broader and more sophisticated than it had been in 1941. That is not to say that it could be characterized as a constructive force – this was an angry society, and not necessarily a virtuous one; but it was less easily manipulated by the political elites, and recognition of Khomeini's authority did not entail unquestioning obedience. Indeed, many of the political groups that had fought for the revolution remained indifferent to Khomeini's leadership, and some retained more than a hint of suspicion, regarding him as no more than a titular head who would gracefully retire to Qom once the revolution had been won.

Competing movements

Of the three major movements which engineered and orchestrated the revolution, it was the left that proved the greatest thorn in the side of the religious leadership. Indeed, of the four major ideological camps that had

[10] BBC SWB ME/6056/A/7, 2 March 1979, speech by Khomeini, 28 Feb. 1979.

emerged from the oil nationalization crisis in 1953, the monarchists had been routed and the secular nationalists, on account of their limited popular appeal, were rapidly marginalized or accommodated, leaving the religious and leftist factions to mobilize their supporters against each other. This conflict ended in a brutal 'civil war' between the two factions which lasted into 1981 and the scars of which remain today.[11] That the religious factions prevailed is attributable not only to the existence of positive support but also to the widespread suspicion among the generally conservative society of the implications of an 'atheistic' red revolution.[12]

While the religious factions gained dominance in the early republican state, it should be remembered that Iranian factions were and remain fluid collections of individuals whose corporate identity is little more than the sum of these individuals; and, in a dynamic environment where ideas were being reformulated, it was not unnatural for individuals to realign themselves. This process, which was just beginning to settle twenty years later, is often considered opportunistic and pragmatic in an unprincipled sense. It may, of course, simply be the realistic way to proceed under the circumstances, and reflect the complex internal dialectic of revolutions. It is arguable that the left was an exception to the pattern of shifting allegiances, but even so left-wing sympathies permeated all factional groupings, while the main leftist faction, the Mujahideen-e Khalq organization, described itself as 'Islamic Marxist', explicitly revealing its 'Islamic' leanings.

The religious factions tended to be collections of individuals often associated with key ayatollahs who leaned in differing political directions. Thus, for example, Ayatollah Taleqani was widely supported by those with left-leaning sympathies, particularly for his emphasis on social justice and public welfare. Indeed, just as some avowed Marxists acquired Islamic clothes, so there were many cases of religious groups leaning towards the left. These tended to reflect the widespread support enjoyed by lay religious intellectuals, such as the recently deceased Ali Shariati, who himself had been influenced by French socialists. Far from being anti-Marxist, some clerics had a keen sense of the political and social value of Marxist thought; they might not agree with it, but they were certainly well versed in it. Ayatollah Khomeini himself, for instance, was widely criticized by his colleagues for teaching Western philosophy to his students – albeit in an

---

[11] The scale of the 'reign of terror' launched against the left, in particular after the bombing of the headquarters of the Islamic Republican Party, effectively eliminated the left as a distinct political force, if not as an ideological force.

[12] Indeed, it is worth bearing in mind that key social groups, including the traditional aristocracy (those who lost most in the land reform) and the bazaar, undoubtedly moved to support the religious factions against the left.

attempt to disprove the tenets of materialism. The chief ideologue of the Islamic Revolution, Ayatollah Motahhari, went further. He made it quite clear that he had more patience for Marx and Engels than the average Muslim, because at least they had tried to understand and change the world. This is a remarkable statement for one so commonly considered a pillar of the 'fundamentalist' establishment.

Religious nationalism

There were also significant ambiguities in the relationship of the revolutionaries with Iranian nationalism. Opponents of the revolution have been keen to paint the movement which overthrew the shah as anti-nationalist and to claim authentic nationalism for themselves. Yet it is quite clear that many, if not all, of the groups that had participated in the revolution had fought on the basis of highly nationalistic slogans. Indeed, the shah's fatal flaw was not necessarily his irreligiosity – although this was clearly held against him – but his apparent dependence on the United States and his failure to defend Iranian national culture, which included Islam. It is certainly true that the shah's unilateral decision to change the calendar of the country from the Islamic to an invented 'imperial' calendar in 1976 caused grave offence, but this had simply compounded the crisis of legitimacy that had surrounded him since the coup of 1953. The tendency to paint the shah as irreligious belies much of the 'Islamic' character of his political discourse in the late 1970s, just as the reverse characterizations of the revolutionaries tends to disguise their core nationalism. Of course, the nationalism espoused by the revolutionaries was more inclusive of religion than the narrow Persian chauvinism displayed by the Pahlavis; but in sanctifying the nation, the revolutionaries gave it greater ideological potential. In this they simply re-established the link between Shi'ism and Iranian identity noticed by E. G. Browne in the nineteenth century and developed by Kashani in the twentieth. Even the renowned Shi'a scholar Motahhari, in his study on Iranian contributions to Islam, revealed a certain sympathy for the achievements and contributions of the Iranians to Islam. Islam was good, but Iranian Islam was a potent combination. For all the universalism of the revolution, this distinction was assisted by the reality of Shi'a Islam as the dominant sect in Iran.

Nothing reveals this complicated inheritance better than the Constitution of the Islamic Republic adopted in 1979. Drafted by French-educated lawyers, it essentially drew upon the constitution of the French Fifth Republic, with additional layers intended to reflect the multiple traditions

45

which had cooperated in the revolution.[13] Much attention is given to the contradictory tensions expressed by the superimposition on its almost liberal democratic values of the authoritarian *velayat-e faqih* (Guardianship of the Jurisconsult). The latter is often interpreted as the first major 'coup' by a somewhat monolithic religious faction against the more secular groups, although this view tends to lump the religious groups into a single authoritarian parcel. Nevertheless, many members of the *ulema* and their supporters preferred an authoritarian political structure, and they were encouraged in this view by the perception of continued social anarchy. The concept of the governorship of the religious jurist had been debated among Shi'a theologians, somewhat erratically, for several centuries, and revolved around the notion that, in a nation faced with increasingly irreligious kings, supreme authority within the state should reside with the jurists. In the characteristically competitive environment of Shi'a academia, Khomeini's somewhat contentious and innovative (if logical) proposal was that this authority should reside with a single individual. In the absence of the Hidden Imam,[14] this jurist would exercise supreme authority within the constraints of the law – although it says something of the 'nationalization' of religion this process entailed that Khomeini later argued that even Islamic law could be suspended if the interests of the state were threatened. During the discussions on the constitution, vigorous debates took place concerning the 'nationality' of any future president, or indeed of the *velayat-e faqih*. Significantly, Khomeini sided with those who insisted on Iranian nationality for the president. What is remarkable about this development is the effective Iranianization of Islam: this was in essence an *Iranian* Islamic Revolution. Far more worrying was the fear, indeed recognition, of many quietist clerics that the process of politicization and nationalization would result in the removal of the *sacred* from Islam.

An unorthodox legacy

Many of these contradictions were reflected in the personality of Ayatollah Khomeini, and were both consequence and cause of his traditional charismatic authority. His relationship with his constituents may be characterized as both reciprocal and dialectic. As noted above, he was never in complete control of his situation, reacting to events as well as seeking to dictate them, and in order to establish at least a semblance of authority he

---

[13] See Abrahamian, 'Fundamentalism or Populism?', p. 33.

[14] In 'Twelver Shi'ism' there are twelve Imams descended from the Prophet, the twelfth of whom went into hiding in the ninth century – hence the Hidden Imam, who will return at the end of time.

had to appeal to a wide range of often disparate constituents. Inevitably, this process of ideological accommodation could go only so far, and many remained beyond the pale; but, by and large, Khomeini was able to appeal to democrats and nationalists through his overt populism, and to the orthodox *ulema* through theocratic authoritarianism. It is the latter image which has dominated, in part reflecting the many traditional religious constituents within the country, and the fact that many of his exiled opponents (some of whom had initially supported him) sought to emphasize his religious credentials to an astonished and credulous secular Western audience. The reality, which many in the West may find difficult to accept, is that Khomeini was a highly complex character who valued and understood the importance of popular participation. His neoplatonic conceptions of government allowed for the foundation of an Islamic Republic in which, in theory at least, free and fair elections would be held, and governments held accountable. Crucially, and much to the consternation of his orthodox opponents, he confirmed the right of women to vote. Sovereignty resided with God, but 'the affairs of the country must be administered on the basis of public opinion expressed by means of election.'[15] Further, it is important to recognize that for all its hegemonic tendencies, the Islamic Republic neither pursued nor in any way achieved totalitarian dimensions. Arbitrary power in Iran is a reflection less of ability than of inefficiency.

It is also important to recognize that Khomeini's attraction for the young was not based on naïve assumptions or on an unusual predilection for authority. The young were attracted less by subconscious Calvinistic leanings and more by the fact that Khomeini was an extremely unorthodox *mullah* who frequently came into conflict with his more austere colleagues. Indeed, he rebuked his fellow *ulema* on more than one occasion for their tendency, as he saw it, to stay in the Middle Ages:

This old father of yours had suffered more from stupid reactionary mollahs [*sic*] than anyone else. When theology meant no interference in politics, stupidity became a virtue. If a clergyman was able and aware of what was going on [in the world around him], they searched for a plot behind it. You were considered more pious if you walked in a clumsy way. Learning foreign languages was blasphemy, philosophy and mysticism were considered to be a sin and infidelity. In the Feiziyeh my young son Mostafa drank water from a jar. Since I was teaching philosophy, my son was considered to be religiously impure, so they washed the jar to purify it afterwards. Had this trend continued, I have

---

[15] Constitution of the Islamic Republic of Iran, Article 6.

no doubt the clergy and seminaries would have trodden the same path as the Christian Church did in the Middle Ages.[16]

Indeed, according to his son Ahmad Khomeini, 'What made him the Imam and led to the historic and victorious Islamic movement was the fact that he fought the backward, stupid, pretentious, reactionary clergy.'[17] This, he argued, was a far more important distinction for his father than opposing the United States. Far from being an austere ayatollah in the guise of Fazlollah Nuri, the firebrand of the Constitutional period who was subsequently executed, Khomeini seemed more akin to personages such as Jamal al Din al Afghani, Mudarris and Ayatollah Kashani. Indeed, much to the horror of his clerical colleagues, Khomeini seemed most in tune with the philosophical traditions in Islam, as his preference for heterodox Islamic philosophers such as Mulla Sadra indicated.

The ideological dimensions of power

Yet Khomeini was also driven by a hegemonic conception of the struggle in which he was involved, and it is this which has led critics to accuse him of totalitarian tendencies.[18] Khomeini himself appropriated language from left-wing ideologies, notably the concept of the oppressed struggling against the oppressors. As Abrahamian points out, much of Khomeini's political rhetoric 'would have been used by secular leftists rather than by clerical leaders'.[19] It seems reasonable to speculate that he was familiar with, if not influenced by, the ideological discourse of social revolutionary theorists, as seemingly borne out by his quest to uproot and replace not only a political structure but its accompanying world-view. Khomeini, of course, was not the first Iranian figure to harbour such ambitions: Mosaddeq had talked of the historical importance of the National Front, whose aims were a total regeneration of the country; the shah had established the Resurrection Party and talked of the revitalization of Iran. But the sanctification of the nation under Khomeini meant that this process could be implemented with a righteous ferocity and indignation arguably unimagined by his predecessors. The new discourse appealed not only to those who sought a restoration of authoritarianism, but also to youth bred

---

[16] Quoted in B. Moin, *Khomeini: Life of the Ayatollah* (London: I. B. Tauris, 1999), p. 276.
[17] Ibid.
[18] For an excellent discussion of the concept of 'hegemony' see Mouffe, 'Hegemony and Ideology in Gramsci', pp. 168–204.
[19] Abrahamian, 'Fundamentalism or Populism?', p. 27.

on the idealistic socialism of the Parisian Left Bank. In any event, the ideological dimension of the factional power struggles was never resolved; politically, the religious parties may have achieved dominance, but ideologically, the field remained open.

Causes of authoritarian domination

The dominance of the authoritarian tendency in the early stages of the revolution can be attributed to a number of factors. One was clearly a tendency towards authoritarianism among many of the *ulema*, who not long before had been staunch pillars of the monarchy for similar reasons. The principle of interpretation, important in philosophical and theological terms, also encouraged elitism: only those qualified to interpret could do so, and those properly qualified were a limited number of religious scholars. This principle also encouraged a paternalistic attitude towards the people. There was a clear tension here between the desire for a genuinely popular revolution which could claim considerable legitimacy – a desire that undoubtedly underpinned the republican aspects of government – and the fear that such popular movements were democratic in the worst Aristotelian interpretation of the term. On the one hand there developed a cult of the *sans-culottes*; on the other, many in the elites worried about how to control them. Some measure of control could be exercised through religion and religious order, but left-wing 'atheistic' groups lacked even this mechanism. In 1953, the establishment rallied behind the monarchy for fear of the consequences of a red revolution; in 1979, in the absence of the monarchy and in the presence of political transformation, the new, somewhat dislocated establishment (in particular the bazaar) rallied behind the *ulema* as the only source of familiar order in an otherwise bewildering maelstrom. Authoritarianism returned on the back of two durable fears: that of national disintegration, and that of a communist revolution. Iraq's invasion of Iran in 1980 compounded the sense of urgency.

The war

The war with Iraq encouraged authoritarianism but prevented the resolution of the many contradictions inherent in the political structure. In effect, the government was granted extraordinary powers as factions set aside their disputes to focus their attentions on the invader. The country was provided both with a respite from the internecine and seemingly inter-minable quarrelling and with a tangible enemy, on a par with the shah, on whom the nation could focus its hostility. In this way, the war truly was, as Khomeini argued, a blessing. In the short term, it allowed the government to settle scores; but as time passed, the prolongation of the war and the social discontent that accompanied it also forced a moderation in policies. The Iran–Iraq War was the first modern war fought by the Iranian state, and the first war of any type fought by Iran in 150 years. Nor was it a localized experience limited to the war front; it affected society at large, through conscription and through the targeting of civilians in the war of the cities. With casualties numbering over one million, few communities were left untouched. The war, along with the revolution, had profound social consequences.

In general terms the war taught Iranians political moderation and cynicism towards authority. Those who had rushed to enlist in the general euphoria of the revolution discovered that the brutality of war could have a dampening effect on zeal. The exhortations of the clerical leadership, taken with the realization that, contrary to previous conviction, the leadership could indeed be wrong, proved a difficult pill for many to swallow. For those who remained to the end convinced of victory, the fact that the Imam could accept the UN-inspired armistice after previously rejecting it was shocking evidence of the fallibility of man. Almost immediately people criticized Khomeini for taking so long to accept a cessation of hostilities, and the search was on to apportion blame. Khomeini was forced to respond by arguing that while the war had fault, there was no one to blame. Others, having fought for their country, were more demanding of the state on their return to civilian life; the social contract would have to be renegotiated. In short, the war began the final stages in the transformation of Iranians from 'subject' to 'citizen'.

Yet, for all that it moderated zeal, the war also left an economy ravaged and a society that was in some sense militarized and unable for economic reasons to demilitarize. This was to have serious consequences on the subsequent development of the state, in two respects. First, not only did a huge section of the population undergo military training and combat experi-ence, many also retained their arms. In this sense the postwar state never enjoyed a monopoly of coercive power over society. In addition, the great militia which had been called for by Khomeini, the *basij* (Islamic militia, literally 'mobilization'), in which it was hoped people of non-military age might volunteer in order to fight in the war, remained 'mobilized' for the simple reason that there were no jobs for its members to go to. Indeed, the *basij* proved a useful reservoir for absorbing much of the youthful population, which had expanded exponentially during the war years due to Khomeini's exhortation to procreation. The *basij* became by default a necessary tool of social control. But in ideological and psychological terms, demilitarization became a grave problem: cases of shell-shock were innumerable, and many veterans were unable to adjust to the realities of peace.

Secondly, and more profoundly, the central lesson of revolution and war alike was a simple one, and it confirms the status of the two combined as a historical watershed: for the first time, Iranians appreciated that political structures are not eternal and that even the most powerful of rulers, with the backing of the world's greatest superpower, could be confounded by an exercise of the popular will. Moreover, this popular will, in the right circumstances, could resist and inflict defeat upon invading forces, and territory so often lost by Iranian shahs over the previous two centuries could indeed be defended and retained. The importance of this realization for the psychological transformation of Iranians should not be underestimated. There was a palpable sense that a corner had been turned. Nothing was eternal, and nothing was predestined; even ayatollahs, as Khomeini was to show with devastating effect against Ayatollah Shariatmadari,[20] who suffered the unprecedented indignity of demotion, were not immune to this new political reality. Unsurprisingly, few within the new power elites of the Islamic Republic fully appreciated this change, and, having suppressed and contained social tensions throughout the war, these elites nurtured little expectation or indeed anticipation of the social and intellectual renaissance that was to follow.

---

[20] Ayatollah Shariatmadari was a leading member of the *ulema* who regularly disagreed with Ayatollah Khomeini. Following allegations of political subversion, Khomeini 'demoted' Shariatmadari, issuing an unprecedented decree to this effect.

4 Rafsanjani and the Ascendancy of the Mercantile Bourgeoisie

When Ali Akbar Hashemi Rafsanjani, then the powerful speaker of the Majlis (the Islamic Consultative Assembly or parliament), was elected president in 1989, he announced that the era of reconstruction had begun, thereby signifying that a new phase of the revolution had been inaugurated. Most studies have focused on the literal implications of this change, assuming the economic aspects of the reconstruction to be an extension of the political settlement of the 1980s. Yet far more significant were the changes that Rafsanjani inaugurated not only in political structure but in political substance.[1] It will be argued here that the 'reconstruction' alluded to by Rafsanjani, while signifying a concerted effort at economic development, was far more emphatically the construction of a mercantile *hegemony*,[2] in which Rafsanjani sought to compensate for the absence of Khomeini's charismatic authority by developing a sustainable political structure founded on, but not exclusive to, the commercial power of the bazaar.[3] In this sense, Rafsanjani, himself a pistachio trader and former property developer, oversaw the construction and consolidation of what can be characterized as a 'mercantile bourgeois republic', founded upon an alliance with the traditional merchants and administered through a large bureaucracy dominated, in true patrimonial style, by himself.

---

[1] Ehteshami has forcefully argued that Rafsanjani's presidency marks the beginning of the second republic: A. Ehteshami, *After Khomeini: The Iranian Second Republic* (London: Routledge, 1995), esp. pp. 114–15.

[2] It is important to note that what is being stressed here is the development of a tendency dictated by a particular world-view, rather than by a 'class' in a socio-economic sense. This is by definition intended to be not a rigorous categorization, but an expansive ideological tendency, possessing a core but continually extending, with varying degrees of success, towards the periphery.

[3] For a definition of 'bazaar', see ch. 2 above, n. 19.

The roots and development of the 'mercantile bourgeois republic'

While the roots of this particular political configuration are to be found in the revolution itself, it was not until Rafsanjani's presidency that the mercantile bourgeoisie, as a social and ideological force, came to dominate the Iranian state and to reap the rewards of their support for the Islamic Revolution. The role of Rafsanjani in their passage to prominence warrants closer examination than it has generally received.

It is often argued that the Islamic Revolution and overthrow of the shah brought about the replacement of the comprador bourgeoisie with the traditional Iranian bourgeoisie as characterized by the bazaar.[4] In this thesis, which bears scrutiny, the 'capitalists' who emerged following the White Revolution were tied to foreign interests, an affiliation reflected in their cultural tastes and inclinations. The traditional bourgeoisie (represented by the bazaar), who had seen their interests eroded by this new bourgeoisie and feared further attacks by the shah on their social and economic position, mobilized to challenge and ultimately remove him, in the process enabling themselves to regain their own position. As a group, then, they had much to gain and much to expect from a revolutionary victory; and indeed they did achieve a great deal in the first few years thereafter. However, they were but one of the many groups and one of the many reasons behind the success of the revolution; and so, while they enjoyed a slice of the cake and their interests were protected, during Khomeini's time they were not the dominant force in the new state, which remained, as a result of revolution and war, politically centralized and socially fluid. Khomeini might preach in favour of private property and the rights of the bazaar, but this did not necessarily entail uninhibited capital accumulation. The leader of the revolution had other constituents too. Furthermore, the exigencies of the war meant that the public sector dominated the economy, leaving little room for mercantile manoeuvre outside the remit of the state, and those with immediate access to the levers of power. It was only with the war over, and Khomeini dead, that Rafsanjani's economic liberalization policies allowed the mercantile bourgeoisie to participate in capital accumulation relatively unfettered by the state.

---

[4] See e.g. Ehteshami, *After Khomeini*, p. 5; and, for a left-wing perspective, B. Jazani, *Capitalism and Revolution in Iran* (London: Zed, 1980). For an excellent exposition of the comprador bourgeoisie see A. Ehteshami, *Political Upheaval and Socio-economic Continuity: The Case of Iran*, Research Unit for the Study of Economic Liberalisation (RUSEL) working paper no. 6, Exeter University.

As the name suggests, Iran's *mercantile* bourgeoisie must be distinguished from the industrial bourgeoisie familiar to Western discourse. The former term applies in those societies where capitalist development is dominated by merchants, whose principal form of capital accumulation is trade. It is their need to dominate this trade that leads them to extend their activities into production. This line of progression is contrasted by Marx with that in which industrialists accumulate capital for the purposes of production and move from there to dominate and control trade. Thus, as Giddens argues:

> there are two contrasting historical modes of progression into capitalist production. The first is where a segment of the merchant class moves over from purely trading operations to take a direct hand in production ... However, this form of capitalist formation soon becomes 'an obstacle to a real capitalist mode of production and declines with the development of the latter'. The second avenue of capitalist development is, according to Marx, 'the really revolutionary way'. Here individual producers themselves accumulate capital, and move from production to expand the sphere of their activities to include trade.[5]

The revolution opened up production, previously dominated by the Pahlavi state and its allies, to the merchant classes; but it was only under Rafsanjani that they were able to take serious advantage of these opportunities. The parastatal organizations, such as the vast religious foundations, effectively became vehicles by which the bazaar and the broader revolutionary establishment gained access to the economic resources of the country. The shift in this direction by the Foundation of the Oppressed (a vast religious foundation-cum-conglomerate formed on the back of the Pahlavi Foundation, and other assorted confiscated assets, whose stated function was to assist the 'oppressed') was most marked under the management of Mohsen Rafiqdoust, whose domination of this conglomerate lasted from 1989 until the summer of 1999. Indeed, this foundation in many ways has come to epitomize the ascendancy of the mercantile bourgeoisie and its dominance over the country's economy. Its desire to gain a foothold in the oil industry is a good example of the mercantile bourgeoisie's attempts to extend its activities into production (the oil industry in this case being the ultimate type of production and thus revenue), while the oil ministry's protests against such a move represent attempts to restrict this expansion.

[5] A Giddens, *Capitalism and Modern Social Theory* (Cambridge: Cambridge University Press, 1971), p. 33.

Mercantile interests in production also extended to the Persian carpet trade, where a trader will commission a carpet and farm out its production to rural artisans and weavers, whose pay for this sophisticated work is usually a minuscule fraction of the sale price. If ever there was a case of the alienation of labour, the Iranian carpet trade must be it! Another less obvious example is Rafsanjani's own hold on the pistachio trade. In this case, Rafsanjani, a producer, was not in control of the country's entire production of pistachios, but he did establish the mechanism by which he could dominate their sale and export and consequently indirectly determine production.

What might thus be described as a 'bourgeois republic' did of course develop incrementally over a decade, and the process was not without its challenges and tensions. It is not the purpose of this analysis to reduce the Iranian political economy to but one of its facets. Yet the commercialization that took hold during the 1990s, as well as the opposition it engendered, overrode other tendencies in a pluralistic society. The accumulation of capital driven by the merchants has indeed become the dominant motif of Iranian society, encouraging the belief that every Iranian is a trader at heart. Arguably, this development is to a great extent a consequence of economic necessity and personal insecurity rather than of some inherent genetic impulse. Certainly there exists a curious interdependence between patrimonial insecurity and mercantile capitalism. The traditional networks of patrimonialism and the absence of a rational/legal framework allow the informality of mercantile capitalism to flourish without fear of accountability. At the same time, the absence of transparency and the fear of extralegal measures encourage the rapid accumulation of capital and, crucially, its export to safe havens overseas. So explicit has this commercialization become that Iran has adopted the unusual, perhaps unique, practice of broadcasting commercial advertisements 'within' television programmes, in the form of streaming banners.

The ascendancy of the mercantile bourgeoisie has been accompanied by the reinstitution of patrimonial politics, dominated in his own ascendancy by Hashemi Rafsanjani, who extended, presided over and manipulated the bureaucracy developed by the erstwhile prime minister, Mir Hussein Musavi. It is important to bear in mind that it is the juxtaposition of these two distinct political structures which has resulted in the peculiar characteristics of post-Khomeini Iran, defined here as the 'mercantile bourgeois republic'. The patrimonial ruler requires mercantile support, while the mercantile bourgeoisie require the political protection of the sympathetic patrimonial ruler in order to flourish. The conjunction represents an alliance of vested interests in which each side encourages the development and prosperity of the other, within specific spheres of influence. Should one seek to intrude into the sphere of the other, as occurred in 1997, then the alliance is likely to come under extreme pressure and may indeed dissolve. In many ways, therefore, each has also proved a *constraint* on the development of the other.

So effective was Rafsanjani's man-management that in many ways the bureaucracy has been moulded to his own image and in effect become an extension of his household. It must be borne in mind, however, that these ties reflect a particular image which he has been able to cultivate and develop. This image has not been without its critics. The emphatic re-establishment of patrimonialism was a consequence of the routinization of charisma which followed Khomeini's death in 1989. While Ayatollah Khomeini embodied both the authority of charisma and that of patrimonialism, after his death these characteristics were divided between his two political heirs: Ayatollah Khamene'i, the new Supreme Leader, was expected to inherit and extend the charismatic qualities while, in the presidency, Rafsanjani became the quintessential patrimonialist. That is not to argue that each exclusively sought to use one particular source of authority, simply that each had one dominant technique.

In the event, of course, Khamene'i was unconvincing as a 'charismatic' leader largely because his theological credentials were viewed with derision by most clerics. He had not, for instance, submitted the required thesis (*resaleh*) necessary for consideration as an ayatollah, and his promotion to the lofty status of Supreme Leader was regarded as essentially political. Khomeini himself, contrary to tradition, had in effect announced Khamene'i's promotion, and there was no general acclamation. This political appointment was later turned to good effect by his supporters and apologists for the system, who acknowledged his theological weaknesses but argued that an ayatollah could be 'made' for a number of reasons, in this case because of Khamene'i's expertise in the field of politics.[6] The weakness of Khamene'i's position deepened when it became apparent that old age would begin to take its toll on a number of the most senior clerics in the country – the venerable objects of emulation whose quiescence in the absence of positive endorsement was interpreted as general approval for the political order.[7] Their deaths would leave the field dangerously open for mavericks, in much the same way as Khomeini had benefited from the vacuum left by Ayatollah Borujerdi's death in 1960. In the end, the new generation of aspiring senior clerics came to an understanding with the

---

[6] View conveyed to the author by a senior ayatollah.
[7] Khomeini had always argued that no two ayatollahs were ever likely to agree on points of acute dispute and that disagreements with respect to the concept of *velayat-e faqih* had to be expected. He, of course, could ride out any such criticism.

political establishment – but not before some attempts were made, however imprudently, to parachute in Khamene'i as the new object of emulation. This possibility was generally greeted with incredulity, and eventually an uneasy compromise was reached by which Khamene'i was allocated responsibility for the faithful beyond Iran's borders while Iranians themselves were free, as tradition dictated, to choose their own object of emulation. This peculiar division of responsibilities did little to enhance the prestige of the Supreme Leader, and Khamene'i, by nature inclined to the moderate wing of the revolutionary establishment, found himself having to be more harsh than Khomeini, having none of the room for manoeuvre of the latter, in order to overcome this credibility gap.

In personal terms, the general outcome was not unwelcome to Rafsanjani. While he had to compensate for the absence of charismatic authority by extending the tentacles of patrimonial domination and cultivating the financially important constituency of the mercantile community, the fundamental weakness of the leadership by extension enhanced his own position within the system. In addition, it allowed him to cultivate a charismatic persona of his own – an exercise endowed with credibility by his political confidence and theatrical flair. In short, Rafsanjani was a showman with the populist touch, and he was well aware that the Iranian public was anxious for something different following the war years. So, while Khamene'i tried to outdo the public austerity of Khomeini, Rafsanjani, in contrast, portrayed himself as easy-going and relaxed. Above all, as his own accumulating wealth indicated, it was seemingly acceptable to earn and enjoy the fruits of wealth.

In social terms Rafsanjani was a moderate, encouraging more relaxed attitudes to religious mores and cultivating the youth vote by unwisely suggesting that sexual frustrations could be allayed by indulging in 'temporary marriage', for which, he argued, all that was required was a verbal contract. The near-scandal this produced forced a hasty revision of the idea; but it serves as a reminder that in the aftermath of the war Rafsanjani was widely regarded as something of a cosmopolitan, 'enlightened' *mullah*. In political terms too, Rafsanjani talked the language of democracy, although it was never quite clear what he meant by this. Certainly, those who worked for him commented on his enlightened views, while foreign correspondents, attracted by his obvious charm, felt that there was more to him than met the eye. There was much reason, then, to believe that Rafsanjani was the enlightened leader people were waiting for. Yet while it would be going too far to call him an autocrat, there is little doubt that Rafsanjani's dominant political philosophy was that of a bureaucratic centralist in the Weberian mould, and that this in time would foster a patronizing attitude towards the general populace.

There is also little doubt that Rafsanjani believed in political reform and that his reading of history encouraged him, among others, to believe that political repression is incompatible with economic development. The consequences of such unbalanced development would lead, as Rafsanjani himself pointed out, to the sort of revolutionary upheaval that resulted in the overthrow of the shah. He was anxious in particular to loosen some of the restrictions which had been imposed during the war years, in particular with respect to freedom of speech and the legality of the political parties. But, to an even greater degree than his social pronouncements, his political inclinations were never effectively extended beyond rhetoric. He found some of his initiatives constrained by social inertia and political opposition; but fundamental to his failure to address the structural problems facing the state was his own lack of political will, shaped by the conviction that economic reform must take first priority and, crucially, that his own myriad interests should not be threatened. Indeed, much like the shah before him, Rafsanjani's good intentions were hampered primarily by his own weaknesses, principally an appreciation of wealth and the desire to be a historic figure. Both these weaknesses made him vulnerable to flattery and ultimately were to alienate him from the populace from whom he had derived so much initial support.

Not that Rafsanjani ever sought to relinquish the popular support he craved. Indeed, his disposition to populism was ultimately to invite criticism from the traditional mercantile community. In his first administration, between 1989 and 1994, Rafsanjani oversaw a major redirection of the economy away from state control and towards trade liberalization. In the aftermath of the war, supported by ministers who favoured the free market and reintegration into the international economy, Rafsanjani encouraged an import boom that was ultimately to hamstring his administration. He also orchestrated the removal of the left-wing statist deputies in the Majlis during the 1992 election – a move which at the time was seen to confirm his moderate image. The religious leftists were, after all, generally regarded as unreconstructed revolutionaries at least a decade adrift in the political progress of the revolution. In their place came a raft of right-wing free marketeers. At the same time, Rafsanjani inaugurated a period of *pak-sazi* (literally, 'clean-up') within the administration, intended to remove some of the diehard dogmatists from sensitive posts in the government (a process whose limits have since become all too apparent). In essence, Rafsanjani was seeking to *demobilize* politics and society following the war, and to *rationalize* them in the service of economic reform.

How effective this could be in the absence of serious political reform was soon to become apparent. What seemed, in fact, to be taking shape was a society and economy directed not so much to the service of reform as to the servicing of the commercial community. This commercial community was small and regarded by many Iranians as a reconstructed elite on the Pahlavi model. Indeed, by the mid-1990s a number of commentators were arguing that a new 'thousand families' were emerging in Iran. For many revolutionaries, on the left or otherwise, this was exactly what the revolution had fought to avoid. It seemed that the Pahlavi monarchy had returned, albeit with different actors and an indigenous bourgeoisie.

Rafsanjani was himself well aware of the political dangers of acceding too completely to the wishes of the mercantile community; but he found himself increasingly trapped by what may be described as a paradox of sultanism. Since the bazaar had funded the right-wing election victory of 1992, it was quite clear that they wanted to reap their rewards. After 1992, Rafsanjani's patrimonial populist leanings led him into further clashes with his mercantile backers, who wanted political and social order to facilitate their control of the economy. It soon became clear that their definition of the 'free market' really meant a market free from the state and controlled by them. Rafsanjani found it difficult to obstruct this monopolistic tendency because in essence he was part of it, and everyone knew it. Indeed, his second administration, from 1993 to 1997, was characterized by clashes with a Majlis originally thought to be supportive of his programme. The result was an embattled and virtually lame duck president eager to compensate for his inability to push through fundamental reform by highlighting various grandiose infrastructural projects which his administration had inaugurated. These all cost more money than the government in fact had access to, and it was apparent to close observers of the administration that claims of a balanced budget were pure spin. Wry commentators noted that Rafsanjani had a penchant for inaugurating projects but there was little evidence of their ever being completed. Nevertheless, those within the Rafsanjani political orbit, including many bureaucrats, remained loyal to a politician who appealed to their patrimonial sensibilities, and Rafsanjani retained popularity among both the bureaucrats and, to a greater or lesser extent, the business community. Rafsanjani was, and remains, very much the businessman's president.

Among those outside this hallowed circle, views were not quite so sympathetic. Rafsanjani's failure to deal with the challenge posed by the right was seen as a reflection of his own political views and his concern to retain as much as possible of the financial fruits of his efforts. The unreconstructed left found that the political wilderness was an excellent school for popular politics, and drew closer to those who had been excluded altogether from the political life of the country since the early days of the revolution. These two groups, reformed and reconstructed as a 'new left', were convinced of the need for social justice and appalled at the direction being taken by the revolutionary movement under Rafsanjani and his mercantile allies. Far from serving the interests of the 'oppressed', the revolution was being redefined in the interests of a mercantile elite whose access to the corridors of power provided them with access to capital. Rafsanjani himself was seen less as patrimonial and more as patronizing and imperious, while his political leanings were interpreted as essentially centralist and monopolistic. His attempts to liberalize the press were seen as little more than an effort to control and manipulate an emerging public sphere[8] – reflecting the salient fact that the extended political consciousness that had emerged from the revolution, though subject to containment during the war years, had not been suppressed. Rafsanjani's populism was seen as an acknowledgment of the need to address this new political reality and to control it through manipulation rather than suppression. This would also legitimize and strengthen his position with respect to the monopolistic right. Thus the left saw Rafsanjani presiding over the quintessential 'bourgeois public sphere'.

Their distaste for Rafsanjani's half-hearted attempts to win popular favour turned to contempt when they contemplated the mercantile elite he seemed to represent and reflect. Here stood the financial pillars of the new authoritarian establishment – the new 'thousand families' – whose accumulation of capital and exhibition of wealth contrasted with the general impoverishment of the majority of Iranians, many of whom had returned from the war expecting something better from the state they had fought for. Indeed, the disparities in wealth distribution had become so stark that they began to affect loyalties within the bureaucracy, and many civil servants began to try their hand at trade. While it was well known that the Revolutionary Guards were involved in commerce, there was growing displeasure at the commercial ventures afoot in other governmental circles. The charge of corruption was becoming widespread; and it says much about the commercialization of society that when the Ministry of Intelligence was instructed to investigate these allegations (and make some high-profile arrests), the result was that ministry employees themselves proved more inclined to join the trend than halt it! Mercantile capitalism, it seemed, took few prisoners in its quest to dominate Iranian society, and commentators lamented the corruption not only in financial but in moral terms. The materialism that had made Rafsanjani popular in the years after the war now appeared to be accelerating beyond anyone's control.

[8] See J. L. Cohen and A. Arato, *Civil Society and Political Theory* (Cambridge, MA: MIT Press, 1992), p. 50.

This was an even starker problem, indeed a blatant contradiction, when contrasted with the avowed 'Islamic' intentions of the government; and yet the 'Islamic' pretensions of the new order made the situation considerably worse. Economic greed, it seemed, had forged a political alliance among the leadership, the presidency and the mercantile community, and a dogmatic and authoritarian interpretation of Islam would be used to sustain this particular relation of domination in public life. Politics in many ways became a three-way contest among these groups, with both Rafsanjani and Khamene'i playing to the mercantile constituency while competing with each other.

While some clerics viewed involvement in politics with trepidation, others saw political activity as one of the chief legacies of Khomeini. It would, they conjectured, ensure that Islam remained relevant to the needs of society. Yet others regarded political activism less as a tool of popular emancipation than as a means of control. These authoritarian clerics, who have since been labelled 'conservatives', drew on the authoritarian legacy of Khomeini and the war years and tended to ignore his more populist pronouncements. Their interpretation of the state was elitist but not modernist, and their patronizing attitude towards the bulk of the population complemented the patrimonialism of Rafsanjani, notwithstanding differences in detail between the two approaches. Arguably, the Islam they espoused had more to do with the exercise of power than with the extension of faith, and this was growing more apparent to both lay and religious observers on the outside of the establishment. In Iran, religion really was in danger of becoming the opium of the masses.

The extension of the mercantile bourgeois hegemony and the drive towards the construction of a bourgeois republic can be seen as an attempt to reconstitute the bureaucratic–authoritarian political structure of the Pahlavi era with different beneficiaries. In many ways, it can be argued that it represented the 'normalization' of revolutionary Iran. But these developments did not take place in a social vacuum. On the contrary, society was more politically conscious than it had ever been, and although many were exhausted by the trauma of revolution and war, few were willing to return to the *status quo ante bellum*. If political consciousness did not immediately translate into constructive coordinated activism, this had much to do with the tools of state control and the widespread anticipation that the Rafsanjani administration would deliver to the mass of the people. Certainly the rhetoric emanating from leaders seemed to suggest that the establishment was aware of the importance of popular support, and people were constantly being reminded that the difference between the Islamic Republic and the monarchy was that the former enjoyed deep social roots:

it was, in short, sustained not only by divine providence but by popular legitimacy. This was, after all, the meaning of the dual heritage of the 'Islamic Republic', bringing together in a miraculous synthesis the divine and the popular.

Yet while it was true that the Islamic Republic enjoyed social roots and social penetration on a scale which would have been envied by the Pahlavis, it was increasingly clear to many people that attitudes towards the masses among the elite of the bourgeois republic differed little from those of the Pahlavis and their courtiers. Indeed, while Khomeini had exhorted his followers to stay with the people and not become alienated from them, the new bourgeois elite were proving just as detached and uprooted from their social context as their forebears. One tale relates how a Revolutionary Guard officer at a wedding banquet complained that the influx of 'common people' into his neighbourhood had 'forced' him to move further into north Tehran.[9] This new political and economic elite increasingly took the view that while the masses might be useful to acclaim or affirm the policies of the leadership, they had no place in guiding or directing policy. Simply, the elites knew better. So developed did this perspective become that some right-wing deputies in the Majlis insisted that the *velayat-e faqih* was in fact absolute, a distinction which had not been afforded Khomeini – although arguably his charisma precluded the need for any formal distinction. Others questioned the need for elections at all and challenged the concept of the 'republic', arguing instead that what should be instituted was an Islamic state. These may have been arguments on the margin, but they served notice to many on the left and the populace at large that the dual legacy of Ayatollah Khomeini was being interpreted with a view to contemporary political needs. Indeed, in many ways they simply reflected the contest between Rafsanjani and Khamene'i, with any elevation of the latter being seen as a challenge to the power of the former.

Nevertheless, beyond this exclusive circle at the head of the regime, social forces were at work. Throughout the Rafsanjani administration society was mobilizing, partly for ideological reasons and partly as a result of material changes. Beyond the impacts of the revolution and war, which were profound, there was the demographic impact of a dramatic increase in the birth rate throughout the 1980s. Rising to a peak of some 3.9% per year, this increase has effectively doubled the size of the Iranian population since the Revolution; moreover, the proportion of young people has risen dramatically, with an estimated 70% being under the age of 30. This development, along with the social and economic role of women during the war

9 Recounted to the author.

years, has had an enormous impact on social attitudes. The position of women was particularly important in socio-political terms, especially since they not only had the vote but were seen as pragmatic in their use of it. Rafsanjani was well aware of this factor in electoral politics and sought to capitalize on it, but others of a more authoritarian slant were dismissive and argued that women should be denied the vote, since it was un-Islamic to grant it to them. Rafsanjani, much to the irritation of these groups, on the contrary seemed to encourage female participation in political life, particularly through the activities of his increasingly outspoken daughter Faezeh Hashemi, whose advocacy of Islamic women's rights offended conservative sensibilities.

This points to another material determinant of social change, in that the politics of the elites frequently spilled over into society at large. In short, while Khomeini's charisma had drawn the factions towards him, the absence of charisma and the growing crisis of legitimacy in the bourgeois republic encouraged the various groups to seek support and legitimacy elsewhere. During Khomeini's lifetime the Islamic sources of legitimacy were emphasized; after his death, greater attention was focused on the republican and popular sources of legitimacy. The effect of this redirection was to enlarge the sphere of popular political activity – to encourage the development of civil society. As Cohen and Arato point out, 'While this effort from above is always expected to stay within careful limits, it cannot amount to a complete farce if the goal of legitimacy is to be attained, and the elements of democratisation that are established in this way are by definition unpredictable and cannot be kept within any predefined limits.'[10]

In 1990s Iran, this dilemma was compounded by the need to co-opt the populace into the economic development package. It was quite clear to most economists, for instance, that Iran's dependence on oil revenues was not a satisfactory basis on which to plan for economic and industrial development. Government revenue could not be held hostage to the fluctuations in the oil price, and indeed some considered that its reliance on the sector made Iran vulnerable to manipulations in the oil market. Other sources of revenue had to be discovered, and it was generally agreed that private sources should be tapped, either through taxation or through the issue of bonds and shares. Both attempts show the limits of the mercantile bourgeois state and its traditional approaches. In order, for instance, to inculcate a tax culture, it was important to be able to audit and assess private wealth, the vast majority of which resided with the mercantile bourgeoisie. There was little chance that the state would be able to extract

---

[10] Cohen and Arato, *Civil Society and Political Theory*, p. 50.

tax revenue from this group, especially since many considered the payment of Islamic taxes to be sufficient. In the absence of any success here, others were less willing to oblige, and indeed found it incredible that they should be made to pay while others much better off would get away with paying nothing. So long as only those who work for the government and whose pay can be docked at source generally pay income tax, the impact of this burden is not likely to be a positive one. Coming increasingly to see their relationship to the state as one of citizenship, Iranians could not be expected to feel much obligation to an economic elite which resisted political change. While some in the government accepted this corollary, many refused to accept the obvious logic of taxation.

The attempt to distribute shares and raise money through bond issues also reflected the limits of reform. Rafsanjani was keen to pursue privatization as a means to raise revenue and also to enable the distribution of economic largesse to a consequently grateful populace. The scheme was modelled on the notions of the 'share-owning democracy' conceived in the Thatcher-Reagan era, and as if to emphasize the link a number of Iranian-American economists were drafted in to set it up.[11] The political priorities soon became apparent when it was noted that the shares had to be cheap enough to be within the reach of the 'average' purchaser, even though this would make the whole scheme uneconomic. Of even greater concern to the government was the belief that the shares could be bought up by 'undesirables'. The solution to this perceived problem was ingenious, if somewhat self-defeating. It was decided to establish unit trust bodies, run by members of the political establishment; these would buy and sell on behalf of the people, who would place their savings at the disposal of the trusts. Not surprisingly, given the growing gulf between society and its rulers, few people were attracted by the proposition. Nevertheless, at the very least the exercise convinced a number of government officials and economists that political reform was a necessity that could not be delayed much longer.

Developments in intellectual life

Another development which broadened the intellectual horizons of society as a whole, and those of the intellectual elites in particular, was the impact of globalization and the information revolution it had brought with it. The establishment had sought to control the flow of knowledge and information,

[11] Interview with author.

but this had repeatedly proved to be too difficult a task, emphasizing once again that whatever the 'totalitarian' pretensions of some sectors of the political establishment, control of this kind was far from ever being achieved. Thus, for example, in the 1980s the government had sought to restrict the use of fax machines, but it discovered that there was a flourishing illegal trade, and subsequently legalized their use. Similarly, an initial ban on video cassette recorders was soon lifted when it became obvious that members of the establishment were themselves using the machines, ostensibly to watch the 'speeches of the Imam'. Videotapes themselves were restricted, until this too was found to be a losing gambit; today officially licensed video outlets rent and/or sell sanctioned videos. The illicit trade, of course, continues and has been encouraged by the technological advances which have made it easier. Thus the advent of DVD drives has made monitoring well-nigh impossible, and Majlis deputies have recently argued that people should be allowed to watch what they want in the privacy of their own homes. Some argue that this is a legitimate right, pointing to the admonitions of Ayatollah Khomeini (see above, page 43), while others increasingly accept that there is little point in attempting to resist the march of technology. It is this view which has resulted in positive encouragement of internet use. Indeed, in contrast with the somewhat half-hearted attempts to ban satellite dishes, there has been no attempt to ban use of the internet, and it was striking that both presidential candidates in the 1997 election used websites to convey their messages.

While it may be argued that internet access would in any case be limited to those members of the political and economic elites who could afford access to computers, there is considerable evidence to suggest that technological penetration of society is far deeper than might be expected. This, of course, reflects the integrated nature of society. Western films and satellite programmes, for example, would be watched not only by relatively wealthy owners but also by poorer members of the extended family, as well as servants and employees. In south Tehran, for instance, prior to the official ban on satellite dishes, it was well known that collectives sprang up to facilitate the purchase of dishes, while tickets were sold for particular programmes. Bouncers would guard the entrance against interference from representatives of the state, and indeed there was little that the state could do. Computer access is in some ways more restricted, and there is a world of difference between the internet cafés of north Tehran and circumstances in the south, but nevertheless many ordinary people have access to both satellite television and computers in their places of work. Many ministries allow access to international news channels on the pretext that government business necessitates it. Indeed, the very notion that Iran was in some ways isolated from the information revolution is incorrect. While the revolution and war hindered and definitely delayed development, the 1990s witnessed a burst of energy intended to close the gap. As one consultant commented, 'Iranians are technology hungry', and as ministries and businesses sought to close the technology gap, computer consultancies, as in other countries, mushroomed.[12] There were of course limits to what could be done; imports, especially from the United States, remained restricted; yet it is remarkable, under the circumstances, what was achieved. True to their nature, Iranians were proving uniquely able to copy, imitate and in some cases improve on technology they acquired.

Foreign correspondents have not surprisingly been most struck by the enthusiasm shown by the clergy for this new technology, reflecting perhaps the continued popular misperceptions regarding the Shi'a *ulema*. While the image of turbaned clerics accessing the internet undoubtedly makes good copy,[13] it should also serve as a reminder that the perception that they are opposed to science and technology is one that Khomeini himself rejected.

> The claim that Islam is against modern (technical) innovations is the same claim made by the deposed Mohammad Reza Pahlavi that these people (Islamic Revolutionaries) want to travel with four-legged animals, and this is nothing but an idiotic accusation. For, if by manifestations of civilisation it is meant technical innovations, new products, new inventions, and advanced industrial techniques which aid in the progress of mankind, then never has Islam, or any other monotheist religion, opposed their adoption. On the contrary, Islam and the Holy Qoran emphasise science and industry.[14]

Indeed, it can be argued that internet use has been given a boost in the belief that it is the ideal vehicle for 'exporting the revolution'. Moreover, it reveals a significant shift in attitude, from one of internalization to one of externalization. Far from advocating an insular purity, many clerics began to argue that by embracing the new technology and harnessing it to good use as they saw it, a more confident Islamic Revolution would be better able to spread the word. This was in many ways the intellectual version of Rafsanjani's dictum that economic success would best sell the revolution to a sceptical public, both at home and abroad. Thus Rafsanjani also

---

[12] Interview with author.

[13] It is worth remembering that this peculiar sartorial identity is a direct consequence of the dress reforms imposed by Reza Shah, and as such the distinctive image is itself a consequence of modernization.

[14] Khomeini's last will and testament, quoted in D. Eickelman and J. Piscatori, *Muslim Politics* (Princeton: Princeton University Press, 1996), p. 22.

encouraged the development of 'popular' television and its broadcast abroad. Critics on the right argued that this was polluting the purity of the revolution; the left viewed it simply as a further extension of the bourgeois public sphere. However interpreted, it did begin a process of liberalization. Yet in the long term the impact of greater accessibility to religious texts, uploaded to the internet and available on CD-ROM, is likely to be more profound. More people than ever will have direct access to material that was once the exclusive preserve of the *ulema*. One ayatollah responsible for the computerization of sacred texts admitted, 'This silent revolution will have incalculable consequences.'[15]

This aside, one of the most interesting developments in the seminaries has been the development of the study of Western philosophy, in the belief that in order to defeat your opponents you must first know and understand them; accordingly, in order to confront the West one must appreciate the challenge and provide intellectual alternatives. As Mojtahed Shabestari argued in 1988:

The fact that our seminaries have separated their path from that of the social sciences and are minding their own business without any aware-ness of the developments in these disciplines has brought us to the present condition in which we have no philosophy of civil rights or philosophy of ethics. [Furthermore] we have neither a political nor an economic philosophy. Without having a set of solid and defendable theories in these fields, how can we talk of universal or permanent laws and values? How can we [even] gain admission to the international scientific communities?[16]

This argument underlines the hegemonic and ideological nature of the Islamic Revolution, and the conviction of many revolutionaries that the revolution was as much an intellectual renaissance and challenge to the 'West' (including in this case Russia) and its overriding philosophy of materialism, as it was a political struggle. The concept of 'independence' was at least as much an ideological project as a political and economic goal. This crucial conviction, which remains vital to any understanding of Iranian political development since 1979, also sheds more light on the growing animosity between the left and Rafsanjani during the period of his presidency. His emphasis on economic development was regarded by

[15] Ayatollah Kawrani, quoted in E. Rouleau, 'The Islamic Republic of Iran: Paradoxes and Contra-dictions in a Changing Society', *Le Monde Diplomatique*, June 1995.
[16] Quoted in M. Borujerdi, *Iranian Intellectuals and the West* (New York: Syracuse University Press, 1996), p. 168.

many as a return to the material corruption of the late monarchy and a failure to address the fundamental reason behind the revolution.

In coming to know an intellectual opponent, of course, one may tend to appropriate and adapt those elements of his or her arguments which appeal. In Iran this process began first with the attempt intellectually to refute communism and socialism. Khomeini himself had sought to do this in his own lectures on Marxism, and, as noted above, he was not averse to appropriating language he found useful. As also noted, this was even more obvious in the writings of Ayatollah Motahhari. After the revolution, the assault on the left was not limited to political retribution; it also involved intellectual scrutiny of the rival philosophy. One of the key architects of this intellectual assault was Abdolkarim Soroush, who sought to deconstruct the dogma of the left as he saw it, and in the process became more familiar with social theory and epistemological tools which would prove useful in a later intellectual contest. Another aspect of this activity was the growing familiarization with the broader sweep of Western philosophy, to begin with principally anti-Marxist texts, but eventually covering a broad range of material. Roleau recounts the following curriculum at a seminary: 'The curriculum, according to the philosophy professor who invited me to his class, runs the gamut from the ancient Greeks to Heidegger and including Kant, Hegel and Marx. Some of his students, who say they have read Saint Simon and Auguste Comte, expressed regret that Foucault had not yet been translated into Farsi.'[17] Indeed, if Western philosophy was considered impure by many *ulema* prior to the revolution, the opposite was increasingly true afterwards. Some senior clerics were positively proud to exhibit their knowledge of the Western tradition; one ayatollah spent the better part of two hours articulating his views on Nietzsche to the author.[18]

Nevertheless, some observers have criticized the level of understanding attained and have argued that a lack of access to texts, or even an inherent bias, has ensured that any such investigation into Western philosophy remains incomplete. This judgment has been used as a justification for not taking such developments seriously. Yet the criticism itself is misplaced, and reflects prejudice on the part of Western observers. No philosophical discussion or debate occurs in a vacuum, and while it may be true that textual analysis has been constrained by the inaccessibility of key texts, the debates have been genuine and serious, and if they reflect local concerns and perspectives, this is to be expected. This does not make them any less

---

[17] Rouleau, 'The Islamic Republic of Iran', p. 3.
[18] Interview with the author.

authentic, but it does represent an important instance of the transplantations of Western philosophy from one tradition to another. In any case, whatever the limitations on the availability of texts, it is fair to point out that there are few Western scholars who can lay claim to having read, let alone understood, everything Marx or Hegel (for example) wrote. It is a matter of selection and interpretation.

It is, indeed, in the hermeneutic tradition that the appropriation and adaptation of scholarly texts has been most explicit.[19] There are a number of reasons for this. In the first place, religious scholars empathize with the hermeneutic tradition as a reflection of their own Shi'a tradition of *ijtehad* (interpretation), in particular its emphasis on multiple layers of meaning and the problems inherent in accessing knowledge. The obvious esoteric implications of contemporary hermeneutics appealed to Shi'a clerics anxious to maintain their monopoly on scriptural interpretation. It also helped that many proponents of this tradition were regarded as religious philosophers, and indeed it was pointed out that Western philosophy had tended to ignore or marginalize this vital aspect of its heritage. Hegel, Nietzsche, Heidegger and Ricoeur were hailed as prime examples of thinkers that were accessible to the theological schools in a way that others were not; although, as the passage quoted above notes, such thinkers in many ways acted as a vehicle for wider inquiry and investigation following other intellectual trajectories. Outside the seminaries and in the universities, the range of works studied was of course even broader. While there remained a broad affinity with the hermeneutic scholars in the West, there continued to be an avid interest in the writings of Marx, as well as those of Foucault and Habermas. All three, in addition to those mentioned above, have been pivotal in shaping Iranian attitudes to the outside world. Khatami's 'dialogue of civilizations', for example, is replete with a Habermasian subtext.

It is crucial to recognize that these developments were not a product of the 1990s, although texts did become more widely available then. In fact they were a direct consequence of the revolution and the intellectual ferment it created. Indeed, as Borujerdi has succinctly argued, 'despite the many obstacles and restrictions put forward by the present regime in Tehran, the 1980s and the 1990s indeed witnessed the prospering of political philosophy and jurisprudence in Iran'; and he adds that 'Far from engaging in esoteric and trivial polemics, the discussions now taking place in Iran are

---

[19] Hermeneutics, as well as being the art or theory of interpretation, constitutes, with its variations, a major branch of continental (European) philosophy and can trace its roots to scriptural exegesis. It deals with textual analysis and interpretation and emphasizes the multiple, layered meaning of a given text.

philosophically sophisticated, intellectually sound, socially relevant, and politically modern.'[20] Many texts were being translated and discussed by Iranian academics and scholars in the 1980s, including Kant's *Critique of Pure Reason*, Nietzsche's *Beyond Good and Evil* and *Thus Spoke Zarathustra* and Durkheim's *Rules of Sociological Method*. It is certainly true that the circle of debate was a limited one, and only gradually expanded to permeate both the universities and the seminaries; but it was a dynamic one which reflected the political upheaval which had given birth to it.

The intellectual revitalization of the myth of political emancipation

The intellectual dynamism and plurality of Iranian society reflected the political realities of the Islamic Republic, and in turn came to influence those realities. Abdolkarim Soroush, the man most often identified with the intellectual renaissance, or indeed reformation of Islamic thought, sharpened his analytical faculties in the service of the revolutionary state against the perceived threat of Marxist ideas. As a lay religious thinker, he was one of a number charged with deconstructing and neutralizing the ideas of the Iranian left, in particular the Tudeh party, reflecting the state's wish not only to eliminate the palpable threat but to remove the ideological challenge as well. The Marxist thought he sought to challenge bore much of the hallmarks of Soviet communism: dogmatism, authoritarianism and domination by an unsophisticated economic determinism. This was not a dynamic, living ideology, and many of its elements would have been no more acceptable to Western Marxists than they were to Iranian Muslims.

Soroush came away from this encounter with a suspicion of the totalizing aspects of Hegelian philosophy and a dislike for historicism. His curious predilection for Popper and the positivism associated with him has been widely noted[21] – curious because Popper would seem to be as far removed from traditions of hermeneutics as one could possibly get. Yet here it is important to remember that the predominant intellectual environment was one in which an authoritarian, totalizing tendency was pitted against a more decentralized pluralism. In essence, philosophers such as Soroush were using Popper's thought and epistemology to deconstruct and break down the restrictive dogma of the Iranian left. In so doing, many of

---

[20] Borujerdi, *Iranian Intellectuals and the West*, pp. 156–7.

[21] It is worth noting that a major influence on Soroush's early intellectual development was Thomas Kuhn's *The Structure of Scientific Revolutions* (Chicago: University of Chicago Press, 1962), which was written as a riposte to Popperian theories of scientific development.

the critics came away with a better understanding and knowledge of Marxist thought, and this was subsequently appropriated and adapted by the religious left. This accomplished, it was only a matter of time before the same intellectual arsenal was turned against that other bastion of dogma, the authoritarian Islamists.

Indeed, by the late 1980s and early 1990s Soroush and others, perturbed by the authoritarian tendencies of the developing 'mercantile bourgeois hegemony', were writing damning critiques of the insular dogmatism of the clergy, who were arguing that political authoritarianism and elitism mirrored and were justified by theological authoritarianism. Concerned by the lack of charismatic authority in the new leader, the ideologues of the right were busy seeking to provide intellectual justification for his supremacy by depicting his position as a reflection of the supremacy of the clergy as a whole and thus as an extension of their collective capacity to manage and direct the affairs of the state. There were two levels to this process: the broader philosophical justification of the state and the *velayat-e faqih* and a more tactical competition with Rafsanjani. The latter tended to preoccupy the political establishment – to the extent that, one suspects, some of the highly critical views expressed were tolerated as a reflection of elite rivalries. Thus Rafsanjani cannot have been upset by vigorous criticisms of 'reactionary clergy', since he identified his political opponents with this category and was undoubtedly unaware that many on the new religious left had also placed him within this same reactionary group. Indeed, the general intellectual challenge this process posed for the political elite was not, and arguably still has not been, taken seriously by the members of that elite, of whichever political tendency.

Soroush's argument was essentially simple, but devastating. It was that Islam the religion should be distinguished from those who interpreted it, and that much that had been handed down through the generations and articulated as the faith was in fact little more than human interpretation and therefore subject to human fallibilities.[22] This was, in effect, the application of critical hermeneutic philosophy to Shi'a theology. Shi'a Islam, of course, contained within it the principle of interpretation (*ijtehad*), and it was well known that the first Imam, Ali, had exhorted the faithful to interpret the scriptures in accordance with their own age. But, argued Soroush, what had occurred over the past few centuries was a contraction of knowledge and its constraint within narrow, insular, dogmatic bounds. This contraction of knowledge, he argued, mirrored the development of a

[22] It can be argued, of course, that 'Islam' is essentially an exercise in hermeneutics. See Turner in the excellent introduction to his translation of the Quran: C. Turner, *The Quran: a new interpretation* (London: Curzon, 1997), pp. ix–xiv.

formal and formulaic *ulema*, whose very organization and ritual encouraged consensus and the stagnation of creative, innovative thought that emerged during periods of what Soroush described as 'expansion'. The Islamic Revolution marked a time of renewal and expansion, but recent developments indicated that the forces of contraction were earnestly resisting these trends, and this situation, for the safety of religion if nothing else, had to be addressed.

The current resistance to expansion, argued Soroush, had little to do with scholarship and religion and more to do with power. In a lecture entitled 'What the University Expects from the Hawzeh' (religious seminary), Soroush criticized the tendency of the seminaries to reproduce the ideological positions which best justify their political power. He urged the seminaries to

> abandon the habit of stealth and concealment in matters of religious knowledge; desisting from treating questions as scandalous; and refraining from expedient speech and action that subserves political power. It must also abstain from regarding human knowledge as superhuman. The Hawzeh must not replace demonstrative arguments with rhetoric. Abandoning religious cosmetics, it must renounce arbitrary selectiveness in the presentation of religion, which must be presented in a scholarly manner.[23]

In a now famous article first published in 1995 in the bi-monthly magazine *Kiyan*, entitled 'The Roof of Livelihood on the Pillar of Religion', Soroush was even more scathing about the role of the *ulema* in debasing religious thought. This article was in fact in response to a critique of an earlier article, and reveals something of the intensity of the debate which was taking place in Iran at this time. Soroush began by stating his argument that the association of religious scholarship with political and economic power was bound to affect that scholarship and could not be considered in the best interests of theological and philosophical investigation. He went on to argue that religion was greater than the *ulema*, that Islam as a faith was greater than jurisprudence (*fiqh*),[24] and that its interpretation could not be dependent on a class who were themselves dependent on maintaining a particular interpretation which would sustain them. In short, the *ulema*, whose very existence as a class depended on their retention of a peculiar

---

[23] A. Soroush, 'What the University Expects from the Hawzeh', in M. Sadri and A. Sadri, trans. and eds, *Reason, Freedom and Democracy in Islam: Essential Writings of Abdolkarim Soroush* (Oxford: Oxford University Press, 2000), p. 183.

[24] This was a particularly contentious argument under the circumstances.

authority to interpret religion, were unlikely to argue themselves out of a livelihood. He added, most damningly, that the *ulema* in any case could not be considered universally worthy of respect, because 'The truth is that among the *ulema* (or those who call themselves *ulema*) those who are impious, poorly educated ... are not few.'[25]

Soroush's project is a familiar one to those acquainted with Afghani or, more immediately, Ali Shariati, who had also argued that Islam had to be liberated from the incompetence of the *ulema*.[26] Soroush, however, was joined by some clerics, who could see the danger of dogma and its consequences for religion, and whose knowledge of Islamic theology and philosophy was profound. For their part, this critique simply reflected the ideas of the Imam himself and his noted battle with the reactionary clergy. Soroush, Kadivar, Shabestari and others were not only articulate and literate; they were also prolific, and there was both a market and media to transmit their ideas. In this respect these writers served the interests of the 'bourgeois republic', in so far as they provided Rafsanjani with ammunition to attack his more conservative opponents in the establishment, in particular those who wanted to encroach upon his own political and economic interests. But in their challenge to authoritarianism, they were also undermining Rafsanjani's own patrimonialism.

The theoretical foundations of an Islamic democracy

Just as the challenge posed by the West had to be met not only by critique but by the development of theoretical and practical alternatives, so too the deconstruction of the authoritarian and dogmatic Islam so popular with Western orientalists and oriental potentates alike had to be accompanied by the construction of a viable alternative. As Soroush argued, an autocratic God was a reflection of an autocratic system and was indeed a flawed interpretation based upon the political needs of that system.[27] In other words, in a classic Marxist sense the bourgeois establishment was reproducing an ideological system intended to support and sustain their relation of domination. Some members of the *ulema* remained vehemently opposed to any innovation in religious doctrine, but also accepted that the ideal religious

---

[25] A. Soroush, 'Saghf Mashiat bar Sotoun Shariat' (The Roof of Livelihood on the Pillar of Religion), *Kiyan*, vol. 5, no. 26, Mordad–Sharivar 1374/Aug.–Sept. 1995, p. 27.

[26] See e.g. A. Soroush, 'Shariati va falsafeh' (Shariati and Philosophy), *Iran-e Farda*, no. 26, Tir 1375 (June–July 1996), pp. 16–19. Shariati was to enjoy a considerable revival; see e.g. the translation of Abrahamian's article, 'Ali Shariati: Ideologue of the Iranian Revolution', *Jame'eh*, 26 Khordad 1377/16 June 1998, p. 7.

[27] A. Soroush, 'The Idea of Democratic Religious Government', in Sadri and Sadri, *Reason, Freedom and Democracy in Islam*, p. 128.

society, governed by a neoplatonic philosopher-king, could not be sustained in an imperfect world. In short, utopia could not be achieved in the absence of the Mahdi, and thus all that could be done in this life was to hasten his arrival. This was best done by retreating from the damaging experience of politics and preparing the community spiritually. This quietist tradition remained authoritarian but was not interventionist. Their justification was simple. While the Sunni community might be able to espouse democracy, no such thing was possible within the Shi'a community, who had placed their faith in the leadership of the infallible Imams. As one ayatollah noted in an interview with the author, if Shi'as were democratic, then they would have supported the election of Abu Bakr as the first caliph rather than supporting the hereditary right of the Prophet's cousin and son-in-law Ali, the first Imam (and fourth caliph). Significantly, even the quietists were keen to view the revolution in Iran as the latest in a sequence of movements beginning with the French Revolution, leading to the Russian Revolution and culminating (so far) with the Islamic Revolution. In a curious marriage between Western revolutionary movements and religion, these three upheavals were seen not as a process of progressive popular emancipation but as the build-up to the emergence of the Mahdi (described to the author in terms of the Nietzschean 'superman'). Thus the French Revolution was 75% people, 25% leadership; the Russian Revolution was 50:50; the Islamic Revolution was 75% leadership and only 25% popular will, and the next upheaval (wherever it occured) would prove to be 100% leadership-based.[28]

Most political clerics rejected both quietism and the incompatibility of Islam with democracy; but they also sought to emphasize the political role of the Imam. Indeed, for those who participated in political activity within the framework of the 'Islamic Republic' it was difficult to argue against the compatibility of Islam with democracy; but rather than arguing for a synthesis of the two, they were quite clear that Islam predominated, and that democratic activity operated within an Islamic framework that was defined by the few. In challenging the right of these clerics to interpret, Soroush and others sought to deny their claim to define the boundaries of democratic practice and to prevent those boundaries being interpreted with an increasing inflexibility that would eventually suffocate democracy altogether. Such a consequence, they argued, would result (as indeed the quietists acknowledged) in damage to popular religion. But they also argued, in contrast to the quietists, that the Islamic Revolution was a powerful exposition of the myth of political emancipation, which had yet

[28] Recounted to author.

to be fulfilled. The democratization of Islam was its chief source of salvation, and a pious people, enthused with religion, would themselves form the foundations and constituent parts of an Islamic democracy. Soroush's argument was in fact that by imposing a harsh and unforgiving Islam upon the people, the conservative clerics were themselves secularizing society.

The argument is both interesting and subtle. Soroush is contending that secularization is a product of the contraction of religious knowledge and its containment within a religious and intellectual elite – in other words, a distinct clerical class. By depriving ordinary people of access to religious knowledge you secularize society by default; thus, conversely, in a true Islamic society in which Islam is democratized, secularism cannot emerge. As Soroush argued: 'An irreligious government is the product of an irreligious society and in a religious society even if someone wanted to, they would not be able to make the government secular or irreligious. In the West too, first society became secular and then government, not the other way.'[29]

Yet Soroush also challenges the notion that 'secularism' implies irreligiosity, arguing that

Secularism has been understood as a deliberate effort to exclude religion from worldly affairs. But the truth is that secular governments are not opposed to religion; they accept it but not as a basis for their legitimacy or as foundation for their actions ... One may think of two possible motivations for secularism's insistence on the separation of religion and government: the belief in the fundamental falsehood of religion, coupled with the fear of its deleterious effects on politics, or the belief in the fundamental truth of religion coupled with concern over its contamination and profanation by political concerns.[30]

Soroush and other writers have sought to reclaim 'secularism' and legitimize it within Islamic discourse by reasserting its original meaning.[31] Thus a distinction is drawn between the irreligiosity of 'laicism', a practice more familiar to France and Turkey, while secularism is defined as this-worldliness and responsibility for the affairs of the temporal world that can be exercised by believers.[32] When the term is understood in this sense, it becomes a self-evident truth that political Islam follows a secular logic, in

[29] A. Soroush, 'Saghf Mashiat bar Sotoun Shariat' (The Roof of Livelihood ...), p. 31.

[30] A. Soroush, 'The Sense and Essence of Secularism', in Sadri and Sadri, *Reason, Freedom and Democracy in Islam*, pp. 56–7. For the original article see *Kiyan*, vol. 5, no. 26, Mordad–Sharivar 1374/Aug.–Sept. 1995, pp. 4–13.

[31] See e.g. M. Farhadpour, 'Nokati peeramun sekularism [Points in Search of Secularism]', *Kiyan*, vol. 5, no. 26, Mordad–Sharivar 1374/Aug.–Sept. 1995, pp. 14–21.

[32] Soroush and others use the term 'secularism' in both positive and pejorative senses, which only encourages confusion.

that its remit is not simply the hereafter but the organization of the present.[33]
Paradoxical as it may seem, therefore, Islamic thinkers and activists such
as Afghani, Shariati, Khomeini and latterly Soroush have been actively
seeking the secularization of Islam – its critical reintegration into contemporary society. Khomeini's irritation with the reactionary *ulema* and their
social irrelevance, which he saw as leading them down the same path as the
medieval Christian clergy, can be understood in this light.[34] Political Islam
is therefore a means to the socialization of the faith, a process facilitated by
its association with the institutions of government. Islam is secular, in that
it deals with the present temporal world, and in order to be relevant it must
be critically scrutinized. For this is the other essential aspect of secular
societies: demystification and scientific scrutiny. Indeed, for Islam to
prosper it must return to its scientific rigour and dynamism.

> The notion that the new world gradually rids itself of religion is only
> half true. It is true insofar as the modern world condemns ignorant and
> vulgar religiosity to extinction. However it also shows a different kind
> of religiosity, a learned and examined religion, to prosper on a higher
> level. Scientific treatment of political and economic affairs does in no
> sense preclude a well-defined role for God and religion in political, social
> and natural affairs. Determining the limits of that role and the exact form
> of that relationship remains to be worked out by scholars. The least we
> can say in this respect is that religiosity or the lack thereof do not enter
> the essence of government. However, as an external reality, government is
> subordinate to society and constitutes one of its forms of realization. If a
> society is religious, its government too will take on a religious hue.[35]

In this view, the centrality of society and social forces predominates over
the role of elites and leaders. This was to be an organic Islamic democracy
growing from below, not imposed by an oligarchy above. For this to work,
argued Soroush, Islam must recognize individual rights, and not simply
confer obligations upon the people. In other words, the relationship between
authority and the people must change, and the people must *assert* their rights.

> [A] religion that is oblivious to human rights (including the need of
> humanity for freedom and justice) is not tenable in the modern world. In

---

[33] See e.g. C. Tripp, 'Islam and the Secular Logic of the State', in A. Ehteshami and A. Sidahmed,
eds, *Islamic Fundamentalism* (Oxford: Westview Press, 1996), pp. 51–69.
[34] Hence Khomeini's exhortation that Iranians must prepare this world in order to hasten the arrival
of the Mahdi.
[35] Soroush, 'The Sense and Essence of Secularism', in Sadri and Sadri, *Reason, Freedom and Democracy in Islam*, p. 61.

other words, religion needs to be right not only logically but also ethically. The discussion of human rights is hardly cosmetic, superfluous, blasphemous, or easily dismissed. Nor is it merely grist for scholastic and casuistic discussions within seminary walls. Simply put, we cannot evade rational, moral, and extra-religious principles and reasoning about human rights, myopically focussing on nothing but the primary texts and maxims of religion in formulating our jurisprudential edicts.[36]

He adds, 'A rule that is not just is not religious.'[37]

Critics of this thesis came from two predictable sources: the Western (and Western-educated) intellectual elite, and the authoritarian Islamists within Iran. Both held to a definition of the 'secular' which viewed it in contradistinction to religion. Since democracy could develop only within a secular environment, it followed that Islam and democracy were incompatible. In adhering to this view, the critics within Iran accused Soroush and his colleagues of submitting to the West, a view encouraged by Western intellectuals who were keen to portray the debate in Iran as a tacit acknowledgment that sustainable development necessitated a 'return' to familiar 'Western' trajectories of development. Soroush argued that both Western and Islamist critics of Islamic democracy were 'feeding from the same trough' of assertions that these traditions were exclusive and incompatible. This mutual exclusivity, he insisted, had to be challenged and deconstructed. It was inconceivable to imagine the West as a unified totality with clear, definable boundaries. Challenging his critics, Soroush asked: 'Where do you draw the boundaries of the West? Is this moral decline present wherever there is the West, or wherever there is the West is there moral decline? Should we know the "Western spirit" based on the West or should we distinguish the "West" from the Western spirit?'[38] The notion of conceiving of the 'West' as a totalizing whole was as simplistic and irrelevant as the orientalist notion of the Orient. It was a reaction to a negative historical experience which had to be overcome. Indeed, Soroush went further: 'We Iranian Muslims are the inheritors and carriers of three cultures at once. As long as we ignore our links with the elements in our triple cultural heritage and our cultural geography, constructive social and cultural action will elude us ... The three cultures that form our common heritage are of national, religious, and Western origins.'[39]

[36] Soroush, 'The Idea of Democratic Religious Government', ibid., p. 128.
[37] A. Soroush, 'Tolerance and Governance', ibid., p. 132.
[38] Quoted in Borujerdi, *Iranian Intellectuals and the West*, p. 161.
[39] A. Soroush, 'The Three Cultures', in Sadri and Sadri, *Reason, Freedom and Democracy in Islam*, p. 156.

One way of countering the assertion of incompatibility has been suggested above in the redefinition of the meaning of 'secular'. But Soroush also sought to refute these challenges on their own terms. First he pointed out that most critiques were based on a version of Islam which was dogmatic and legalistic. This version, as reflected in the disputations which had occurred within Iran, and with which he was intimately involved, could not stand. Islam was larger than legalistic Islam, and Islamic government was larger than its identification with 'jurisprudential rule'. Indeed, argues Soroush, Islam contains more intellectual components than jurisprudence alone, and to extend jurisprudential methodology to the entirety of the faith is incorrect. 'The truth ... is that religious law is not synonymous with the entirety of religion.'[40] Moreover, Soroush challenges the notion that democracy is synonymous with extreme relativism and entails that all things come under scrutiny. Taking the argument that no society is entirely 'secular' in the sense of allowing scrutiny of all things according to public whim, Soroush points out that even Western societies have their sacred cows which tend not to be subjected to critical enquiry.

> In other words, although the state in liberal governments stays neutral toward religious claims, it does not remain impartial concerning scientific achievements. It is true, then, that the liberal society is no longer a religious society but a scientific one. The same status accorded to religion and religious certitude in religious societies is ascribed to science in liberal societies ... had religion enjoyed as popular an epistemological niche as science and had it not been weakened by the philosophical and scientific forays of Western scholars, the society could have conceivably remained both 'religious' and democratic, just as it has remained 'scientific' and democratic.[41]

In other words, Western societies too have their certainties built upon theoretical foundations.

> The idea that religion and democracy are mutually exclusive has its roots in another illusion as well: the belief that in a democracy everything is subject to referendum and debate and that nothing has a solid and a priori 'foundation'. This is false. Is it not true that democracy is built upon a particular vision of humanity and history, elaborated by social and political philosophy and science? Take the principle of voting. Is it arrived at through voting? Can one start with no presuppositions

[40] A. Soroush, 'Tolerance and Governance', p. 134.
[41] Ibid., pp. 136–7.

and still achieve all the wondrous blessings of justice, right, and wisdom? Of course not.[42]

In support of this view, Soroush draws on both Montesquieu and de Tocqueville, and indeed directly from the latter to show that religion has a foundational role in the political system of the United States.[43] By thus redefining both Islam and Western conceptions of both secularism and the parameters of democracy, Soroush propounded a forceful argument which was ultimately justified by its ability to protect, enhance and enrich the spirit of religion. Religious democracy moves from being a luxury to being a right and a necessity, and as such the necessary goal of all true believers. Thus Soroush appeals both to supporters of democratic development and to the pious.

> In democratic societies, the path of examined religiosity is more open and inviting. Those who appreciate the value and sanctity of religion and the glory of investigation will never doubt that a single examined faith is nobler than a thousand imitated, shaky, and weak beliefs. 'The religious despotism,' a term perceptively coined by the knowledgeable jurisconsult, logician and theologian of the last century, Ayatollah Naini, is indeed insurmountable except by the help of such rational democracy. Religious despotism is most intransigent because a religious despot views his rule [as] not only his right but his duty. Only a religious democracy that secures and shelters faith can be secure and sheltered from such self-righteous and anti-religious rule.[44]

Social responses to the bourgeois republic

While Soroush was the most prominent of the lay religious thinkers to impact upon intellectual life in the post-revolutionary period, he was by no means the only one. Nor were his writings the preserve of an exclusive intellectual elite. On the contrary, many of his views struck a chord not only with the increasingly frustrated young filling the expanding universities but also with many young *mullahs* (*talabehs*, or trainee *mullahs*) who found that the unpopularity of their profession was having a negative impact on Islam as a whole. They, along with some of their mentors,

[42] Ibid., p. 151.
[43] Ibid., p. 153.
[44] Ibid., p. 155.

agreed with Soroush that a legalistic religion was replacing the spirit of the faith. According to Hojatoleslam Mohsen Kadivar, speaking in 1995, 'Today, the central question facing the clergy is to determine how it can preserve its independence, fiercely defended for centuries, in the face of an Islamic state. The clergy does not want its fate to be that of Marxist parties in the former communist states.'[45] This intellectual ferment, when combined with the social, political and economic changes which had taken place, was to prove an explosive brew. In short, politically disenfranchised, socially marginalized and economically under pressure, Iranians now discovered that they still had something to fight for, rather than simply to fight against.

There is little doubt that in the early stages of the bourgeois republic thinkers such as Soroush were tolerated by members of the political elite anxious for intellectual ammunition in their internecine contests. Others found that the promotion of the illusion of democracy was useful for their own legitimacy, the legitimacy of the system and the image of the Islamic Republic abroad. Certainly there was a powerful internal logic to the arguments. The Islamic Revolution, after all, as the leaders consistently said, was founded on the popular will and did not triumph by force of arms. In these ways, even a cynical leadership supported and extended the myth of political emancipation while seeking to strip it of any real political muscle.[46] By the mid-1990s, however, social tensions were beginning to boil over, with riots in a number of major urban centres. The most serious occurred in cities as disparate as Mashhad, Isfahan and Qazvin, where rioters, many of whom were armed and had fought in the war against Iraq, took to the streets in protest at a central government they found alien and distant. The government's response was to attempt to quash the disturbance through force; but, significantly, both the army and the Revolutionary Guards refused to participate in what they saw as a policing action. In the end the government resorted to sending in local militias, but the result was very much a compromise, and the state realized that it had effectively lost the monopoly of violence. While Islamic vigilantes might be useful in harassing people (for example, intellectuals such as Soroush), large-scale repression was no longer a reliable option.

Within governmental circles, not only was elite rivalry fracturing into serious divisions about the best course of action, with Rafsanjani and the Majlis moving in different directions, but the activities of people such as Soroush were increasingly being viewed with irritation – especially when

---

[45] Rouleau, 'The Islamic Republic of Iran', p. 5.

[46] See e.g. Ayatollah Meshkini's sermon concerning 'people power' in the run-up to the 1997 presidential elections, Iranian TV, 1 March 1997; BBC SWB ME/2857 MED/14, 3 March 1997.

it became apparent that Soroush was attracting the attention of foreign correspondents.[47] At the end of 1995, when asked whether Soroush had become a problem for Iran in terms of the country's international relations, the Iranian foreign minister Dr Velayati answered unequivocally: 'Yes, if someone is in a position where he is serving the people, he must bear in mind that, when he says something which will be reported in the community and the world and when he knows that this nation's enemies will use his words against our country, reasonableness and fairness dictate that he should not say those things.'[48] Comparisons were also being ominously drawn between Soroush and Ahmad Kasravi, a popular nationalist intellectual who had originally trained as a cleric and who was assassinated by religious extremists in 1946.

Soroush felt compelled to answer Velayati, and did so in the space provided by the popular leftist Persian daily *Salaam*, then edited by Abbas Abdi:

Mr Foreign Minister: I advise you not to join your voice in unison with anti-freedom groups that distort the lofty name and good image of this country in the eyes of foreigners and future generations or with those who insist on propagating violence and distorting truth. They have nothing to offer this nation and cannot bring it glory. Cling to freedom because God has not created anything more beautiful than it. Do not fabricate pretexts for plucking the petals off the flower of freedom, but make sure that there are no thorns on this flower. Do not put this blessing in the hands of evil forces; show the Iranians and the world that the words and deeds of Iran's politicians and statesmen are one, that they are serious advocators of freedom, and that they do not overtly or covertly collaborate with the enemies of freedom. It is this thought and this freedom which will ultimately uproot the evil enemy from this land. Appreciate those who speak justly and who do not expect anything in return.[49]

---

[47] See e.g. R. Wright, 'Iran's new revolution', *Foreign Affairs*, Jan./Feb. 2000, vol. 79, no. 1, p. 139.
[48] BBC SWB ME/2495 MED/18, 28 Dec. 1995; IRNA (Islamic Republic News Agency), 26 Dec. 1995.
[49] BBC SWB ME/2510 MED/11, 16 Jan. 1996; *Salaam*, 2 Jan. 1996.

5 The Failure of the Mercantile Bourgeois Republic and the Election of Khatami

By the mid-1990s it was clear that the bourgeois republic that had emerged was not delivering on the expectations and aspirations of the majority of Iranians, and for all the hype about economic development, the disparity in wealth distribution was growing at an alarming rate.[1] While there was some truth in the argument that infrastructural investment was not likely to yield immediate results, and that the people should be patient while Rafsanjani sought to apply a long-term and durable reconstruction and development programme, government protestations to this effect could not assuage a growing sense of frustration at the continued poor performance of the economy. Some went so far as to argue that the situation had been considerably better during the war, and the more cynical became nostalgic![2] Undeluded by all the grandiose visions and speeches, economists criticized the short-term populism of the Rafsanjani government.

More damagingly, disillusionment with the failure to address fundamental political reforms was growing. Some argued that this failure was the result of conservative obstructionism in the Fourth Majlis (1992–6) and the assertiveness of the Majlis deputies following the debt crisis of the early 1990s. Increasing numbers of others argued, with greater efficacy, that Rafsanjani had made a compromise with his opponents and was not serious about political liberalization. On the contrary, it was argued, as long as the fruits of economic development continued to flow into the right coffers, few members of the elite were serious about adjusting, let alone reforming, the status quo.

---

[1] See E. Rouleau, 'The Islamic Republic of Iran: Paradoxes and Contradictions in a Changing Society', *Le Monde Diplomatique*, June 1995, p. 7.
[2] Interview with author.

Parties and personalities

Rafsanjani, undaunted by his critics, displayed a single-minded, somewhat idiosyncratic interpretation of his own role in Iranian history, and in the development of the Islamic Republic in particular. He saw himself as a central, directing, if somewhat paternalistic influence; and it was an image that many of his supporters agreed with and wholeheartedly encouraged. Greatly influenced by his hero, the nineteenth-century prime minister Amir Kabir, Rafsanjani imagined himself as the 'saviour' of Iran, a figure (again, not unlike the self-perception of the last shah) whose historic achievements would outweigh in the public eye any personal weaknesses he might have, especially for good living. Hubris and avarice were to prove Rafsanjani's crucial personal weaknesses, despite his considerable political acumen. Given the similarities between him and the last shah, it should come as no surprise that he scrutinized, assessed and sought to learn from the mistakes of Mohammad Reza Shah. Indeed, this historical world-view played a fundamental role in the divisions that were to emerge between Rafsanjani and the conservative 'mercantile' establishment reflected in the Majlis.

Rafsanjani was increasingly convinced that the shah had fallen because, while his economic reforms were on the whole positive, they were not matched by any significant political reforms. It was this crucial imbalance that had made the fall of the monarchy inevitable and served notice that an economically dominant position was still vulnerable to the consequences of political intransigence and inflexibility. There were considerable debates throughout the 1990s as to how far political reform should go, and while his rivals on the right objected to political liberalization, critics on the left contended that Rafsanjani was unlikely to take any measures that would harm his personal grip on power and the hegemony he had carefully sought to construct. In so far as Rafsanjani supported a measure of political liberalization, those on the left of the political spectrum were willing to support him, but this was a tactical decision which simply reflected a superficial commonality of purpose. Suspicions as to Rafsanjani's real motives ran deep, and most on the left were pushing for a level of reform which far exceeded Rafsanjani's intentions. Distrusted on the left and at odds with the increasing authoritarianism of the conservative right, in both political and ideological terms, Rafsanjani and his supporters moved to take the centre ground.

This division in the political (and bureaucratic) establishment became increasingly apparent in the run-up to the 1996 elections for the Fifth Majlis, when Rafsanjani's supporters issued a statement in his support and

demeaning to the activities of the Majlis.[3] In arguing that 'to point out the glory, rank and status of the Majlis it is sufficient to say that it began work with Hashemi [Rafsanjani] and developed and matured with him', the executive not only exposed the bitter rivalry which had emerged but evinced a vulnerable arrogance. While many people enjoyed the rivalry and tended to sympathize with Rafsanjani, the pomposity of it all cannot have been lost on observers. The Majlis itself considered the statement 'a great insult and injury' and its members appealed to the Leader, Ayatollah Khamene'i, to adjudicate in the matter, since they did not consider that the officials responsible would provide the apology they demanded.[4] This statement, they argued, somewhat belatedly, would encourage division prior to the all-important Majlis elections. The statement, as it turned out, was the opening salvo in the public phase of a dispute which had hitherto been simmering away discreetly for some time, and it indicated that many pro-Rafsanjani administrators and officials were preparing to establish an institutional framework for their political activities, distinct from the Jame'eh Ruhaniyyat-e Mobarez (Militant Clergy Association) to which Rafsanjani himself belonged, as it became increasingly right-wing.

The new organization, entitled the Servants of Iran's Construction (generally shortened to Servants of Construction), was composed of senior technocrats and officials. A notable member was the mayor of Tehran, Gholamhussein Karbaschi, whose no-nonsense approach to politics in the capital had captured the imagination of the young and irritated the wealthy merchant elite. Karbaschi had acquired a controversial reputation on account of his dictum that illegality would, and indeed should, be confronted by all means possible – including, if necessary, reciprocal illegality. Thus bazaar merchants who failed to pay their taxes found their shops walled in overnight, and the demolition of these walls by curious coincidence cost the same as the original tax request. Protected by his mentor Rafsanjani, Karbaschi had pursued his task of making Tehran both habitable and self-sufficient with considerable enthusiasm. It was also apparent that Karbaschi was a useful tool with which to put pressure on the recalcitrant bourgeois republicans, who saw no reason to share their wealth while the president was accumulating it at an accelerating rate. For all Karbaschi's zeal and undoubted sincerity, his close association with Rafsanjani was to prove something of a double-edged sword. Nevertheless, it was by no means a one-way relationship. Karbaschi, who had made his name in Isfahan, proved a highly effective manager and became extremely popular among

---

[3] BBC SWB ME/2513 MED/8, 19 Jan. 1996; IRNA news agency, 17 Jan. 1996.
[4] BBC SWB ME/2522 MED/1, 30 Jan. 1996; IRNA news agency, 27 Jan. 1996.

ordinary people. In providing this essential link he was to prove an immensely useful political ally to Rafsanjani, who was becoming increasingly alienated from the people. Furthermore, Karbaschi provided the vital service of keeping the capital quiet. Indeed, it is worth noting that throughout the 1990s, while other cities erupted in occasional violent protest, Tehran was relatively quiescent. This was no mean achievement; arguably, Karbaschi provided the fundamental stability on which the bourgeois republic was built. But he achieved this by pursuing policies and espousing rhetoric which in the medium term would prove damaging to the hegemony he helped to sustain.

The formation of the Servants of Construction, and the prominence in the group of Karbaschi in particular, represented a political watershed: it not only exposed the political fractures among the elite but apparently set out to widen them. While other groups had proved ultimately consensual, the Servants seemed to be ready and willing to engage in a genuine political contest. Their emergence was also the first serious indication of the cracks in the patrimonial system; for, while Rafsanjani viewed them as yet another tool in his general policy of divide and rule, enabling him to avoid a damaging level of political dependency on his mercantile allies, the members of the new group saw themselves as a genuine political organization with explicit aims. Rafsanjani himself had previously argued in favour of the establishment of political parties: 'From the early days of my executive work, I have repeatedly emphasised that our constitution demands a pluralist system of parties. If parties were formed seriously, I would support them.'[5] Yet while he regarded his association with the Servants as politically useful, he remained ambivalent and non-committal towards them, preferring instead to speak of 'transcending' politics. At the same time, as he and members of the Militant Clergy Association were to stress, Rafsanjani had not left that organization.[6] Rather than align himself with the new group, Rafsanjani argued, he would remain impartial in the forthcoming Majlis elections, noting that in any case the Servants should not be considered 'a split or a new faction'.[7]

Nevertheless, the differences in emphasis between the old and the new groups were increasingly apparent, especially when it was decided to issue separate lists of nominated candidates, and some journalists saw in this split a real opportunity for the emergence of pluralistic politics.[8] The English-language daily *Iran News* commented in its editorial that the splits

[5] BBC SWB ME/2471 MED/1, 27 Nov. 1995; Iranian TV, 24 Nov. 1995.
[6] BBC SWB ME/2518 MED/8, 25 Jan. 1996; IRNA news agency, 24 Jan. 1996.
[7] BBC SWB ME/2522 MED/2, 30 Jan. 1996; IRNA news agency, 28 Jan. 1996.
[8] BBC SWB ME/2523 MED/1, 30 Jan. 1996; IRNA news agency, 30 Jan. 1996.

should be viewed as a positive development which would enhance the stability and credibility of the system. It argued: 'Since we consider our system of government to be based on popular support, then all political factions loyal to the system must consider the opposition as political and election rivals rather than personal enemies, and must refrain from character assassination and any other unethical and religiously abhorrent acts concerning their opponents.'[9] Others, including Rafsanjani, recognized that political parties were a valuable means of control and essential for channelling political energies into constructive activities. The *Tehran Times*, for instance, commented that political parties were the surest way to consolidate democratic government, adding: 'If the major Islamic groupings do not form political parties, there will be further defections ... in the absence of political parties, such groupings will mushroom, endangering the whole political system.'[10] However, while many on the left were willing to work with the Servants of Construction as the only available way of posing a credible challenge to the right,[11] there was also a growing view that whatever pluralism was allowed would be heavily controlled and essentially would reflect the needs of the mercantile bourgeoisie.

A number of groups decided to participate in the Majlis elections, and the authorities sought to encourage popular involvement by stressing the fairness of the electoral process.[12] According to the interior ministry some 80% of the electorate voted, and Ayatollah Khamene'i congratulated the people on a successful election, noting that officials were duty-bound to investigate any complaints.[13] Not surprisingly, there were a few. The most astonishing attempt at manipulating the result was the protest lodged by the *right wing* Majlis Speaker Ali Akbar Nateq Nuri, who claimed that people had 'mistakenly' voted for the leftist Abdullah Nuri when they had meant in fact to vote for him. This remarkable claim received a sympathetic hearing from the accommodating authorities, who decided to divide the votes allocated to Abdullah Nuri and reallocate half of them to the Majlis Speaker. As a result, Faezeh Hashemi, Rafsanjani's energetic and popular daughter of the centre-left, was displaced by Nateq Nuri as the candidate winning the largest number of votes in the Tehran poll, while Abdullah Nuri's share of the vote declined correspondingly. Overall, while some on the left expressed satisfaction that the election had seen the 'traditional right' lose their majority in the Majlis, others were less impressed.

[9] BBC SWB ME/2517 MED/6, 24 Jan. 1996; IRNA news agency, 23 Jan. 1996.
[10] BBC SWB ME/2517 MED/7, 24 Jan. 1996; IRNA news agency, 23 Jan. 1996.
[11] BBC SWB ME/2528 MED/13, 6 Feb. 1996; IRNA news agency, 4 Feb. 1996.
[12] BBC SWB ME/2512 MED/10, 18 Jan. 1996; Iranian TV, 17 Jan. 1996.
[13] BBC SWB ME/2563 MED/1, 18 March 1996; Iranian TV and IRNA news agency, 15 March and 17 March respectively.

The newspaper *Salaam*, known to be left of centre in its political orientation, was emerging as one of the most vocal critics of the bourgeois republic. Owned and managed by Hojjatoleslam Khoeiniha, a radical revolutionary who had been the chief point of liaison between the students occupying the US embassy and Ayatollah Khomeini, its editor was one of those student leaders, Abbas Abdi. It retained a strong connection with the student community, and in making the link between the student movement and the press it constituted the most explicit example of the highly integrated nature of the emergent Iranian 'civil society'. *Hamshahri*, the newspaper of the municipality of Tehran, was bold, colourful and entertaining; *Salaam* made up for its lack of colour with political bite. Whereas *Hamshahri* supported the Servants of Construction and was perceived as centrist, *Salaam* was the standard bearer of the new left, and its guiding philosophy was Islamic social democracy. Indeed, Abdi described himself as a social democrat, borrowing effortlessly from the language of continental European politics.[14]

The newspaper encouraged controversy and popular participation with a column devoted to readers' views, some of which were incisive. One reader called to complain that the Militant Clergy Association had in fact manipulated the elections, to which the paper replied with customary sarcasm: 'The Militant Clergy Association considers itself above the law and considers it below its dignity to ask permission from the law for its campaign.'[15] On another occasion, when one of the Friday prayer leaders in Tehran condemned an arson attack against a bookshop in Pakistan by a radical Sunni group, a reader called to ask why he had not condemned similar attacks by extremists in Iran. *Salaam*'s answer was uncompromising: 'The justification may be that if a wicked group like the Sahabah Corps sets libraries, bookshops and books on fire, their action also becomes wicked and it is a sin and a crime; whereas if a group of people carry out this act with pure intentions and in order to win God's favour, then there is nothing wrong with it!'[16] Comments such as these earned the paper and its staff a huge following, and one writer has credited *Salaam* with the vital function of raising public awareness and fostering hope that social justice could prevail.[17] But there was a price to be paid for such outspokenness; having earned the enmity of the authorities, the paper found itself being suspended before the elections, and Abdi himself was imprisoned, on one

---

[14] Interview with Abdi.

[15] BBC SWB ME/2563 MED/2, 18 March 1996; *Salaam*, 13 March 1996.

[16] BBC SWB ME/2834 MED/12, 4 Feb. 1997; *Salaam*, 29 Jan. 1997.

[17] H. Kaviani, *Ramz peerozi yek rais jumhur* (The secrets behind a president's success) (Tehran: Zekr, 1378 (1999/2000)), pp. 66–7.

occasion for eight months. The relationship was therefore anything but smooth, and the left were under no illusions about the limits of Rafsanjani's enthusiasm for political reform.[18]

Of particular concern were the rumours that Rafsanjani was seeking a third term as president, in contravention of the constitution.[19] Not that constitutional prohibition was necessarily a serious obstacle; Rafsanjani had engineered an amendment to the constitution before, in 1989, when the post of prime minister had been abolished and its powers transferred to a much-strengthened presidency. Given the centrality of Rafsanjani to the revolution and the apparent predilection for authoritarian rulers among Iranians, it seemed natural that Rafsanjani would seek, like other Middle Eastern chief executives, to extend his term indefinitely. Some supporters argued, as indeed they still do, that in periods of social and economic reconstruction it was important to have a strong man at the helm who could guide the nation at this particularly difficult time.[20] This characterization obviously appealed to Rafsanjani's self-image; but there were two problems to this master plan. Those on the left opposed any amendment to the constitution which would affect its democratic components, perceiving any such adjustments as a betrayal of revolutionary principles, while those on the right were horrified that Rafsanjani might in fact monopolize the presidency and therefore deny one of their own an opportunity.[21] Neither side was particularly convinced by the representation of Rafsanjani as the best and only man for the job, and for differing reasons, either ostensibly democratic or definitely oligarchic, both were determined to oppose it.

It is not clear how serious Rafsanjani was in seeking a third term, although speculation was rife for several months, and one official commented that it was 'entirely possible' that people would spontaneously write the name Rafsanjani on their ballot papers, leaving the incumbent 'no choice' but to return reluctantly to the helm.[22] It seems, however, that the rumours were encouraged in order to gauge public opinion, which was, for the reasons stated above, overwhelmingly negative. It was generally believed that Ayatollah Khamene'i intervened in private to settle the issue and effectively

---

[18] Another cause of consternation was the broadcast by state television of a programme which claimed to 'expose' political traitors. It was widely condemned for its poor taste and vindictiveness, and seen as an example of right-wing extremism; see *Baz ham Hoviat?!* (Hoveat again?!), *Iran-e Farda*, no. 26, Tir 1375 (June/July 1996), pp. 2–4.

[19] BBC SWB ME/2558 MED/13, 12 March 1996; IRNA news agency, 11 March 1996.

[20] One of the initial proponents of this view was Abdullah Nuri; see Kaviani, *Ramz peerozi yek rais jumhur*, p. 81.

[21] Bahonar called such a move the greatest service to the enemies of the revolution; see Kaviani, *Ramz peerozi yek rais jumhur*, p. 83.

[22] See Rafsanjani's negative reply in ibid., p. 84.

to deny Rafsanjani the chance of a third term. The consequent damage to the credibility of the system, it was argued, would be too great.

Rafsanjani's elimination as a candidate, however, created a problem for the left and the centrist political forces: they now had to find a replacement candidate to take on the challenge from the right and the political establishment, which seemed to favour the Speaker of the Majlis, Ali Akbar Nateq Nuri. The nomination of Nateq Nuri as a candidate for the presidency in many ways reflected the confidence of the mercantile bourgeoisie and their dismissive attitude towards the patrimonial and bureaucratic elements of government. Indeed, the antagonism between these two aspects of the (incomplete) Rafsanjani hegemony was palpable in the year leading up to the presidential election in May 1997, and it is important to remember that many bureaucrats, whose political attitudes were often anathema to the left, nevertheless shared more in common with the latter than with the wealthy merchants. Rafsanjani enjoyed a certain appeal among bureaucrats because of his management skills and political astuteness, as well as his sense of history; but the right, as represented by Nateq Nuri, possessed all the associated vices and few of the virtues. Furthermore, many bureaucrats, at most levels of government, while firm believers in the Islamic republican system, did not believe that their efforts were intended to serve a new commercial oligarchy. Also, and significantly, on account of their own relatively low wages they had little in common with the mercantile bourgeoisie. On the contrary, they often looked in disbelief at the disparity in lifestyles, and many began privately to question whether their sacrifices in revolution and war had been made simply in order to line the pockets of this new elite.

For many, Nateq Nuri was an explicit and somewhat crude representation of the political interests of the mercantile bourgeoisie. He was neither charismatic nor especially intelligent, and many of his public comments revealed a man alienated from the reality of life in Iran, though very much in tune with the demands of his constituents. Many baulked at the prospect of his representing the Islamic Republic of Iran abroad, while at home his election would simply confirm and consolidate the dominance of the mercantile bourgeoisie and their authoritarian allies among the *ulema*. The prospect horrified many outside the increasingly narrow right-wing establishment. As the editor of the magazine *Iran-e Farda* (and a former minister), Ezatollah Sahabi, stated bluntly in an interview with the London-based Arabic-language newspaper *Al-Hayat*: 'The presidential elections may be the last and if the bazaar branch controls the government they will not take place again.'[23]

---

[23] BBC SWB ME/2842 MED/17, 13 Feb. 1997; *Al-Hayat*, 11 Feb. 1997.

Two factors exacerbated this political tension. One was the obvious arrogance of the right and of Nateq Nuri himself, who in the run-up to the election effectively behaved as if he had already won it. One wit pointed out that while Western election results were announced within twenty-four hours, Iran had improved on this substantially by announcing the results some three months prior to the election! His style became increasingly presidential as the elections approached, but even more galling was his ill-concealed enthusiasm for the role. As early as January 1996 he had announced his readiness to 'serve sincerely at any post'.[24] The other exacerbating factor was the apparent shift in political loyalties as technocrats realigned themselves, often in contradiction to their avowed political leanings. This shift in loyalties of course was and is nothing new to Iranian politics – indeed, it makes the task of factional categorization a process of continuous definition – but it was of especial significance in this case because the machinations smacked of blatant opportunism, laying the foundations of a deep enmity between former allies. Men such as the foreign minister Ali Akbar Velayati or Javad Larijani (along with his brother Ali Larijani) were considered pillars of the moderate wing of the establishment, and the ease with which they shifted well to the right was seen by many as a grotesque case of political prostitution.

His personality and political acumen excepted, Nateq Nuri seemed to have much going for him. He was supported by both the right-wing political establishment (including, apparently, the leadership) and the mercantile bourgeoisie, with all their financial muscle. More importantly perhaps, the right, partly as a consequence of their confidence, seemed united and resolute. In contrast, their opponents seemed a disparate bunch, well-meaning and idealistic but disorganized; and, critically, there seemed to be no obvious candidate to lead the challenge. Yet the left and centrist allies possessed a number of advantages which were not immediately apparent. Clearly, they now enjoyed the support, financial and otherwise, of Rafsanjani and of many of the bureaucrats and administrators within the government, notably including the mayor of Tehran. Less obvious was the philosophical and ideological cohesion they enjoyed as a result of the intellectual climate which had been taking form. Their message of 'social justice' and popular participation in government was, as noted earlier, a powerful myth which resonated with the public, and it was not (as some had feared) limited to the urban centres or Tehran in particular. The politically and economically disenfranchised were many and receptive, and the social mechanisms established to ensure national cohesion and dominance from the centre in

[24] BBC SWB ME/2510 MED/8, 16 Jan. 1996; IRNA news agency, 13 Jan. 1996.

fact ensured that the message was disseminated throughout the country. Students from the regions, for instance, would often study in Tehran and vice versa, while conscription often took youngsters to postings away from home for some part of their service.

If this social cohesion and determination was to be politically effective, the left and centre would have to have a prominent candidate to challenge Nateq Nuri. While some had expressed interest in the mayor of Tehran, Gholamhussein Karbaschi, many on the left were less enthusiastic and sought instead to encourage the former prime minister Mir-Hussein Musavi to stand. Musavi was popular both with the bureaucracy, many of whom could date their employment to his premiership, and among leftists, who recognized his commitment to social justice and a fair distribution of wealth. Certainly, as noted above, there was a view that the controlled economy of the war years had been much more beneficial and constructive to the Iranian economy than the boom and bust years overseen by Rafsanjani. Indeed, it was observed that while Musavi had steered the economy through the war and out the other side without incurring serious foreign debt, Rafsanjani had effectively squandered that inheritance. Musavi, however, refused to stand, despite a poll showing that he would win handsomely.[25] Many hoped that his reluctance could be overcome, while Rafsanjani held back in the hope and expectation that somehow the absence of a serious contender would allow him to return through the back door. Meanwhile, the conservatives, increasingly worried that Musavi would indeed stand, and pose a genuine threat to their candidate, began to argue that the constitution in fact demanded that only a cleric could be president.[26] In the event, the nominated candidate of the leftist political groups was the former minister of culture and now head of the National Library, Seyyid Mohammad Khatami.

Khatami had been nominated by the Militant Clerics Society (Majma-e Rohaniyun-e mobarez or MRM), the most prominent leftist faction – not to be confused with the Militant Clerics Association, which represented the right and had nominated Nateq Nuri as its candidate.[27] The MRM, whose leaders included a former Speaker of the Majlis, Mehdi Karrubi, had a difficult relationship with the centrists and in particular with Rafsanjani, but were sufficiently concerned with the possibility of a Nateq Nuri victory to enter into negotiations, eager to avoid splitting the opposition vote. By

[25] For the prolonged discussions intended to persuade Musavi to stand as a candidate, see Kaviani, *Ramz peerozi yek rais jumhur*, pp. 60–100.
[26] Ibid., pp. 70–1.
[27] BBC SWB ME/2848 MED/9, 20 Feb. 1997; IRNA news agency, 18 Feb. 1997. See comments on the crucial meeting by Mohammad Salamati (leader of the leftist Islamic Mujahideen Organization) in Kaviani, *Ramz peerozi yek rais jumhur*, pp. 108–12.

early March most of the main leftist groups were on board, and the Servants of Construction had also announced their willingness to back Khatami.[28] This alliance was important in that it not only brought on board the administrative might of the Tehran municipality but also meant that the two most popular daily newspapers, *Salaam* and *Hamshahri*, would now be backing the same candidate.

There were two other important groups that needed to be brought under the Khatami umbrella: women voters and the vibrant but militant student organizations. The standard-bearer of the latter was the outspoken Heshmatollah Tabarzadi, at that time secretary general of the Union of Islamic Associations of University Students and editor of the banned *Payam-e Daneshjoo* (The Message of the Student). Tabarzadi's Islamic credentials were impeccable – two of his brothers had been killed in the war with Iraq – and he was in many ways representative of the student body. This credibility allowed him a degree of outspokenness from which others would have shied away; but his publication was finally banned after he had penned a particularly critical piece against the corruption of the then head of the Foundation of the Oppressed, Mohsen Rafiqdoust. Taking his cue in some measure from the writings of Soroush, Tabarzadi called on whoever would be president to implement the constitution and to observe people's rights. He also criticized the ambiguity of current interpretations of freedom of speech, arguing that 'At present, as soon as one speaks about freedom of speech, press freedom or respect for people's views, he is accused of weakening the status of the *vali-e faqih*[29] and revolutionary values.' He reserved his greatest criticism, however, for what he termed the growth of 'sanctimonious piety' in society: 'The constitution has not allocated any section to sanctimonious piety, and this issue has no place in state civil law. Whenever a group tries to express its views openly, it is labelled as anti-Islamic and against the aspirations of the revolution and religious sanctities. Of course, we must always respect our national and religious aspirations.'[30]

Women, as noted above, had been agitating for a more central role in politics and society, in part as a consequence of their increased social and economic importance during the war years, but also because of the activities of such prominent 'Islamic feminists' as Faezeh Rafsanjani. As a result, politicians in the Islamic Republic tended at the very least to pay lip service to women's issues, and indeed candidates' attitudes to these would

---

[28] BBC SWB ME/2865 MED/11, 12 March 1997; *Hamshahri*, 9 March 1997; on the decision of the 'Hezbollah Assembly' (not to be confused with the Ansar-e Hezbollah) to support Khatami see also BBC SWB ME/2864 MED/16, 11 March 1997; IRNA news agency, 10 March 1997.

[29] The person embodying the concept or principle of the Guardianship of the Jurisconsult (*velayat-e faqih*).

[30] BBC SWB ME/2872 MED/15, 20 March 1997; *Kar va Kargar*, 11 March 1997.

prove crucial in the run-up to the election. In the early stages of preparations for the poll, as a clear indication of this new confidence on the part of women, Azam Taleqani, secretary of the Women's Society and daughter of the prominent revolutionary ayatollah who had died in 1979, announced her decision to stand for the presidency, declaring: 'I have accepted the presidential candidacy in order to restore women's rights and exercise social justice.' While some scoffed at the very suggestion that a woman could be president, the determined Ms Taleqani pointed out that

> 'article 115 of the constitution … states that the president must be from among the country's political and religious figures, and in no Islamic document has it been mentioned that women cannot be among the political figures.'[31]

The Guardian Council, which was charged with vetting the candidates (there were over 230 in total), reflected the wishes of the right-wing conservative establishment, including the leadership, and was quite clear about its remit in this matter. Put bluntly, there were to be as few obstacles to the presidential progress of Nateq Nuri as was possible without irreversibly damaging the credibility of the political system in the eyes of the people. The secretary of the Guardian Council, Ayatollah Jannati, in one of the Friday prayer sermons, made clear his views when he pointed out:

> Some of these people [who have registered their names] make one laugh. How come such a person, with such a background, has registered as a candidate? I mean certain unknown people, the people that one has to look at with a magnifying glass to see or recognize them. Such people intend to become a president of a country and receive votes from all of the people …
>
> In any case, there are issues which the law does not refer to but we should pay attention to them. These are the conditions which the people should be aware of. One of those conditions is that the presidential candidate should not be a liberal.[32]

Azam Taleqani fell into neither category, but here the Guardian Council proved more ingenious, by arguing that the word *rajal* in article 15 (referred to by Ms Taleqani) was an Arabic loan word with a masculine gender. As a result, the interpretation was clear: only important male candidates could

---

[31] BBC SWB ME/2898 MED/11, 21 April 1997; IRNA news agency, 19 April 1997.
[32] BBC SWB ME/2857 MED/13, 3 March 1997; Voice of the Islamic Republic of Iran, 28 Feb. 1997.

stand. While clever, this was not convincing, and the female constituency went in search of a candidate that would reflect their political and social ambitions.

The election campaign

Seyyid Mohammad Khatami, one of the four candidates remaining after the vetting procedure had been completed, was regarded by many as a political lightweight. Indeed, few took seriously his prospects as a contender for the presidency, and his candidacy was largely dismissed by those on the right. In the event, this proved to be one of his most significant strengths: not only was his apparent weakness a major reason for allowing him to stand, it also meant that his opponents became complacent.[33] Indeed, it would be fair to say that until February 2000, when the reformists finally captured the Majlis, few on the right took either Khatami or the reformist movement seriously at all. While they had reacted to events, they had failed to form any coherent political strategy to challenge Khatami. In 1997, however, the bitter recriminations against Khatami that were later to surface were not yet thought of, and the right in their confidence allowed themselves a modicum of magnanimity. According to the journalist Babak Dad, who subsequently wrote a highly popular book about the Khatami campaign, Khatami was perceived as little more than a figurehead of the shallow literati, though his candidacy was to be welcomed in so far as it would draw more people to the ballot box.[34] Khatami had himself justified his candidacy on these grounds, arguing to a sceptical establishment that if he could increase electoral participation by a mere 10 per cent he would have fulfilled his revolutionary duty.

Yet it is important not to exaggerate Khatami's apparent political illiteracy. It is certainly true that he was little known outside Iran, though a quick investigation would reveal that he had been minister of culture for some ten years between 1982 and 1992, in the first Rafsanjani administration. His resignation in the face of parliamentary pressure was greeted with dismay by the intelligentsia, but it also meant that he was not tainted with the excesses of the Rafsanjani era or associated in any way with the growing power of the mercantile bourgeoisie. Khatami was an intellectual,

---

[33] Kaviani, *Ramz peerozi yek rais jumhur*, p. 199.
[34] B. Dad, *Sad Rooz ba Khatami* (One hundred days with Khatami) (Tehran: Sahafi, 1377 (1998/9), pp. 20-1. Kaviani (*Ramz peerozi yek rais jumhur*, p. 119) notes that Khatami was as yet not a 'national' figure.

94

and as such appealed to the students and the press and was disdained by the commercial community, while his political integrity was viewed as naïveté by those operating within the patrimonial framework. In short, while he might be well-intentioned and 'nice', few considered him capable. Yet his political experience was extensive. Like a number of key reformers, such as Mojtahed Shabestari and Abdullah Nuri, he had served in the influential Hamburg Islamic Institute, where he became familiar with German and extended his knowledge of Western philosophy. For a member of the *ulema* he was most definitely unorthodox, having no difficulty in performing his military service under the shah (considering it a useful experience) or in extending his theological training at Qom by studying for a degree in Western philosophy at the University of Isfahan. Above all he was inclusive. As Ata'ollah Mohajerani, then a member of the Servants of Construction, said revealingly: 'Dr Khatami's status as a Seyyid [descendant of the Prophet] will have an effect on the people's perception of him, his image, his remarks and his status, and will make him popular ... Khatami is the kind of person who can create national harmony. A president will find it difficult to create national harmony if he relies on a [certain] faction or group.'[35]

The presentation of Khatami was a vital ingredient to his electoral success. As a Seyyid, unlike Nateq Nuri, he would appeal to traditional voters while his intellectual credentials won him approval among the intelligentsia and students – key elements of the ideological vanguard. While his opponents mocked the fact that he was head of the National Library, this hardly made him a 'librarian'; but his obvious love of books appealed to the artistic and literate heart of Iranian culture and was effectively contrasted to the financial materialism represented by Nateq Nuri. Khatami represented the non-commercialized purity of Iranian culture; but, as he was to prove in his campaign, he was also an articulate proponent of the myth of political emancipation, and in this lies the secret of his (continued) political success. For, as Hegel argues forcefully, 'herein lies political genius, in the identification of an individual with a principle. Given this linkage, the individual must carry off the victory.'[36]

Khatami's campaign revolved around a number of principles, each of which constituted a key element of the myth of political emancipation. In

---

[35] BBC SWB ME/2875 MED/22, 24 March 1997; *Akhbar*, 18 March 1997.
[36] G. W. F. Hegel, *The German Constitution* [1802], in *Hegel's Political Writings*, trans. T. M. Knox (Oxford: Oxford University Press, 1964), p. 216. See also Hegel's comments in his 'Introduction' to *Lectures on the Philosophy of World History*, trans. H. B. Nisbet (Cambridge: Cambridge University Press, 1975). Hegel's philosophy of history is particularly pertinent because of its similarities with reformist views in respect of the unfolding of the freedom of consciousness.

short, his campaign was both ideologically coherent and relevant.[37] Central among these principles was the implementation of the 'rule of law', a popular motif which could trace its antecedents to the nineteenth-century Qajar reformers, such as Malkom Khan, and was given explicit expression during the Constitutional Revolution when the initial demand had been for a House of Justice. The equal and universal application of the law would result in a fairer society, the curtailment of state arbitrariness and the expansion of social justice. This latter idea was itself a central platform of the campaign, which argued that society as currently constituted served the interests of the minority over those of the majority and generally exacerbated disparities in wealth, which were indeed growing. Majority interests could be better served by the extension and development of 'civil society', which would operate as a balance against the intrusions of the state not only in the fields of politics and economics, but also on a day-to-day basis in the social and cultural aspects of life. In short, people had 'rights' which lay beyond the interference of not only the state but even the Supreme Leader – hence, by extension, his power was not 'absolute'. The people were 'citizens' who enjoyed a social contract with the state, and it is significant that in announcing his candidacy Khatami described himself as a 'citizen'.[38] This was a bold proposition, but one that resonated. More controversial was Khatami's central philosophy, reflected in Soroush's writings, that 'freedom' and 'religion' should work in harmony, and that conflict would result in defeat for the latter.

These principles encapsulated the broad but attractive platform developed and built upon by Khatami and his supporters. Like all effective political slogans, they harboured a degree of imprecision which would allow a wide range of interpretation, deflect direct attacks and facilitate inclusivity.[39] In the words of Behzad Nabavi: 'The factions which support Mr Khatami hope to bring about the possibility of expression and thinking, to expand and promote political freedoms and to institutionalize these things. If we fail to have these things we will not be able to say anything about other issues. We believe that capitalism without freedom is much worse than capitalism with freedom.'[40]

Not only did Khatami successfully identify with the socially resonant myth of political emancipation, he sought also to communicate this message effectively to the people. One of the criticisms of the Khatami campaign was its obvious lack of financial and logistical infrastructure.

---

[37] Kaviani, *Ramz peerozi yek rais jumhur*, p. 220.
[38] Ibid., p. 117.
[39] See Kaviani's comments, ibid., pp. 226–7.
[40] BBC SWB ME/2905 MED/8, 29 April 1997; *Salaam*, 17 April 1997.

Nateq Nuri had all the advantages of the Speaker, with the resources this brought with it. Yet, ironically, the presidential manner in which this was used proved a huge liability, while Khatami's modest bus proved much more effective and appealing, He did not give the impression that he was alienated from the people. Nateq Nuri, on the other hand, suffered a series of public relations disasters, not least being the revelation that he had spent some 1.4 billion rials on publicity materials and posters. While Khatami's trips around the country to address the people were somewhat erratic and had the appearance of spontaneity, Nateq Nuri's campaign was organized with military precision, down to the scale and design of welcoming decorations and the slogans that the crowds were 'encouraged' to chant. His trip to Mazandaran, his native province, was set up in this manner and proved disastrous, at least partly due to the efforts of some of the many establishment figures who came to his aid. His brother Ahmad Nateq Nuri, the chief of the Iranian boxing federation, proved particularly inept in rousing the crowds in Mazandaran in support of his brother, and his rallying speech did not impress listeners – especially his peculiar decision to depict his brother as a latter-day Reza Shah![41]

Khatami, by contrast, decided to deliver his first speech to students at the Office for the Fostering of Unity (Daftar-e Tahkim Vahdat), where he outlined his views on the importance of the constitution and the idea that government was a gift from God entrusted to man. He stressed, by reference to the precedent of the government of Imam Ali, that tyranny could only be opposed through the institutionalization of rights.[42] To students who had been agitating for greater intellectual and political freedom, not only was Khatami's decision to address them first a good sign, but his comments and philosophy seemed at one with their own. In cultivating the loyalty of the country's students, Khatami both provided his campaign with momentum and gained valuable compensation for the inadequacies of his administrative network throughout the country by being able to tap into the nationwide network of student organizations. Kaviani argues that it was Khatami's popularity with the students that first alerted people to the possibility that he might do better than many had expected, and he pinpoints an enthusiastic rally held for him at the Sharif University in Tehran. Certainly, one must not underestimate the importance of either students (and the young in general) or women to the Khatami campaign. Apart from having presence, Khatami also seemed to be far more in tune with the demands of women, and he certainly appeared more

[41] Kaviani, *Ramz peerozi yek rais jumhur*, pp. 131–2; Dad, *Sad Rooz ba Khatami*, pp. 86–7, also pp. 74, 77.
[42] Kaviani, *Ramz peerozi yek rais jumhur*, pp. 120–21.

relaxed taking questions about them, in stark contrast with Nateq Nuri who always seemed to be in search of Islamic political correctness.[43]

Not surprisingly, Khatami also garnered support among the artists and intelligentsia, many of whom had fond memories of his work at the Ministry of Culture. The renowned film director Mohsen Makhmalbaf declared his allegiance publicly, and was followed in late March 1997 by an open letter of backing signed by twenty-two film-makers.[44] While his opponents were dismissive of support from such quarters, it did provide the Khatami camp with some of the best artistic talents in the country, and in an election campaign in which television was to prove an important medium – a medium which Khatami fully understood – this was to be a much more important qualitative asset than had hitherto been appreciated. Khatami proved much more telegenic than his opponent, much more relaxed in front of the camera. A comparison of two rival campaign films, conducted by a cinematic magazine in the month after the election, sums up the distinctive styles of the two men.[45]

> Khatami's film begins with 'beautiful epic music', during which we see the candidate, in different towns with pious clerics, and representatives of the various religious minorities, along with various ethnic minorities, and the enthusiasm and excitement of the people in his company is clearly shown; an image of a child who tries to enthusiastically kiss his hand, but Mr Khatami prevents him … Mr Khatami in this film, is at one moment a poet, at times a statesman, or a family man, and at other times a popular and revolutionary personality … The interviewer (Mohandess Hojjat) and the producers of the programme knew well, that simple conversations, friendly, with little politics, in a half hour television programme, would better present the subject. For this reason the programme went after his human dimension; with questions such as: How many children do you have?; Are you good with children?; Do you want to be president at home too?; Is your wife happy with your candidacy? … To which Mr Khatami would provide suitable and agreeable answers. For instance in answer to a question regarding his suitability, he relates a night in the desert [*kaveer*]: 'The most exciting memory which comes to my mind relates to my childhood and adolescence in the desert. In the summer nights when you sleep on the roof, the star littered sky seems so close that you think that by extending your hand just a little, you can

---

[43] Ibid., pp. 131, 217–19, 224.

[44] Dad, *Sad Rooz ba Khatami*, pp. 55, 70.

[45] Kaviani, *Ramz peerozi yek rais jumhur*, p. 241. This excellent comparison, quoted in ibid., pp. 242–50, was originally published in the monthly magazine *Film*, Tir 1376/1997, no. 205.

pick out the stars. This itself creates such a feeling of exaltation and excitement in a person. Looking at the sky and its proximity to the ground is a source of a type of love and excitement and sense of life.' The answer to this question is such that even the most ordinary person in society can empathise with his candidacy. When one considers that all the ratified candidates have revolutionary credentials, or were among the companions or supporters of the revolution or founders of the Islamic Republic of Iran, and that the viewers know this, in this short time, the viewers are seeking undiscovered facets of their characters; things that are less obvious in political personalities. In the section of the film, when the question is asked, 'What are your own feelings with respect to the Imam?' the director, in contrast with the usual way of projecting the image of the questioner from the beginning to the end of his question, instead focuses on the emotional face of Mr Khatami, which at the moment of hearing the question belies sadness and admiration, and after a short pause, he begins his answer. This short image is one of the most powerful segments of the film ... The image of a bus which has been used for the first time for a national figure has also allowed the projection of an attractive image from within the bus, distinct from what people would have expected; an image which would not have been possible from a car or limousine.

In short, Khatami is depicted as affable, approachable, pious, comfortable with people and, crucially, in his description of 'reaching for the stars', as a man full of aspiration and hope.

This skilful election broadcast can be contrasted with one for Nateq Nuri which begins somewhat differently and essentially gives the viewer an image of business as usual.

After the announcement of the name and qualities of Mr Nateq Nuri, the film begins with an image of Ayatollah Javadi Amoli who forcefully says at the beginning of the film, direct to the television screen, the words which should have been left to the end of the film, and these are that voting for Mr Nateq Nuri is better ... The fundamental problem of beginning a film in this manner is that the rest of the film becomes uninteresting to the viewer; it would be like beginning a film or television serial with the words: 'The aim of our story is tell you that good will conquer evil.' ... In the limited time of a half hour film, inter-viewees allude to Mr Nateq Nuri at least 60 times and do so expressly exactly 25 times. The use of titles such as 'His highness Mr Nateq', or 'his eminence' ... or 'his excellency', by most of the interviewees, has more of a negative rather than a positive impact ... Mr Nateq Nuri [then] introduces himself, 'I am Ali Akbar Nateq Nuri, born in 1322', the image is then switched to one of his identity card. What is the point of an image of his identity card? Documenting the above statement serves what purpose to the viewer? ... Afterwards the image switches to Dr Shebani, 'I think it is necessary for him to highlight Mr Nateq Nuri's uniqueness for the benefit of our younger people.' This scene has begun with a suitable conversation. Undoubtedly viewers, in particular the younger generations, are keen to hear Mr Shebani's words but this scene is suddenly cut to Mr Nateq Nuri, 'In my opinion, I don't see any real value in making myself known.' What is the point of this sentence? If this film was intended to introduce a candidate to the public, why has the producer used a scene where the candidate regards such an introduction as of little use? Of course, if in the continuation of this dialogue Mr Nateq explains the reasons why, this may still prove interesting for the viewers, but unfortunately the scene immediately cuts to Mr Shebani, 'One of his characteristics is that he is not really in favour of publicising himself.' This statement, in a political election broadcast, contradicts the purpose and aim of such a film.

A number of factors rapidly become apparent from this graphic comparison of the rival films. In the first place, it is evident that however novel an experience a truly competitive election might have been, the political sophistication of the electorate cannot be doubted. Khatami's election broadcast shows all the technical skill, political nuances and subtlety of an effective Western-style election broadcast. Unlike his rival, he neither takes popular support for granted nor underestimates the voters' intelligence or political discernment. Nateq Nuri's broadcast, in contrast, is somewhat two-dimensional and bland, repeating messages that are both uninteresting and largely irrelevant to the general public. He also misjudged by recounting his revolutionary experiences and time spent in the shah's prisons. This would mean little to a sceptical youth, for whom the revolution, while undoubtedly significant, is part of history. For those who do view the revolutionary inheritance as important – and it should be remembered that these formed the core of the ideological vanguard of the Khatami movement – Nateq Nuri was the last person they would consider representative of its values. Indeed, Nateq Nuri, and what he represented, remained for many the antithesis of revolutionary aims; and his film would not have persuaded them otherwise.

The contrasting films also reflected the fundamental changes which had occurred in the nature of politics during the period of the bourgeois republic, and the failure of the mercantile bourgeoisie to understand this. While some, including undoubtedly Rafsanjani, recognized that there was a 'popular' dimension to politics which had to be considered, few appreciated how far it was driving the political agenda or realized that, far from being passive, it was, principally through student and media agitation, becoming an increasingly active agent for change. The political revolution of the late 1970s was now transforming itself into a social phenomenon of peculiar potency. To recognize and understand this was to harness it; to fight it was to find yourself constantly frustrated. The reformists seized upon this 'higher universal' and made it their own end.[46]

This reality was to become apparent in the election campaign, during which the supporters of Nateq Nuri sought to undermine Khatami's credibility. One such attempt consisted of the allegation that he did not support the idea of the 'absolute' velayat-e faqih or, more contentiously, the idea of velayat at all.[47] There is little doubt that many of Khatami's supporters questioned the nature of the Supreme Leader's authority, though this was nothing new, and certainly there were some who were bold enough to assert that the Leader should be subject to popular election. Exemplifying the views of the authoritarian right, Ayatollah Mahdavi Kani launched a furious attack on those who claimed that the authority of the Leader came from the people rather than God.[48] Far from raising popular doubts as to Khatami's suitability, however, this assault actually raised interest in the election and made the electorate realize that there might be far more at stake than they had thought. At the same time, Khatami was scrupulous in his own statements concerning the leadership and stressed that the velayat-e faqih was the foundation of the political order.

Another tactic was to argue that Khamene'i himself was ill-disposed to Khatami and indeed favoured Nateq Nuri, who made a point of his apparent closeness to the Leader.[49] This association was widely regarded as real, but far from assisting Nateq Nuri only emphasized his links with the establishment. The portrayal of a political alliance between them has stuck in the public imagination and coloured subsequent analyses of Ayatollah Khamene'i's role in political developments, but a closer scrutiny of the record indicates a greater ambivalence on the part of the Leader: Khamene'i was not explicit about his political leanings, though he may have been swayed by those surrounding him, and many of the assertions of his support for Nateq Nuri have come from the latter's camp rather than through

[46] See Hegel, 'Introduction' to Lectures on the Philosophy of World History, p. 82.
[47] Dad, Sad Rooz ba Khatami, p. 129.
[48] Kaviani, Ramz peerozi yek rais jumhur, pp. 127–8.
[49] Dad, Sad Rooz ba Khatami, pp. 159–63.

the office of the Leader. Indeed, there was considerable frustration among certain senior administration officials that the conservatives seemed to have 'hijacked' the leadership, with some emphasizing (in private) that while this affiliation might reflect the views of many of his closest officials, Khamene'i himself was anxious to escape the association. Khatami's view on the relationship, which he kept to himself, reveals an altogether more complex situation. According to Mohammad Salamati, the director general of the Islamic Mujahideen Organization, Khatami recounted a conversation with Khamene'i that took place a full year before the elections during which the Leader 'made it clear that not only am I not against your entry into the elections, but if you are victorious, this would be a source of great happiness to me'.[50]

Attempts to manage institutions in its favour were also to backfire on the Nuri camp, including in particular a quest to monopolize the air time available on the national television network, whose director, Ali Larijani, was the younger brother of Nateq Nuri's key supporter Mohammad Javad Larijani. The latter was to prove an enormous embarrassment to the Nuri campaign following a trip by the candidate to the United Kingdom; in the initial stages of the campaign great irritation was caused by the very public declaration of support the elder Larijani had given to Nateq Nuri, when many had considered that his natural political leanings lay with Khatami. As noted above, the wholesale 'defection' of such technocrats to Nateq Nuri was viewed by many reformists as well as Rafsanjani loyalists as a grave betrayal and formed the basis of much of the vitriolic antagonism which was to follow, giving the electoral contest an edge it otherwise might not have had. The initial protests against IRIB, the state broadcasting organization (Islamic Republic of Iran Broadcasting), came from centrist politicians such as Abdullah Nuri and Mohammad Hashemi, Rafsanjani's brother and former head of the IRIB. Hashemi was particularly scathing in attacking the 'presidential' service IRIB offered Nateq Nuri, some six months before the electoral contest was meant to begin.[51] And yet, given Nateq Nuri's poor screen presence, his constant presence on the television proved to be only another handicap,[52] while Khatami's relatively limited

---

[50] Quoted in Kaviani, *Ramz peerozi yek rais jumhur*, p. 112. Khatami was apparently reluctant to mention this conversation for a full year after the election, in case people took advantage of it. One suspects that this reticence owes something to political prudence as well as personal integrity.

[51] Kaviani, *Ramz peerozi yek rais jumhur*, pp. 129, 132. Ali Larijani emphasized the impartiality of the IRIB; see BBC SWB ME/2864 MED/16, 11 March 1997, IRIB, 9 March 1997. There were frequent charges and countercharges of media bias; on allegations of bias against *Hamshahri*, a newspaper run by the mayor of Tehran, Gholamhussein Karsbachi, see BBC SWB ME/2912 MED/ 10–11, 7 May 1997; Iranian Radio, 5 May 1997; *Hamshahri*, 6 May 1997.

[52] Dad, *Sad Rooz ba Khatami*, p. 181.

exposure, often cut short by 'freak' power cuts, only served to heighten interest in him.

Again and again, the apparently amateur nature of the Khatami campaign served to accentuate his image as a man of the people, while the presidential presentation of the Nateq Nuri campaign only served further to alienate him from them. Some provincial governors well disposed to Nateq Nuri saw to it that various items of literature were laced with Nateq Nuri motifs. Much of this represented political hedging by those who thought Nateq Nuri's victory was a simple formality and expected that if they had expressed loyalty earlier in the day they could be expected to reap the rewards later. Thus the governor of Ardabil province, for instance, used a quote from Nateq Nuri to grace his official letterhead.[53] Other governors saw to it that extensive resources were allocated for Nateq Nuri's impending trips, in an obvious attempt to impress the future president.[54] Nor was such behaviour limited to the domestic arena. In a now infamous 'state' visit to Moscow, Nateq Nuri was fêted as the next president and received by Yeltsin, as well as being allowed to address the Russian Duma.[55] Not surprisingly, there was much recrimination in Russian diplomatic and political circles following the election.

There were other more or less trivial ways in which the conservative-dominated institutions inadvertently encouraged support for Khatami. For example, the Guardian Council suddenly decreed that candidates must not be called by titles to which they were not, strictly speaking, entitled, such as 'Dr' or 'engineer'. Despite Nateq Nuri's accumulating collection of honorific epithets, the only candidate to be popularly known as 'Dr' was Khatami, on account of his philosophical leanings and substantial writings. This move, popularly seen, therefore, as a slight against Khatami, simply tended to draw attention to his education in contrast to his rivals.[56] More controversial, perhaps, was the decision by the Guardian Council and the ministry of the interior not to announce the names of the valid candidates in alphabetical order, but to place Nateq Nuri first and Khatami third.[57] This caused such an outcry that the Guardian Council was forced to make a public response. The protest itself may be put down to two factors: first, it was a reflection of how suspicious political activists had become of the Guardian Council, so that even a small irregularity such as this could evoke the charge of institutional bias; second, there was a genuine concern

[53] Ibid., p. 178.
[54] Kaviani, *Ramz peerozi yek rais jumhur*, p. 149.
[55] BBC SWB ME/2891 MED/3, 12 April 1997; Interfax News Agency, 11 April 1997.
[56] Kaviani, *Ramz peerozi yek rais jumhur*, p. 147.
[57] Ibid., p. 150; Dad, *Sad Rooz ba Khatami*, p. 206.

that the roll-call of names reflected the order in which the names would appear on the ballot paper. In an interview with the BBC, Nateq Nuri had somewhat implausibly attributed his poor performance in the Majlis elections to the fact that his name had appeared so far down the ballot paper. This, he argued, was the chief reason why he had not garnered enough votes.[58] As a justification for failure this was not a good response, making the electorate appear both lazy and stupid, but the action of the Guardian Council seemed to many to be responding to Nateq Nuri's complaint.

Another counterproductive tactic was the use of Islamic vigilantes, most of them belonging to a group known as the Ansar-e Hizbollah, to heckle and often violently disrupt meetings being addressed by Khatami. The chief target of this group tended to be student gatherings, the conservatives having taken note of student agitation and the potential force this had given the Khatami campaign.[59] Few gatherings were untouched by the violence; but, far from quelling enthusiasm for Khatami, it galvanized support, encouraging supporters in the conviction that they were engaged in a worthwhile, even historic, movement. Many protested that the Law Enforcement Forces and the interior ministry were not doing enough to safeguard their security, reinforcing the belief that the 'forces of conservatism' had penetrated all parts of government.

Two particular attempts at disruption stand out as examples of how Khatami was able to turn ostensibly embarrassing and distasteful encounters to his advantage. During a visit to Mashhad on which he was to address members of the *ulema*, members of the Ansar-e Hizbollah infiltrated a meeting and began chanting slogans. When an old man from within this group sought to have his say, Khatami invited him to take the podium, which he did, presenting his case against Khatami with some gusto. Having finished, the 'Ansar' then tried to prevent Khatami responding, despite the protestations of the crowd, which finally silenced the hardliners. One cleric who witnessed the scene commented afterwards: 'Up till half an hour ago I was determined not to vote for Mr Khatami. However with the events that these people [Ansar-e Hizbollah] have this night created, and the humility of Mr Khatami which I witnessed with my own eyes, I am now resolved to think seriously about voting for Mr Khatami.'[60]

As time went on and Ansar-e Hizbollah incursions became more frequent and regular, Khatami, whose popularity was increasing, was able to answer his critics without interruption. During a subsequent trip to the University of Isfahan, a group of Ansar began to heckle and at one point

[58] Dad, *Sad Rooz ba Khatami*, p. 79.
[59] E.g. BBC SWB ME/2908 MED/5, 2 May 1997; *Iran*, 27 April 1997.
[60] Dad, *Sad Rooz ba Khatami*, p. 115.

shouted, 'Mr Khatami! You have two weak points. Firstly, you are incompetent. Secondly, if you become president, you will use extremists.' Khatami's response and method of delivery reveal something of his ability to master his audience. He first disarmed his opponents by retorting: 'Of course, I have more than two weak points!' At this the Ansar-e Hizbollah members cheered and congratulated themselves. Only then did Khatami deliver the rhetorical knock-out blow, adding: 'However, the biggest weakness is this, that weak people, possessing few and scanty numbers, should consider themselves absolute [in all matters].' This raised the biggest cheer, and proved a significant humiliation for the fifty or so Ansar-e Hizbollah present.[61]

As the campaign progressed doubts crept into the Nateq Nuri camp, but did not amount to serious concern about the eventual outcome – although there were already signs that Nateq Nuri was having to adjust his rhetoric to take into account the Khatami factor. It was important, after all, to win by a wide margin to ensure that a second round would not be necessary. Accordingly, the issues of women and the young began to play a more prominent role in campaign rhetoric. One speech in particular was devoted almost exclusively to the role of women in society and the efforts Nateq Nuri had made to further gender equality.[62] It revealed a realization both that the women's vote would be important and that most of it was likely to be cast in favour of Khatami. It represented in many ways a belated attempt to snatch the initiative away from Khatami, who had effectively succeeded in establishing the terms of debate. Indeed, in an echo of 1979 it was clear to all but the incumbent establishment that they had lost the ideological initiative and that there appeared to be no political or intellectual depth or sophistication to their campaign. They simply had nothing to offer but more of the same; and in this absence of intellectual stimulus, the Khatami camp was forging ahead with new bold ideas. The consequence of this early loss of the political initiative was that the conservatives found themselves reacting to events rather than dictating them; and the more extreme they became, the more absurd their position appeared. For all Nateq Nuri's protestations, his attempts to 'catch up' simply made him look more inept.

By the end of the campaign, Khatami could afford to ignore some of the questions put to him. The newspaper *Resalat*, for instance, tried to highlight supposed weaknesses by publishing a list of questions attacking

---

[61] Ibid., p. 123; the term 'absolute' in this context almost conveys the meaning of 'totalitarian' in Western discourse.

[62] BBC SWB ME/2920 MED/6–8, 16 May 1997; Tehran Radio, 14 May 1997.

Khatami's judgment and character.[63] A particular point which came up again and again was his resignation from the Ministry of Culture in 1992, which was at that time publicly put down to 'exhaustion'. Although few people believed that this was the real reason, some conservatives clearly thought that this raised issues of ability and stamina. The question remained unanswered. Instead the reformists, as they were to be known, felt confident enough to take the attack to the opposition camp. Here, both their superior political sophistication and the incompetence of their opponents served to provide them with two particularly significant triumphs. One was a trip by Nateq Nuri's campaign manager Mohammad Javad Larijani to London in February 1997, during which he met a senior British Foreign Office official. His meeting with Nick Browne, then head of the Middle East section, had been taped by embassy staff (not a particularly unusual practice). The conversations were gradually leaked from the embassy to the Iranian press at the most inopportune time and effectively exploited to destroy Larijani's political career. During these private discussions Larijani is reported to have been extremely dismissive of the Leader, Ali Khamene'i, to have promised that the Rushdie issue was a detail which would be solved as soon as the election was won, and to all intents and purposes have been fishing for British approval. Needless to say, as news of these remarks seeped into the Iranian press, the reaction was explosive, and Larijani was forced to defend himself in a number of interviews.[64] Whatever the accuracy of the reported comments (and we are unlikely to know for several years), they played on existing fears and suspicions among many Iranians. In particular, Larijani's dismissal of the importance of the Leader and his references to a 'business-friendly' government seemed to confirm views that power was shifting emphatically towards the mercantile bourgeoisie, who not only dictated the domestic pace of events but were now seeking to extend their links abroad. That Larijani should be discussing such matters with the British also hastened suspicions that Britain, the great bogeyman of modern Iranian history, was developing, or had already developed, intimate links with the Iranian conservatives. The magazine *Zanan* (Women) put the incident to good political use when it decided to coin the term 'Lari-gate' to describe this public relations fiasco.[65]

Far more serious was the successful identification of Nateq Nuri as the 'Taleban of Iran', a label devastating in its effectiveness. The Afghan

---

[63] The questions are listed in Dad, *Sad Rooz ba Khatami*, pp. 145–6.

[64] BBC SWB ME/2904 MED/10, 28 April 1997; *Iran*, 19 April 1997.

[65] Dad, *Sad Rooz ba Khatami*, p. 171. See also Behzad Nabavi's comments in *Salaam*, quoted in BBC SWB ME/2905 MED/7–8, 29 April 1997; *Salaam*, 17 April 1997.

Taleban had been growing as the dominant force in the fractured Afghan state since 1995, when they had taken Kabul. These Sunni zealots, who had been trained in Pakistan with Saudi financial help and not insignificant US encouragement,[66] were anathema to the government in Iran, which remains the only state to have condemned them as non-Islamic. Not only were they virulently anti-Shi'a, they also represented a loss of status and influence for Iran in the Afghan state. There were other, more particular reasons for irritation too, including Iran's desire to repatriate the approximately two million Afghan refugees who remained in Iran. The severe policies administered by the Taleban were not regarded as conducive to any repatriation policy; on the contrary, many Afghans were sending their daughters to Iran, both for security and also to secure them an education. In addition, the main source of domestic funding for the Taleban was the production and smuggling of opium, much of which came through the Iranian border and which the Iranian authorities were struggling to contain. Most important as far as the Iranian public were concerned was the harsh image projected by the Taleban, with their rigorous interpretation of Islamic law, epitomized, for example, by cases of modern items such as television sets being 'hanged' from trees.

The record of the Taleban in Afghanistan had a direct impact on the domestic politics of Iran. Not only was an avowedly Islamic regime condemned as un-Islamic by Tehran, thereby confirming that different interpretations could in fact exist, but the 'totalitarian' (absolute) actions of the Taleban seemed to have their parallel among religious extremists in Iran, who complained, for instance, that giving women the vote was 'un-Islamic'. It also further encouraged the establishment of a national distinctiveness and essentially confirmed the localization of the Islamic Revolution. While Iran professed to be the leading light of the Islamic world, it fought hard to distinguish itself from extremists in both Algeria and Afghanistan. As more than one government official argued, 'ours is an *Iranian* Islamic Revolution.' In a curious way, American policy towards the Taleban encouraged this shift, in that by signalling that it did not have a problem with radical Islam but only with radical Iranian Islam, the United States confirmed that the antagonism was at root an anti-Iranian one. While this policy may have been pursued to placate its other Muslim allies, given the policies of the Taleban it was a woefully shortsighted one. As far as Iran was concerned, it reinforced the legitimacy of nationalism and Iranianism;

[66] The US oil company Unocal was keen to pursue the construction of an oil and gas pipeline through Afghanistan, a project regarded as ridiculous by almost everyone, although the US government encouraged it on the pretext that it would circumvent Iran. So close did their relationship become that on at least one occasion Taleban officials were invited by Unocal to the United States.

and it was Khatami, with his inclusive policies, who best represented this resurgent pride in all things Iranian. Nateq Nuri and his Ansar-e Hizbollah 'allies' seemed to be more representative of Islamic extremism, and, as the Taleban made very clear, things could get worse. In short, the Taleban proved to be the looking-glass in which Iranians could see, with some horror, a possible future. It should be pointed out that Nateq Nuri was unlikely in fact to have led the country down such a path, but nevertheless it was a charge that stuck, an effective strategy which capitalized on people's fears; Nateq Nuri's late protestations on television only served to confirm suspicions, and sealed his fate.

The Election of 2 Khordad

So unexpected and so dramatic was Khatami's victory on 23 May 1997 (2 Khordad) that in retrospect it can be difficult to recapture the sense of national euphoria it engendered. There were clear social signs indicating an imminent triumph for Khatami, but right up until the election, few of his supporters were willing to acknowledge the potential scale of the victory, or indeed how receptive the public had been to their message. Polling day proved to be the vital test of the level of political consciousness. Many hypotheses had been advanced; this was the practical trial which would prove or disprove the conflicting views. Some argued that Khatami would win on the second ballot, if the election remained fair. Others hoped that at least he would force a second ballot, thus tempering the scale and scope of a conservative victory. Still others, including most of the diplomatic corps in Tehran, argued that owing in part to election manipulation and the inherent conservatism of the provinces, Nateq Nuri would win. As one diplomat recounted, one of the most satisfying experiences he had enjoyed was the speed at which his colleagues had rushed to rewrite their dispatches.[67]

Right up until the end, there were concerns that the election result would be manipulated. The satirical weekly *Golagha* had printed a cartoon on its front page showing a ballot box with a vote for Khatami going in and being transformed into a vote for Nateq Nuri on exit! There is little doubt that there were attempts to rig the election, with lorry-loads of fraudulent ballot papers being stopped. Rafsanjani himself is reported to have sat in on one count to ensure its fairness. The scale of the victory, with some 70 per cent of the votes, equivalent to 20 million voters, in favour of Khatami, was

---

[67] Interview with author; see also *Jame'eh Madani va Iran-e Emrooz* (Civil society and today's Iran) (Tehran: Naqsh & Negar, 1377/1997), p. 259.

itself a substantial bulwark against fraud: there were simply not enough fake ballot papers to bridge the gap![68] But the greatest insurance against malpractice was the reality of the social basis of Khatami's support, which was duly reflected in the various tiers of the administration, despite the best pleas of senior officials. Foreign minister Velayati, for instance, ordered posters of Nateq Nuri to be placed throughout the ministry building; others simply went around taking them down. Many public posters were defaced with irreverent graffiti. Contrary to the wishes of their commanders, on the night before the election members of the Revolutionary Guards were handing out posters of Khatami to passing motorists.[69]

What had occurred on 23 May was a social phenomenon with profound political consequences, founded on that most potent of myths – hope.[70] It was now up to the reformists to institutionalize their victory; but first they had to begin the arduous task of dismantling and deconstructing the mercantile bourgeois republic.

---

[68] Salamati, quoted in Kaviani, *Ramz peerozi yek rais jumhur*, p. 207.
[69] Recounted to author.
[70] See Kaviani, *Ramz peerozi yek rais jumhur*, pp. 183–95.

6 Contested Hegemonies and the Institutionalization of Power

The landslide election victory of Mohammad Khatami on 23 May 1997 left the assumed front-runner Nateq Nuri personally humiliated and the conservative right emotionally shattered and bewildered. An enormous amount of political manoeuvring occurred in the immediate aftermath of the election result as governors and Majlis deputies alike sought urgently to recover lost ground and realign themselves. Only a few days before the poll, most deputies had a taken a public oath of fealty to Nateq Nuri, while senior officials had publicly voiced support for the 'president elect'. The deputies quickly backtracked and, much like prodigal sons, returned to the fold admonished. But others were to be less fortunate. Mohammad Javad Larijani discovered that there was to be no recovery from the political wilderness, but probably the greatest venom was directed at Ali Akbar Velayati, whose unusually long tenure at the Ministry of Foreign Affairs was, many conjectured enthusiastically, about to end. Velayati, whom some commentators had considered a potential president himself, had increasingly been described as a 'lay cleric', a technocrat whose 'sanctimonious piety' had placed him beyond the pale. His fate was to be dispatched as an adviser to the Leader; this allowed him to save face, although few people were in any doubt that the move was equivalent in British terms to being sent to the House of Lords, in essence signifying the end of his political ambitions.

Despite the euphoria, however, doubts remained – about Khatami's ability and, more seriously, about the willingness of the conservatives genuinely to relinquish power.[1] To paraphrase Winston Churchill, most reformists considered the electoral victory the end of the beginning rather than the beginning of the end. The difficulty of the task ahead was not underestimated, and such was the scale of the victory that there was a palpable sense of being in uncharted territory. While some argued that Khatami

---

[1] See e.g. H. Amirahmadi's comments in a roundtable discussion for the journal *Etela'at Siyasi-Eqtesadi*, in *Jame'eh Madani va Iran-e Emrooz* (Civil society and today's Iran) (Tehran: Naqsh and Negar, 1377/1997), p. 242.

should be careful not to underestimate the conservatives, others argued that on the contrary he might overestimate their strength and join forces with them.[2] There is little doubt that hope was accompanied by considerable trepidation, if not outright fear, among many ordinary people at what the conservatives might do in retaliation. This fear soon transformed itself into a depressingly characteristic, if reassuring, fatalism, which the reformists sought to dispel, while for obvious reasons their opponents sought to cement it. Fatalism, raised to the status of a philosophical virtue by many Iranians (though by no means unique to them), has been the bane of all managers of change – constitutional, monarchical or republican – throughout the country's modern history, and in so far as it is characterized by a belief in the unchanging nature of things, it can be regarded as a variant of orientalism. More precisely, though, it can be considered as the quintessential 'false consciousness' in the classic Marxist sense. Fatalism is encouraged in order to quell hope and to justify the status quo – often, as in this case, as a manifestation of the divine order.[3]

This fatalistic attitude, which persists to this day, was encouraged by an unusual 'unholy alliance' of conservatives, exiled opposition groups and foreign commentators unwilling to come to terms with the social changes convulsing the country and to concede that such things could happen in a country which was ostensibly the epitome of 'fundamentalist' dogma. A running commentary on the first three years of the Khatami presidency (and there is little sign of it petering out) has been the oft-repeated refrain *plus ça change*, with emphasis on the continuation of poor economic performance, the apparent institutional dominance of the conservatives and the alleged inactivity of the reformists on what are considered 'substantive issues'. Much of this is prejudiced nonsense which, preoccupied with detail, fails to see the wood for the trees – or indeed, on occasion, arises from looking at the wrong wood altogether. Put simply, if you don't see change, it may be because you are looking in the wrong place. Another frequently repeated mantra is the concern that Khatami is about to fall, to be removed, or simply to be assassinated. While such threats are very real,[4] they detract from the process of consolidation which accelerates with every day that Khatami remains in place. As the president said himself before the Majlis elections in February 2000, people are constantly predicting his imminent political demise, yet somehow he is still here.

[2] See comments in *Jame'eh Madani va Iran-e Emrooz*, p. 256.

[3] Hence the title of the book (by various authors) *Beem-ha va Omid-ha* (Fears and expectations) (Tehran: Hamshahri, 1378/1999–2000).

[4] The recent *fatwa* (religious judgment) issued against the president is a case in point.

The reformist world-view

Many of the reformist groups which occupied the centre and centre-left of the political spectrum were no less surprised than their opponents by the scale of their victory. Khatami's new chief of staff, Hojjat-ol Islam Abtahi, recounted in an interview how he had not appreciated the receptiveness of society to the message which Khatami sought to impart. Nor, however, did anyone have any illusions about the potential fragility of the victory. Not only would expectations be high, but the scale of the electoral victory meant that Khatami now headed a coalition composed of many and various partners, all agreed on the need for change but differing on the nature and speed of that change. In addition, the government inherited a flawed economy, an unhelpfully low oil price, and a conservative faction entrenched in many government institutions and undoubtedly eager for revenge. The walls of the bourgeois republic had been breached; now a strategy for consolidation and institutionalization had to be both formulated and implemented.

One advantage the reformist camp did enjoy was ideological cohesion: while differences existed in detail, there was a broad consensus on what may be termed the 'meta-narrative' of Iranian political development. Broadly speaking, the Islamic Revolution, as a movement for political emancipation, was not dissociated from the movements which had preceded it in the twentieth century, and its origins were generally located within the Constitutional Revolution of 1906; hence the continued vigorous debates about the nature of that political upheaval. Similarly, while strict Islamists might debunk and reject the secularism of Dr Mosaddeq, most reformists encouraged his rehabilitation as a democratic hero undermined by foreign allies and their conservative allies in Iran. The analogy being drawn was obvious. The Islamic Revolution itself was the third significant attempt of the century to achieve political emancipation, stability and democratic order.

This may seem an odd assessment for those Iranians who were victims of revolutionary purges and subsequently witnessed the dominance of the authoritarian tendency, yet it is one adhered to by most reformists. Indeed, there is a fundamental misconception which needs to be addressed, and that is that Khatami's victory represented a rejection of the Islamic Revolution by an oppressed society finally given an opportunity to speak. While there is little doubt that some cast their votes with such an intention, that tendency should not be exaggerated. Nor should it be assumed that the earnest desire for serious reform can be easily translated into one for another revolution. Most wanted a reform of the current system, not its removal, if only for the simple reason that most Iranians deemed one revolution per individual lifetime quite enough.

What was being rejected was a particular interpretation of the Islamic Revolution – the authoritarian tendency – and its patrimonial offspring, the 'mercantile bourgeois republic'. On this view the Islamic Revolution itself, as a manifestation of the popular will, was a legitimate event that had been hijacked by the authoritarians exploiting the circumstances of the conflict with Iraq, when political development came a poor second to the exigencies of the war; thus the opportunity to institutionalize popular participation was missed during the first decade of the revolution.[5] While the election of President Rafsanjani was initially seen as an opportunity to get the revolution back on track with serious attempts at political development, hopes were disappointed by the erratic and haphazard nature of reform under that regime, to the point that by the end of his presidency many reformists considered that Rafsanjani had betrayed the cause in favour of his own personal financial and political interests.

It should also be borne in mind that Ayatollah Khomeini, while on occasion viewed with a critical eye,[6] is nevertheless regarded as a source of legitimacy by many reformers, who regard the construction of the bourgeois republic as a betrayal of his legacy.[7] Even among those who have little affection for him, many respect his achievements. He remains a dominant figure, and it may come as a surprise that reformists have been much more enthusiastic in quoting him in defence of their cause than conservatives, who have been much more muted. This is to some extent a reflection of his ambiguous legacy, but also of the intellectual rigour of the reformist camp. Khatami himself is related to the Khomeini family by marriage and has enjoyed the support of the ayatollah's grandson, Hasan Khomeini, as well as other members of the Khomeini household, each of whom has stated unequivocally that Khatami is delivering on Khomeini's promise. This may be open to debate, but such backing is a useful advantage in a sometimes bleak political terrain, and it has not been effectively challenged by the conservatives.

For the reformists, then, the victory of Mohammad Khatami heralded in essence a return to the original aims of the Islamic Revolution,[8] which itself had to be situated within the context of successive political developments, and these now had to be consolidated, institutionalized and

---

[5] See e.g. S. Hajarian's comments in *Jame'eh Madani va Iran-e Emrooz*, pp. 310–11.

[6] See the allegations made by the newspaper *Resalat*, BBC SWB ME/2999 MED/14, 16 Aug. 1997; Voice of Israel external service, 14 Aug. 1997.

[7] See e.g. Hajarian's comments in *Jame'eh Madani va Iran-e Emrooz*, p. 316.

[8] For broader discussion see the various articles in *Beem-ha va Omid-ha*.

extended. This latter point is extremely important, because, as some argued, while the change of regime may have spelt a return to the 'spirit of '79', the social and intellectual changes realized politically in the election of Khatami also constituted an extension of those early aims – a social fulfilment of political aspirations and as such a political phenomenon in its own right.[9]

Policies

It is sometimes argued that the reformists are good on theory but not capable in practice: that is, they can win political campaigns but for all their style and sophistication, they have few concrete plans for action. It is certainly true that while they have managed to coin popular slogans with social appeal, they have been weaker on substantive issues of economic reform. Yet many people take the view that political reform is a prerequisite to meaningful and sustainable economic development and that Iran's experience under both the last shah and Rafsanjani have revealed that one without the other is a fragile achievement. Moreover, it will be argued below that the first Khatami administration has indeed witnessed substantive gains in both ideological and political development, which may be less tangible than material gains but which are crucial to the long-term success of the latter. Thus, in assessing the achievements and failures of the Khatami administration and the reformists, it must first be recognized that they are principally involved in what may be termed a hegemonic contest in which the bourgeois republic is dismantled and replaced with an Islamic democracy. This requires primarily attitudinal rather than institutional changes, following the line that if society is not ready for democracy (the favourite refrain of autocrats) then it must be prepared.

The policies of the reformists can be summarized as follows:

- *Political rationalization is a prerequisite to economic development.* Political institutions must operate on rational legal grounds, and everyone, without exception, is subject to the law. A legal framework is a secure environment for social, political and economic development and provides non-violent mechanisms for the resolution of disputes, be they personal or corporate. This is assisted by:

[9] See in particular A. Abdi's interesting interpretation, ibid., pp. 137–44; see also Hajarian's comments in *Jame'eh Madani va Iran-e Emrooz*, pp. 307–8.

- *The institutionalization of civil society* According to Montesquieu, 'virtue' is essential for the functioning of a republic. There must be honesty, integrity and transparency, with a division of powers to ensure that power is not monopolized. Civil society is enhanced and extended by the cultivation of debate within universities and the expansion of the press, along with the subsequent development of associations and parties. In essence, a new public sphere must be developed out of, or indeed in contradistinction to, the bourgeois public sphere. This will be assisted by pulling back the state. Iranians must complete their transformation from subjects to citizens (with rights) and extend a developing social cohesion in a constructive relationship with the state.

- *The enhancement of the Majlis* The Majlis is the greatest single symbol of society's relationship with the state. It is the point of inter-action between people and government, and creates an organic bond between the two. A Majlis which reflects the popular will has more chance of passing laws which will be respected, as well as holding to account those institutions and individuals which society and public opinion feel have transgressed the public trust. There must be a con-sensual approach to law-making; laws cannot be imposed upon an unwilling populace.

- *Consolidating popular participation.* People must recognize that they have a direct influence on government and that their votes count. Public apathy and fatalism are the enemies of democratic develop-ment; people must become accustomed to voting but also must recognize and appreciate the value of their vote.

- *Decentralization.* Power must be decentralized, to give the provinces more say in the running of their own affairs; also, at a local level, people must be able to see the fruits of their political endeavours. This not only encourages a sense of empowerment but assists in prevent-ing the monopolization of power. In many ways, this marks the most significant physical break with the structure of the Iranian state as founded by Reza Shah.

- *Depersonalization.* Power must be depersonalized and institutional-ized. Henceforth the aim would be to centre power within concrete institutions rather than for it to be dependent primarily on individuals.

- *Religion as the handmaiden of democracy.* A revitalized and redefined Islam will provide the social and cultural cohesion for the operation of a democracy, in the same way that Alexis de Tocqueville argued that Christianity was the essential foundation of American demo-cracy. Islam provides the basis of virtue and the value system which guides individual actions, although it should be remembered that the ideological foundation of the Iranian state is *religious nationalism*.

* *Economic restructuring.* Investing in an economy which has been organized to serve the interests of a mercantile oligarchy is a fruitless exercise which only exacerbates disparities in wealth. The frontiers of mercantile capitalism have to be rolled back, though by no means eliminated, if a constructive investment-based economy is to have a chance of succeeding. In calling for an 'entrepreneurial spirit', Khatami is in essence calling for a shift from mercantile to industrial capitalism, while recognizing the need for government mediation of the market, so that social justice can be attended to. Economic pluralism is essential for political pluralism and vice versa.

* *Reintegration into global society.* Isolation serves no purpose. The new administration is keen to establish a broad range of links based on mutual respect and trust. Khatami believes that dialogue is now possible because Iran has matured politically and socially and no longer has a dependency relationship with the West. A constructive relationship will facilitate both much-needed foreign investment and an exchange of ideas.

Given that much of this can be achieved within the framework of the current constitution, which of course was approved by Ayatollah Khomeini, the dominant slogan has been the implementation of the constitution, against which there is little opponents can say. Where the ambiguity lies, of course, is in the role of the Leader; if one follows an authoritarian interpretation, as many conservatives do, then the republican aspects of the constitution become largely irrelevant, since the Leader is essentially above the law. If however, the Leader is subject to the law – at the very least, Islamic law – then the potential conflicts of interest are much reduced. It should come as no surprise, therefore, that one of the first debates that the new minister of the interior, Abdullah Nuri, permitted in Tehran University was a discussion on the political function of the Leader within the context of the constitution. This infuriated the conservatives, and set the tone for the struggle to follow.

Agents of change (1): students

The emergence of the student movement promises a renewal of revolutionary politics as well as the arrival of a new social force. Student insurgents have rejected established models of political action: they refuse to pin their hopes on the remote manoeuvres of parliamentary assemblies or party conferences. The main student movements are quite aware that their struggle is against the social system as a whole; they refuse to participate in it on its own terms.[10]

There are two major engines of change which essentially constitute the ideological vanguard of the reformist movement in Iran: the student movement and an expanded, vigorous press. The student movement has traditionally played a pivotal role in the political life of the country, and indeed, as noted in an earlier chapter, the foundation of the University of Tehran in 1934 by Reza Shah can be counted one of his most significant social and political legacies (although it was not his expectation that students would prove so rebellious).[11] Successive governments have sought to tame and control the student population, in terms both of monitoring intake and of controlling graduates' subsequent careers.[12] Students, in many ways taking their lead from the student demonstrations of 1968 which convulsed western Europe, played a fundamental role in the Islamic Revolution, committing one of its most symbolic and significant acts in the seizure of the US embassy in Tehran in 1979. They were (and remain) idealistic, driven and determined to achieve their goals. While the shah consistently misunderstood the student population, Khomeini actively cultivated their loyalty. Following the Islamic Revolution the new establishment sought not only to purge all that was considered impure from the curriculum but also to control access, ensuring that those students from authentic 'Islamic' backgrounds had priority in gaining admission. On the positive side this was justified on the grounds of widening access to a much broader range of students from throughout the country, but it was also used to deny social and political 'undesirables'.

Very soon, however, the new establishment was to find that the new intake of students were no more willing to submit to higher authority than their forebears, and in the aftermath of the Iran–Iraq War a new generation of students began to take a critical look at their surroundings. With more access to literature, much of it translated into Persian, and benefiting from the impact of global communications, students were better read and more knowledgeable about politics than ever before. Among the authors they knew and were happy to debate were Locke, Hegel, Marx, Weber, Foucault,

---

[10] A. Cockburn, 'Introduction', in A. Cockburn and R. Blackburn, eds, *Student Power, Problems, Diagnosis, Action* (Harmondsworth: Penguin, 1969), p. 7.

[11] See F. Halliday's perceptive essay, 'Students of the World Unite', in Cockburn and Blackburn, eds, *Student Power*, p. 323; for an extensive analysis see also Sadeq Zibakalam, 'The Roots of the Student Movement in Iran', *Payam Azadi*, 30 Azar 1378/21 Dec. 1999, p. 4.

[12] This is of course by no means unique to Iran; see G. Stedman Jones, 'The Meaning of Student Revolt', in Cockburn and Blackburn, eds, *Student Power*, p. 33.

Nietzsche, Habermas, de Tocqueville, Wittgenstein, Gadamer, Ricoeur, Oakeshott and Giddens.[13] They also had a keen sense of history and viewed themselves as the heirs to a powerful tradition of political emancipation which it was their duty to carry forward. Far from being an isolated 'elite' section of society, the student movement in Iran was an intellectual reflection of that society, having emanated from it through a selection procedure which had little to do with social status or economic wealth. The student body thus can be said to enjoy an organic relationship with society, and it is this intimate and integrated relationship which accounts for much of its social and political influence. As Halliday argues, 'A militant student movement will only succeed in revolutionary objectives where it allies itself organically with the major exploited classes of society.'[14]

While Iran cannot be considered a 'post-industrial' society, the centrality of education to the country's culture and the advent of the information age, which has been enthusiastically received in Iran, have combined to give students a central role in political development. Alain Touraine's comments can therefore be seen to have some relevance:

If it is true that knowledge and technical progress are the motors of the new society, as the accumulation of capital was the motor of the preceding (industrial) society, does not the university then occupy the same place as the great capitalist enterprise formerly did? Thus, is not the student movement, in principle at least, of the same importance as the labour movement of the past?[15]

Agents of change (2): the press

As noted above, the press had been steadily expanding during the 1990s, both in number of publications and in scope. Particularly important was the growth of ostensibly cultural magazines and journals, which tended on the whole to deal with matters of political philosophy and sociology.[16]

[13] It is worth remembering that Paul Ricoeur went to Iran at the invitation of the French Institute in the mid-1990s and that his three lectures were packed out. On Oakeshott see e.g. H. Bashiriyeh, 'Andisheye Michael Oakeshott' (The thought of Michael Oakeshott), *Etela'at Siyasi-Eqtesadi*, vol. 10, nos 105–6, June–July 1996, pp. 4–10. Giddens: interview with author. Alas, the 'Third Way' has reached Iran!

[14] Halliday, 'Students of the World Unite', p. 324.

[15] Quoted in Stedman Jones, 'The Meaning of the Student Revolt', p. 26.

[16] See e.g. K. Alamdari, 'Raz Napayedari demokrasi' (The secret behind the failure of democracy), *Adineh*, Shahrivar-Mehr 1374/August–September 1995, pp. 51–3. Another prominent early addition to the intellectual fray was the bi-monthly *Goftegu* (Dialogue); see in particular the special issue on 'Democracy', Winter 1375/1995.

Certainly one should not underestimate the extent of the quantitative expansion during the Rafsanjani administration, although this included many journals which dealt with non-political issues. During the Khatami administration, however, the daily newspapers became an overt aspect of political strategy, with the intention of informing, educating and extending political consciousness. So bold did the press become, with a vibrant corps of investigative journalists the like of which Iran had never seen, that, for the first time in modern Iranian history, Iranians *chose* to get their news from domestic sources as opposed to foreign ones. As one Western diplomat commented, the quantitative growth was matched by a dramatic increase in qualitative output, such that it was often difficult to keep pace with the flow of information.

The function of the press was in essence to set the terms of political discourse and dictate the agenda. They were to define the new hegemony, outline the borders of a new discursive field and force the pace of political development through a simple process of information transparency. People had a right to know, and the more they knew the more effectively they could hold those in government to account. The press was not only a conveyer of ideas; it was to be a central pillar of civil society, mediating views in both directions. Something of the flavour of the press can be gleaned from the following response from the newspaper *Hamshahri* to a criticism from the Majlis Speaker and defeated presidential candidate Nateq Nuri that political development should wait until the country had put its economic house in order. It reveals not only a renewed determination by the press to get the message across but also a more organic understanding of the nature of political change: 'Political development is not an original idea demanding that some people should sit around and define its boundaries for promulgation, in writing, to the nation; it is rather a new approach to political and social relations which has taken shape around two well-known concepts of constitution and civil society.'[17]

Agents of obstruction

Shaken though they may have been by the failure of their candidate to secure the presidency and, by extension, dominance of both the economic and institutional levers of power, in the immediate aftermath of the 1997 election few conservatives were overwhelmed by a desire for serious

---

[17] BBC SWB ME/3274 MED/2, 9 July 1998; *Hamshahri*, 7 July 1998.

reflection.[18] Disregarding the real social forces at work, there was a tendency to remain essentially in a state of denial with respect to the causes of Khatami's victory and to put their loss down instead to the idiosyncrasies of an Iranian population given to occasional reaction. In other words, this was a temporary phenomenon which would pass,[19] and if it proved anything more than ephemeral, then the conservatives would bring their resources to bear to encourage its speedy demise. In terms of being able to obstruct and generally to provide the 'friction' which at all times hinders the process of change, the conservatives had substantial resources at their disposal. Not only did they and their allies permeate the senior echelons of the judiciary, the Revolutionary Guards and the Law Enforcement Forces, they also dominated the largest commercial conglomerate, the Foundation of the Oppressed (discussed in Chapter 4 above). Thus their qualitative influence was far in excess of their numbers. In addition, they were willing to use force where necessary – as had been made very clear during the election campaign. The Ansar-e Hezbollah, while down, were not out, and their willingness to use extra-legal methods was to prove a major frustration to the reformists who sought the moral high ground with their commitment to the rule of law. This frustration was to be accentuated by the fact that the judiciary, and particularly its associated organs, the revolutionary, press and special clerical courts, were not short of judges willing to toe a partisan line. Indeed, for all the potential and real violence of the Ansar, 'institutional violence', as one commentator argued, was a much greater threat to the reform process than 'raw violence', which invariably elicited a very negative public response.[20]

While there was undoubtedly an element of ideological conviction motivating the conservatives, it is remarkable how fragile this was and continues to be. Certainly, the stance of the wealthier mercantile establishment, however dogmatic, seemed to reflect and revolve around their tangible commercial and financial interests. The core of their religious and political philosophy was essentially the principle of the 'absolute' *velayat-e faqih* which had come under substantial criticism, and indeed it was not at all clear whether the Leader himself was partial to such an interpretation.

---

[18] Just as the reformists were made up of numerous groups, so too the conservatives consisted of various elements, although these were fewer in number. By 1997 the term 'conservative' (*mohafezeh-kar*) became current to describe what has been termed in this study the 'mercantile bourgeoisie' and their allies, including the hardline Ansar-e Hezbollah. While ideologically more compact, their inherent rigidity made them more fragile and less cohesive than their opponents. They cannot therefore be considered monolithic.

[19] Very much as de Tocqueville argued; see above, page 9.

[20] H. R. Jalaipour, *Pas az dovum khordad* (After 2 Khordad) (Tehran: Kavir, 1378/1999), pp. 375–7.

While the foot-soldiers of the movement, such as the Ansar-e Hezbollah, undoubtedly harboured determined views, ideological conviction certainly seemed less in evidence higher up the socio-economic ladder. In short, the conservatives had very little to contribute to the ideological and political debate other than arguing that Khatami was not up to the task ahead of him, that he was a closet 'Stalinist', and that the economy should take priority over any quest for political development. Indeed, it was on the state of the economy that the conservatives pinned their hopes – as indeed had Rafsanjani, who, having assisted in bringing about Khatami's victory, was not averse to the possibility of being called back to rescue a faltering economy.

Several reasons were advanced in favour of such an outcome. As an 'intellectual', Khatami could not possibly manage the economy of a country; and, as his resignation from the Ministry of Culture had shown, he was liable to break under pressure. Soon the multitude of problems – some, of course, assisted or manufactured – would prove too much, and Khatami would return to his books. He had in addition inherited a fragile economy, with a low oil price and no sign of immediate recovery, which would prevent him spending his way out of difficulty. Furthermore, the lessons of history seemed to suggest that even popular governments could be undermined through economic pressure – for example, one needed to look no further than the government of Dr Mosaddeq, fatally weakened by economic embargoes and finally terminated through a coup. (The Mosaddeq era was indeed to weigh heavily in the calculations of both sides.) But above all, the conservatives counted on the economy being the sphere in which they could boast overwhelming strength – they had access to capital. This weapon was best seen in action soon after the election, when Mohsen Rafiqdoust, the head of the Foundation of the Oppressed, transferred the bulk of the Foundation's hard currency reserves overseas, thereby precipitating a dramatic devaluation of the rial, which of course would enrich those with access to hard currency (mainly the mercantile bourgeoisie) in the same proportion as it would further impoverish the majority of the population.

Yet even in this area the conservatives suffered from palpable weaknesses, chiefly the absence of a coherent and distinct economic policy. Indeed, it is striking how indistinct conservative economic policy is from that promoted by the reformists; while the latter are less zealous about the market and emphasize social justice, it is apparent that the main planks of policy are not disputed. Both sides support the liberalization of the economy and see the attraction of foreign investment. If anything, the conservatives prefer a more radical implementation of market economics, though they remain vague on the issue of subsidies, and for all their rhetoric they are identified in the public imagination with the status quo. They represent, in short, the interests of the mercantile bourgeoisie, and their call for less government interference is regarded essentially as aimed at the further appropriation and monopolization of economic power by this group. Seen as exclusive and 'class-based', therefore, their criticisms of government economic policy lack popular credibility. Nevertheless, their inability to entrench their hegemony should not detract from the reality that as a consolidated political-economic bloc they remain a powerful obstacle to reform – a reality recognized by the reformists, who have targeted their political strategies accordingly.

A new beginning

The widely held belief in the transient nature of the new presidency was apparent even before Khatami's formal inauguration, as rumour and counter-rumour raised queries about his political longevity, both formally and personally. The widespread euphoria was matched by an unremitting cynical fatalism, which suggested that he would be forced to step down almost immediately, or indeed assassinated. Most people, it seemed, were anticipating some sort of engineered crisis which would result in the overturning of the election result. Then as now, such speculations reflected the tensions born of impending change. In the event, Khatami was inaugurated on schedule and was able to present his first cabinet, which many political pundits viewed as his first serious challenge. The inauguration safely achieved, focus swiftly shifted on to the institutional impediment to change posed by a humbled but re-energizing Majlis.

It was well known that Khatami's cabinet, while including many of Rafsanjani's former ministers, would also place individuals considered unacceptable by the conservatives, in sensitive ministerial posts. In presenting his cabinet, therefore, Khatami was careful to emphasize the meritocratic basis of selection, noting the overall number of candidates and the extensive criteria used to judge their qualities and qualifications for the posts. In a style which would soon come to be characteristic of Iran's new 'philosopher-president', Khatami sought to deflect the criticism expected to arise from the Majlis floor, with the explanation that:

> There is always a great distance between realities and ideals. Mankind's quest for perfection in fact means ceaseless efforts to reach certain ideals. In effect, one can never claim that an achieved end represents

an ideal. However, we should be realistic. Given all the real conditions and circumstances, I am satisfied with my selection and believe that I have submitted to the esteemed Islamic Majlis the names of some noble and competent individuals whom I have chosen as my colleagues.[21]

Two candidates in particular were likely to come under especial scrutiny: Abdullah Nuri as the new minister of interior, and Ata'ollah Mohajerani as the new minister of culture and Islamic guidance. The latter was to prove the most controversial as the Majlis attempted to claim its first scalp, arguing that Mohajerani was a 'liberal', had voiced pro-American views, and had once been a member of the Mojahedeen-e Khalq Organization (MKO).[22] Among the more peculiar objections voiced to his appointment was the criticism that, given the opportunity, Mohajerani would not kill Salman Rushdie. Khatami and his nominee decided to come out fighting, and (not for the first time) used the platform afforded by the conservatives to set out their own stall. Pointing out that Mohajerani's views reflected those of the electorate, Khatami argued that differences in opinion and debate were valuable, and that equally Mohajerani should not be disqualified on the basis of his opinions:

Of course, one can have a critical approach to this viewpoint, but what is certain is that one cannot say that a person cannot occupy an important cultural office simply because he adheres to a certain way of thinking ... I should say that his [Mohajerani's] viewpoints are the closest to the views that were expressed during the election and won the vote of the majority of the people.

In his speech to the Majlis Khatami, much like Mohajerani, also showed his talent for communication by drawing on examples of unorthodoxy from Iran's Islamic past, using the example of Molla Sadra, a prominent religious philosopher from the Safavid era who was persecuted for his beliefs by the orthodox *ulema* of the period. His ideas remain popular and

---

[21] BBC SWB ME/2999 MED/10–14, 16 Aug. 1997; Iranian TV, 13 Aug. 1997.
[22] BBC SWB ME/2999 MED/15, 16 Aug. 1997; Voice of Israel, 14 Aug. 1997. The Mujahideen-e Khalq Organization was an Islamic Marxist guerrilla group which emerged in opposition to the shah and was instrumental in his overthrow. Following the Islamic Revolution in 1979, the members of the group became involved in a bitter conflict with other factions and were driven into exile, eventually settling in Iraq in 1986. From there they have conducted periodic incursions into Iran. For further details see E. Abrahamian, *Radical Islam: The Iranian Mujahideen* (London: I.B. Tauris, 1989).

widely influential among the seminaries and are known to have been central to Ayatollah Khomeini's thought. As such, the example and analogy were unassailable:

> in our Islamic system the freedom of thought and expression has certain limitations and is also dependent upon certain conditions. A precondition for this freedom is that it should not sabotage the tenets of Islam or undermine the rights of the public. We announce in very clear terms that these limitations exist and the people who live under this system should acknowledge and accept them. What is absolutely certain is that the Islamic system must impose these limitations. But the question is: Can everything in the arena of culture be resolved by using either these limitations or the instruments of coercion, or both? If this had been the case, Molla Sadra, who was condemned [by his contemporaries], would not have been revered today and, instead, the ideas of those who condemned him would have enjoyed prominence within Islamic culture.[23]

Noting that he would respect the vote of the Majlis, Khatami nevertheless did not attempt to hide what he thought of the various 'slurs' attached to his nominee, and his anger and irritation at the tactics used by opponents of Mohajerani are very clear:

> Mr Mohajerani, who is an expert in the field, should write several articles and define the concept of liberalism for the benefit of people [...] who do not understand what the term means and are only interested in using it to slam someone else. Perhaps Mr Mohajerani should write and tell us why a religious person who believes that religion effectively runs one's life can never be a liberal. Licentiousness? How can one attach this label to a person who has accompanied me on journeys and other events? How can one accuse him of advocating licentiousness? How easy it is to utter these words. We seek refuge in God's sanctuary … Support for America and Israel? Just like that? What makes it worse is that we say such things about individuals whose characters have always been open to public scrutiny. Mr Mohajerani is one of our assets … It is exactly this kind of Muslim thinker that we need today.

Mohajerani, who was to become the government's official spokesman, showed his own flair for oratory when he too addressed the Majlis to

---

[23] BBC SWB ME/3005 MED/7, 23 Aug. 1997; Iranian TV, 20 Aug. 1997.

defend his nomination. Taking on his critics, Mohajerani explained his youthful interest in the communist Tudeh party, his defence of an officially sanctioned MKO rally in 1980 (which had been violently disrupted) and his call for talks with the United States. Referring to the importance of the rule of law, Mohajerani showed himself to be shrewd, logical and, importantly, literate in Islamic history and religious theory. Relevant analogies and metaphors littered his speeches, giving them an air of religious (and national) authenticity his opponents found difficult to criticize. Thus:

If we take stock of our Islamic and Iranian heritage, a nation with a strong record as a cradle of civilization and culture, then in my view it is a great pity to use swear words and insults at this juncture to reject an idea. This is because it will bring the opposite results ...

I believe that we must value our artists, writers and film-makers, as they deserve our respect. The power of creativity is an extension of God's creativity for mankind. We must create a seedbed which allows these seeds of creativity to blossom. We must create an atmosphere of peace and tranquillity in all centres of art and culture. We shall all serve Islam and the Islamic Revolution. It is, of course, natural that at this juncture we must pay attention to the issue of freedom as a Divine gift. The Imam Jafar al Sadiq ... said that if a person worries about everything but freedom, he is neglecting a major issue, that is, freedom itself. In other words, freedom is the major issue and other matters are minor [Koranic verses omitted] ...'[24]

In the event, the cabinet was approved, and although Mohajerani received the lowest number of votes, the fact that he had overcome the first hurdle was seen by many as a major achievement and a harbinger of things to come. The news was greeted with some relief by both the press and Khatami himself.[25]

The process of ratification also became the first vehicle by which the administration could begin to extend a new public sphere, institutionalizing the process which had led to Khatami's victory and thereby redefining the terms of political discourse and beginning the transformation of Iranian politics. Thus it was important to reiterate the main themes of the campaign and ensure their dissemination throughout society. These included the institutionalization of the rule of law, the expansion of the press, addressing the needs of the young and elevating the role of

[24] BBC SWB ME/3005 MED/12, 23 Aug. 1997; Iranian TV, 20 Aug. 1997.
[25] BBC SWB ME/3004 MED/1, 22 Aug. 1997; Iranian TV, 20 Aug. 1997. BBC SWB ME/3004 MED/2, 22 Aug. 1997; IRNA news agency, 21 Aug. 1997.

women in society. In order to lead by example, Khatami, while surprising some by not appointing any women ministers, did appoint a woman vice president for environmental affairs, Masoumeh Ebtekar, who by virtue of her post was entitled to sit in on cabinet meetings. Contrary to subsequent impressions, he also laid great stress on the importance of the economy. Meanwhile, his belief in the press as a means of communication between government and society was clear:

> The more independent and freer the press, the greater their representation of the public opinion. The press has two main roles: one is the proper transfer of the demands and happenings of the society to the authorities, and the other is the true transfer of the issues which the establishments have to the people: explaining of those issues, and making people understand.[26]

The press enthusiastically pursued this new mandate, as a brief glance at the newspaper *Salaam* reveals. Thus, for example, on the occasion of Women's Week, the newspaper headlined the president's views that more opportunities for the development of women must be found. Women, it noted, were essential to the development of a solid and durable society, and indeed were essential in the search for solutions to social problems.[27] On another occasion, later in 1997, Khatami made the point more emphatically, asserting that the proper defence of women was in fact the defence of humanity, and that it was 'outrageous' that women should be viewed as second-class human beings. Gender differences, argued the president, were not a 'problem' but a blessing.[28] Such views were not limited to the executive: Ayatollah Khamene'i himself, anxious to be seen as progressive and in tune with the mood of the times, announced to a reported gathering of some 100,000 women that 'the law and Islamic society must fight tyranny and oppression against women'.[29]

Other themes that were regularly addressed in the newspaper related to issues of cultural and intellectual freedom, the relevance of the seminaries to contemporary problems, as well as the importance of clerical *service* to the people, and the need to build security for all.[30] Particular emphasis was given to the compatibility of 'freedom' (which many conservatives viewed as suspiciously 'liberal') and religious values. Similar emphasis was given

---

[26] BBC SWB ME/2999 MED/13, 16 Aug. 1997; Iranian TV, 13 Aug. 1997.

[27] *Salaam*, 27 Mehr 1376/19 Oct. 1997, p. 1.

[28] *Salaam*, 9 Azar 1376/30 Nov. 1997, pp. 1–2; see also *Salaam*, 28 Dey 1376/18 Jan. 1998, p. 1.

[29] *Salaam*, 1 Aban 1376/23 Oct. 1997, p. 1.

[30] Intellectuals, students, the press and women were the four main foci of attention; see e.g. *Salaam*, 13 Ordibehesht 1377/3 May 1998, p. 1.

to the concept of the rule of law and its compatibility with the Sharia, a theme again endorsed by the Leader.[31]

For all the positive statements of this initial 'honeymoon' period, persistent underlying tensions were nevertheless apparent. The outspoken and pro-reform Ayatollah Taheri, the Leader's representative in Isfahan, for instance, warned that the 'enemies of the revolution want to make the sweetness of political participation bitter' for the people, adding that officials should remember that their posts were a responsibility and an honour, not a route to easy money.[32] He was also vocal in his criticism of those who were meant to uphold the law but instead abused that responsibility, in particular members of the Ministry of Intelligence and the Law Enforcement Forces, which were widely perceived to be permeated by officers sympathetic to the conservative cause and as a consequence highly partial in their application of the law.[33] Indeed, it was increasingly apparent that members of the Law Enforcement Forces were encouraging, tacitly or actively, the violent disruption of Friday prayer gatherings (in which unorthodox views were aired)[34] and, more explosively, student rallies. As noted above, universities were a focus for political development, both in acknowledgment of their centrality to the reformist cause and also in recognition of their potency as an ideological vanguard. Unsurprisingly, therefore, the campuses became a flashpoint for conflagrations between the rival factions. Students were increasingly incensed at the way in which the spirit of the law was being abused by the conservative establishment, while the latter claimed that, in demonstrating against 'legal procedures', students were acting outside the law: not only did they argue that the conservatives were behaving in a manner contrary to the wishes of Khomeini, but, much more controversially, that the students had taken to chanting slogans which seemed to impugn the legitimacy of the *velayat-e faqih*.[35] That such demonstrations had been sanctioned by the Ministry of the Interior only heightened tensions as institutional battle lines began to be drawn, ranging the Ministry of the Interior against the judiciary, and the print media against state radio and television (the latter headed by Ali Larijani, the brother of the disgraced Javad). The robust response of Abdullah Nuri, the minister of the interior, to the conservatives' bullying was viewed with some astonishment by the latter, and also raised his profile among the

---

[31] *Salaam*, 5 Aban 1376/27 Oct. 1997, p. 2; 6 Dey 1376/27 Dec. 1997, p. 1; 7 Dey 1376/28 Dec. 1997, p. 1; 10 Dey 1376/31 Dec. 1997, p. 1; 7 Dey 1376/28 Dec. 1997, p. 1.
[32] *Salaam*, 4 Aban 1376/26 Oct. 1997, p. 2.
[33] *Salaam*, 22 Azar 1376/13 Dec.1997, p. 1; see also *Salaam*, 25 Bahman 1376/14 Feb. 1998, p. 1.
[34] *Salaam*, 29 Ordibehesht 1377/19 May 1998, p. 1; see also Taheri's comments, *Salaam*, 30 Ordibehesht 1377/20 May 1998, p. 1.
[35] *Salaam*, 12 Esfand 1376/3 March 1998, p. 1.

students.[36] While conservative papers rarely covered such clashes (and never criticized them), the reformist press was unequivocal in its condemnation, stressing their counterproductivity and anti-Islamic nature.[37] Even Khamene'i felt obliged to try to cultivate a more sympathetic image with the students in the aftermath of the confrontations, and much publicity was given to an 'impromptu' visit during which the Leader casually walked and talked with the students.[38]

It would be mistaken to assume that the reformists were reacting to violent provocation from conservative hardliners. On the contrary, it was the reformists' willingness to take their case to the public and to redefine the terms of political discourse that bewildered and disorientated the conservatives. Khamene'i, in particular, seemed to be one step behind the president, whether on the issue of women, students or indeed 'spontaneous' public walkabouts.[39] While economic issues were not neglected, it was political matters that dominated, with Khatami emphasizing the importance of political development, inclusivity (all Iranians were 'citizens' irrespective of their religious persuasion) and pluralism to the health of the nation, while Nuri confirmed what the conservatives feared, that 'political development was central to the work of the interior ministry'.[40] Not only did the debate reveal the divisions among the *ulema*, but the frequency of non-governmental interventions in the debate also reflected the far broader social basis of the movement. Ayatollah Tavasoli, in a speech in Isfahan, for example, lambasted what he described as the 'ignorant' defence of the *velayat-i faqih*, which he argued was no defence at all. While recognizing the fundamental position of the *faqih* to the revolution and the Islamic Republic, he stressed that the basis of the Islamic Revolution was the development of a popular ideology. He warned, 'If one day, we lose the people, then we have nothing.'[41]

Hojjat-ol-Islam Mehdi Karrubi, the secretary general of the Majma-ye Ruhaniyun Mobarez (the Association of Combatant Clerics), pulled no punches when he argued that the 'Islamic Republic' was Khomeini's legacy. Indeed, while his words could be interpreted as critical of those who emphasized republican over Islamic values, they were equally directed at

---

[36] *Salaam*, 14 Esfand 1376/5 March 1998, p. 1. Mohajerani was similarly vocal in the defence of the press; see *Salaam*, 13 Esfand 1376/4 March 1998, p. 1.
[37] *Salaam*, 30 Ordibehesht 1377/20 May 1998, p. 1; see also Nuri's comments, *Salaam*, 28 Esfand 1376/19 March 1998, p. 1.
[38] *Salaam*, 23 Ordibehseht 1377/13 May 1998, p. 1.
[39] Khatami was well known for his 'human touch' and was frequently pictured on 'walkabouts' without the presence of suffocating security; see *Salaam*, 23 Bahman 1376/12 Feb. 1998, p. 1.
[40] See e.g. *Salaam*, 15 Bahman 1376/4 Feb. 1998, p. 1; *Salaam*, 7 Dey 1376/28 Dec. 1997 p. 1; *Salaam*, 5 Bahman 1376/25 Jan. 1998, p. 1.
[41] *Salaam*, 25 Bahman 1376/14 Feb. 1998, p. 1.

those who argued the reverse. Karrubi stressed that 'The first word of the Imam following the development of the revolution was that this system must be founded on an *Islamic Republic*, not one word more nor one word less.' Furthermore, according to Karrubi, Khomeini had stated that no one was entitled to go against the people, and that he was nothing but a servant of the people. Khatami was therefore pursuing the authentic and legitimate legacy of the Imam. As if to emphasize the religious aspects of this legitimacy, Karrubi also drew on the reported discomfiture of Imam Ali at the conflicts following the Prophet's death, and warned that much the same could happen now. This was a bold attempt at mythic characterization, and one which the conservatives can have neither missed nor appreciated. Khatami, after all, was a *seyyid*, a descendant of the Prophet; the implication was clear: the conservatives, much like the immediate heirs of the Prophet, were taking the community away from the wishes of the founder.[42]

All the while, sufficient positive coverage was afforded to Khatami to ensure his personal centrality to the political process.[43] The fact that he opposed the 'personalization' of politics practised by his predecessor (as witnessed on billboards throughout the country) only encouraged the cult of Khatami. Where possible the generous comments of foreign dignitaries and officials were reproduced in press coverage of the president's activities in order to emphasize Khatami's 'global' impact.[44] This impact was soon to be magnified by the opportune occurrence of two events which were to catapult Khatami into the international arena. The first was the transfer to Iran of the presidency of the Islamic Conference Organization, and the hosting of a conference in December 1997, which effectively signalled Iran's return to regional if not yet international respectability; the second, in many ways equally important, was his interview with Christianne Amanpour on CNN. These events took place within the space of a month and in many ways encapsulated the foreign policy strategy to be endorsed and pursued by the new administration.

The foreign policy of reintegration

Rafsanjani and his supporters can be said to have followed a realist conception of international relations in which states operate according to their interests, principally economic. The concomitant world-view tended

---

[42] *Salaam*, 24 Aban 1376/15 Nov. 1997, pp. 1–2.
[43] *Salaam*, 27 Aban 1376/18 Nov. 1997, p. 1.
[44] Space, for instance, was afforded in one issue to report the praise given by the UNESCO chief to Khatami; see *Salaam*, 4 Aban 1376/26 Oct. 1997, p. 2.

to see rational economic choice as the chief determinant of international policy; thus the US intervention to evict Iraq from Kuwait was seen in crude terms of oil politics and US economic interest. Iran too, it was surmised, would soon be restored to the international economic order, because despite the obvious lack of affection for the regime in the West, there were clear interests at stake which no Western power could ignore. To some extent the policies of the European powers and Japan justified this interpretation of the international system. Yet there was also a gnawing frustration that despite Iran's efforts to consolidate a strategic economic partnership with certain European countries, the relationship remained fragile and prone to disruption by 'events'. Investment did not materialize and it was increasingly apparent that the slightest 'misdemeanour' on Iran's part, be it with respect to human rights or through alleged terrorist activities, inevitably and almost automatically led to a diplomatic setback. A good example of this fragile foreign policy revolved around Iran's alleged illegal occupation of the three Persian Gulf islands of Abu Musa and the Greater and Lesser Tunbs, to which acres of print space have been devoted since a ferryload of UAE schoolteachers were denied entry by an over-zealous Iranian official in 1992. Much to Iranian consternation and bewilderment, the latterly dormant island dispute with the United Arab Emirates exploded in the international media as an example of Iranian aggrandizement in Arab territory, and was raised periodically to berate Iran. The government of Abu Dhabi eventually managed to convince its supporters (Western diplomats included) that the simmering dispute was an example of Persian covetousness towards the whole of the Emirates, an expansionist ambition that some took as read, despite the fact that there has never been any evidence to support this assertion. From Tehran's perspective, this was an unfortunate and, it hoped, temporary aberration over which reason would soon prevail. More conservative commentators accepted it as an example of Western duplicity and perennial animosity.

What was missing in this analysis was any conception of how such a situation should be handled, partly because the real depth of the gulf which had emerged between the 'West' and Iran since the revolution had not been fully appreciated. This was not in essence a matter of 'interest' but a matter of 'communication'; to put it simply, the protagonists were no longer speaking the same language. Khatami recognized that the core of the problem had less to do with economic and political interests and more to do with a profound ideological distrust which had emerged through cultural suspicions and subsequent misunderstanding. In short, Khatami adapted internal discourse analysis to international relations and concluded that Iran was doomed to an absence of strategic depth in any of its significant overseas relationships because the protagonists occupied different 'discursive fields'. While the two sides may think they are engaged in 'dialogue', the absence of a common language, or *symbolic field*, meant that even when they used the same vocabulary they meant different things, and this could only accentuate the sense of mistrust. Furthermore, Khatami realized and accepted – probably the first politician to do so since the revolution – that the sphere of foreign relations could provide a useful and constructive ballast for his domestic policy. In other words, foreign policy was not distinguished from domestic policy, nor seen as antagonistic, but viewed rather as inclusive and complementary. Foreign relations were not simply an extension of domestic revolutionary rivalries, egotistic and insular, but a valid sphere of political operations which, if well harnessed, could have a positive bearing on internal developments. Khatami's strategy was in many ways facilitated and prepared by Soroush's argument about Iran's triple intellectual heritage, and could be interpreted as a continuation of Rafsanjani's attempt at detente. But it is important to recognize the significant differences in approach: his emphasis on cultural and ideological sensitivities, as opposed to interest, and the fact that the practice of foreign policy had shifted gear.

Khatami had made clear his stance on foreign relations during the election campaign when he argued that 'In the field of foreign policy, we would also like to announce that we are in favour of relations with all countries and nations which respect our independence, dignity and interests.'[45] When tackled on the issue during a television interview, Khatami acknowledged that care had to be taken when facing up to the 'cultural onslaught', but he also warned against too heavy-handed an approach to the outside world:

As an Islamic government and society, we cannot leave our society vulnerable before threats. We would pass laws and where necessary, discourage people from and warn against corruption and inappropriate influences. This should be undertaken with discretion and finesse. What is important is that we live in this world, where there is aggressive culture and aggressive determination in attacking us politically and economically. What are we supposed to do? We cannot close the doors completely. We might be able to close the doors to a certain extent and in some areas. But, given the way the world is progressing, tomorrow it would be impossible to close the doors. The principal way would be to immunize people.[46]

[45] BBC SWB ME/2917 MED/11, 13 May 1997; Iranian TV, 10 May 1997.
[46] BBC SWB ME/2920 MED/9, 16 May 1997; Iranian TV, 12 May 1997.

Many of these ideas were elucidated at greater length during his opening speech to the Islamic Conference Organization, which held its eighth summit in Tehran in December 1997 and offered an ideal forum for the new Iran to present itself and its new president to the wider world. The final touches to the main assembly hall were made in the very last minutes before the delegates arrived, and there was considerable pride in Iran over the extensive guest list, which contrasted favourably with a US-sponsored economic forum for MENA (Middle East and North Africa) which had been held in Doha a month earlier. Such was the Arab countries' irritation with Israeli moves affecting the peace process and US quiescence that they effectively boycotted the Doha gathering and instead arrived *en masse* in Tehran, a move which was bound in turn to irritate Washington. Iran meanwhile basked in the glory of its football team's almost miraculous qualification for the 1998 World Cup and of the arrival of so many world leaders in its capital. Symbolically at least, the era of 'isolation' seemed to be over.[47]

This was an ideal platform for Khatami to articulate his vision of the Islamic world and its position in the wider international system. His speech, which was contrasted favourably with the harsh tones of Ayatollah Khamene'i, began intriguingly with the comment: 'I do not know if I should begin my speech with the bitter issues that are, or the joyous issues that should be.' He then began a detailed articulation and explanation of his thoughts on the ailments afflicting Muslim societies and cautioned against the tendency to hark back to the glories of the past:

Today, it is not possible to rebuild the civilisation of the past, because its time has passed. And, impossible as it may seem, if it were, it would not be desirable ...

... we should know that between the Islamic civilisation – or more correctly, the civilisation of the Muslims – and our lives today, there stands a phenomenon known as Western civilisation. A civilisation whose effective achievements are not few, and its negative effects are also manifold, especially for non-Westerners. Our age is one of the domination of Western civilisation and culture. Understanding it is necessary. An effective understanding goes beyond the frills of that civilisation and reaches the roots and foundations of its values and principles ... we must understand our past; not for returning to it and stopping in the past, which is truly ossification, but for finding the essence and meaning of our identity and to purify it from preconceptions and habits that are totally dependent on time and place.

[47] See e.g. *Salaam*, 18 Azar 1376/9 Dec. 1997, p. 1; 20 Azar 1376/11 Dec. 1997 p. 1.

Similarly, an understanding of the 'self' was an essential prerequisite for a constructive and mutually beneficial understanding of the 'other':

Inhabiting our common Islamic homeland does not mean being reactionary, negating scientific achievements, isolating ourselves from the contemporary world or falling out with others ... Life in peace and security can only be achieved when one has an in depth understanding of the culture, thoughts and even tastes and interests of others. And a profound understanding of other nations' spiritual and cultural lives requires the establishment of discussion or dialogue with them. True dialogue will only be possible when the two sides are genuinely aware of their roots and identity, otherwise, the dialogue of an imitator who has no identity, with others, is meaningless and is not in his interest.[48]

This concept of 'dialogue of civilizations' was a clear and clever response to Huntington's thesis on the 'clash of civilizations' and represented the appropriation of a discourse familiar in Western intellectual and policy circles. This appropriation gave Khatami's argument immediate relevance and indicated his ability to penetrate and effectively usurp an otherwise exclusive discourse. At the philosophical level the concept of a 'dialogue' and the manner in which it was articulated also revealed the President's exposure to Habermasian influences.[49] He argued that dialogue was now possible because Iran was sufficiently independent and confident of itself to pursue this route constructively and positively.[50]

Given this context, it is not surprising that Khatami decided on using the international media as his vehicle of communication with the United States. Indeed, his decision to appear on the US news channel CNN must be seen as a far more calculated move than is often appreciated, and it shows not only Khatami's mastery of communication but his acute understanding of the *means* of communication in the modern world. In a speech he made in 1995 while head of the National Library, entitled 'Observations on the Information World', he made the following revealing comments:

[48] BBC SWB ME/3099 S1/4–9, 11 Dec. 1997; Iranian TV, 9 Dec. 1997.

[49] See e.g. his comments to Western journalists in New York: 'This is where dialogue between civilizations becomes meaningful; there must be dialogue on the basis of rationality.' BBC SWB ME/ 3344 MED/12, 29 Sept. 1998; Iranian TV, 28 Sept. 1998.

[50] There are of course clear parallels between his approach to conservatives at home and to interlocutors and audiences abroad. Khatami has clearly been frustrated by the failure of some Western commentators to appreciate the seriousness of this policy; see e.g. his address to foreign ambassadors, BBC SWB ME/3763 MED/8, 14 Feb. 2000; IRNA news agency, 11 Feb. 2000.

In its contemporary, complex forms, information technology represents one of the highest achievements of modern culture which uses its control over information to solidify its domination of the world. Thus, inquiry into the nature of the information world is inseparable from uncovering the nature of modern civilisation itself. And until we address this important question we will not be able to muster the confidence and wisdom to understand our relationship to modern civilisation. Otherwise, we will live in a world whose rules have been set by others, at the mercy of circumstance, not as masters of our fate ... The flood of information in our age saturates the senses of humanity so extensively that the ability to assess and choose is impaired even among Westerners who are producers of information, let alone us who have a peripheral role in the information world. Electronic information is the brainchild of modern civilisation. Thus, the power of today's information-based mass culture is tied to the legitimacy of the values of Western civilisation for which the information revolution counts as the most prominent achievement.[51]

Khatami, it may be conjectured, knew full well how to use the opportunity afforded him by CNN; and just as the media and intellectuals (including students) had proved vital to the success of the reformist movement in Iran, so too these very same constituents would serve him well in the propagation of his message abroad. Indeed, pleasantries aside, the target of his interview was the intellectual elite, groups he recognized would be vital to any reassessment of Iran in Western policy circles. Some pundits concentrated on his praise for American civilization and his 'regret' for the hostage crisis of 1979, and on his policy statements, such as his rejection of terrorism in 'all its forms' and his condemnation of American foreign policy 'dependence' on Israel – a criticism which caused almost disproportionate irritation among some Washington commentators. But the real interest of his comments lay in his assessment of US achievements and historical development, as well as US relations with Iran. Khatami sought to redraw the map of US–Iran relations, to place events within 'context' and, crucially, to integrate Iranian political development within a discourse familiar to Iranians. He thus reminded his US audience that US–Iran relations did not begin with the hostage crisis of 1979, and drew their attention to the coup of 1953 which resulted in the overthrow of the nationalist prime minister Dr Mohammad Mosaddeq. There was, he argued:

---

[51] For the full text see M. Khatami, 'Observations on the Information World', in *Hope and Challenge: The Iranian President Speaks*, trans. A. Mafinezam (Binghamton: Institute of Global Studies, Binghamton University, 1997), pp. 61–71.

a bulky wall of mistrust between us and American administrations, a mistrust rooted in improper behaviour by the American governments. As an example of this type of behaviour, I should refer to admitted involvement of the American government in the 1953 coup d'etat which toppled Mosaddeq's government, immediately followed by a $45m loan to strengthen the coup government. I should also refer to the capitulation law imposed by the American government on Iran.

In addition, he argued that the chanting of anti-American slogans was not intended to insult or undermine the US government or the American people. Indeed, 'No one has ever had the intention of insulting the American nation, and we even consider the American government as the legitimate and lawful representative of its people.' On the contrary, the chanting of such slogans had to be seen in the context of a process of purification, a means by which Iranians could restore some balance to a tarnished relationship: 'These slogans symbolise a desire to *terminate a mode of relationship* between Iran and America [italics added].' He added that both he and the Leader were not happy with the practice of burning the American flag, which he recognized caused offence. While Dr Mosaddeq, some forty-five years earlier, had sought to appeal to US sensibilities by comparing the American war of independence with Iran's struggle against imperialism, President Khatami went one crucial step further. He sought to show the similarities between the two narratives and effectively to integrate them. By pointing to America's Puritan roots, Khatami was trying to remind his audience that the United States has a religious foundation, and in fact remains an intensely religious society. His thesis, which clearly resonated with Americans' perceptions of their own history, was that:

> The puritans constituted a religious sect whose vision and characteristics, in addition to worshipping God, was in harmony with a form of republicanism, democracy and freedom. They had found the European climate too restrictive for the implementation of their ideas and thoughts. Unfortunately, in the 16th, 17th and even 18th centuries there was a serious clash between religion and liberty. In my opinion, one of the biggest tragedies in human history is this confrontation between religion and liberty which is to the detriment of religion, liberty and the human beings who deserve to have both. The puritans desired a system which combined the worship of God with human dignity and freedom.

Taking the opportunity to offer generous praise to Abraham Lincoln, 'the strong and fair-minded American president', Khatami then moved on to deliver his rhetorical *coup de grâce*:

This civilisation ... is best described by the renowned French sociologist Alexis de Tocqueville who spent 18 months in the USA in the 19th century and wrote the valuable book entitled *Democracy in America*. I hope most Americans have read this book, which reflects the virtuous and human side of this civilisation. In his view, the significance of this civilisation is in the fact that liberty found religion as a cradle for its growth and religion found the protection of liberty as its divine calling. Therefore in America, liberty and faith never clashed, and as we see, even today most Americans are religious people. There is less war against religion in America. Therefore the approach to religion, which was the foundation of Anglo-American civilisation, relies on the principle that religion and liberty are consistent and compatible. I believe that if humanity is looking for happiness, it should combine religious spirituality with the virtues of liberty.[52]

In drawing this interesting analogy between the democratic experience in the United States and reformist aspiration in Iran, Khatami was seeking nothing less than an ideological revolution to underpin and prepare for a diplomatic revolution. No longer the 'Great Satan', the United States possessed qualities which, if not worthy of emulation, certainly provided common ground on which the two erstwhile antagonists could meet. It was a strategy of integration, which most Americans seem to have missed, if for no other reason than the failure to recognize themselves as a religious society, although this characteristic is apparent to most outside observers, including de Tocqueville, who commented extensively on it. Indeed, such is the dominance of the 'secularization thesis' that de Tocqueville's assertion, 'Religious nations are therefore naturally strong on the very point on which democratic nations are weak; this shows of what importance it is for men to preserve their religion as their conditions become more equal', is rarely quoted.[53] However, if the majority of Americans were more enthralled by his appreciation of American civilization, Khatami's comments did strike a chord with the one group he had intended to target, the media and intellectuals, and indeed this interview marked the beginning of a durable love affair. This effect was almost immediately apparent, for while

[52] BBC SWB ME/3210 MED/2, 9 Jan. 1998; Iranian TV, 8 Jan. 1998. Considerable coverage of the interview was given in the Iranian media, with conservative organs concentrating on Khatami's criticisms of the United States, and the more moderate papers giving more complete coverage. *Salaam*, for instance, printed the complete text; see *Salaam*, 18 Dey 1376/8 Jan. 1998, p. 1; 20 Dey 1376/10 Jan. 1998, p. 8; 20 Dey 1376/10 Jan. 1998, p. 1; 21 Dey 1376/11 Jan. 1998, p. 1.

[53] See A. de Tocqueville, *Democracy in America* [1835] (London: Everyman's Library, 1994), part I, ch. 17, pp. 300–14, and part II, ch. 5, p. 22. Khatami's use of de Tocqueville reportedly led to a surge in sales in the United States.

the US State Department struggled to present a coherent response which did not appear negative or rejectionist, the pundits on CNN were eager to present the event as positively as possible. As a result, any official US response which did not cater for dialogue and some attempt to break down the wall of mistrust would appear mean-spirited and dogmatic. In a curious way, Khatami had seized the moral high ground and the ideological initiative. He had no longer simply 'charmed Iranians' but had also initiated a highly effective charm offensive abroad.[54]

This charm offensive continued with considerable efficacy throughout 1998, and arguably culminated with Khatami's visit to the United Nations General Assembly in September, where expectations among the foreign press corps were high. His apparent success in presenting a different image of the Islamic Republic to the West raised eyebrows not only among his opponents at home but also among opposition groups abroad, who saw in him the greatest single threat to their *raison d'être*. That is not to say that Khatami's strategy bore immediate fruit; the wall of mistrust was never likely to come down overnight, and those who remained suspicious developed new theories to compensate for the Khatami phenomenon. One argument suggested with great urgency that he remained a cleric and merely a sympathetic extension of an otherwise brutal regime, while other, more subtle positions sought to dissociate him altogether from his context, arguing that he was and remains a curious anomaly – in short, he wasn't *really* a cleric. Thus some commentators revealed a curiously persistent ability to make fact fit, however uncomfortably, prejudice.

When Khatami visited the United Nations in September 1998, CNN decided – unusually for such a visit – to broadcast Khatami's speeches live: not only his address to the General Assembly, where he revealed his Hegelian conception of history as the unfolding of truth and the 'realisation of justice',[55] but also his speech to a select group of Iranian expatriates. This latter speech was exemplary in revealing Khatami's ability to target his audience and tailor his speeches in such a way as to draw his audience in. He was very well aware that Iranian expatriates were unlikely to be a sympathetic audience, and acknowledged as much in the opening introduction to his talk before leading into a subject which he was relatively sure would be appreciated: 'It is not easy [for me] to address this

---

[54] See e.g. E. Sciolino, 'The Cleric who Charmed Iranians', *New York Times*, 1 Feb. 1998; see also 'On the Virtues of the West by Mohammad Khatami', *Time Magazine*, vol. 151, no 2, 19 Jan. 1998.
[55] For the full speech see M. Khatami, *Hezareh-ye goftegu va tafahom* (A thousand discussions and understanding) (Tehran: Resanash, 1378/1998–9), pp. 47–59; for more comments on the linear nature of history, see his speech to the Eleventh Islamic Unity Conference broadcast on Iranian TV on 13 July 1998, BBC SWB ME/3279 MED/12, 15 July 1998.

gathering, because of the diversity of tastes and viewpoints. It is a difficult task to make a speech which would suit everyone. I, therefore, thought that it may be a good idea to address this gathering today by saying something about the Iranians' spirit.'

He then launched into a speech which was replete with intellectual and nationalist motifs:

> You, esteemed ladies and gentlemen, are aware of the fact that mythology is a highly vast and complicated subject, which has received much respect, analysis and research in our time. Mythology describes the spirit of various nations. And there is no nation or people whose history is free of myth. Of course in conformity with the weight of civilisation and the history of the nation, the myth of the nation is deeper and more complicated. And civilised nations usually have myths. The ethical myth and the myth epic indicate this spirit of the Iranians ... I do not wish to mention all the specifications of the spirit of Iranians and what has been reflected in Ferdowsi's Book of Kings. However, I believe that at this juncture in time we, the Iranians, need to know two or three points in order to understand the essence of the Iranian spirit. I take these few points from the epic of Rostam and Esfandiar in the Book of Kings.[56]

This speech is interesting on two levels: in his appeal to Iranian nationalism and history for an audience clearly not readily sympathetic to Islamic motifs and also in the highly intellectual language he used, revealing himself to be a cultured and articulate man. It is interesting to note that at this stage CNN abruptly ended its live transmission, with the justification that Khatami was, once again, digressing into philosophy! Yet while this 'digression' may have meant little to CNN's audience, it caught the attention of the two audiences Khatami sought to capture: the intellectual elites among Iranian expatriates and Americans. Thus, in taking questions at the end of his speech, Khatami made a point of praising the various minorities in Iran and their contributions to *Iranian* (as opposed to the particularism of 'Persian') culture. At one stage, when asked a question by an eminent Zoroastrian scholar, Khatami went so far as to interrupt the

---

[56] BBC SWB ME/3339 MED/1, 23 Sept. 1998; IRNA news agency, 20 Sept. 1998. For a fuller account see Khatami, *Hezareh-ye goftegu va tafahom*, pp. 64–76. The IRNA transcript fails to include his mention of 'Islamic myths', which is revealing, as is his choice of words. 'Myth' is used in English, while he also uses the Persian term *ostureh*, which is a historical myth on the same lines as the usage of Barthes in *Mythologies*. In other words, Khatami is drawing on a specifically social science terminology.

questioner, first to praise him, then to note that they came from the same city and then to point out that, as Iranians, 'we all have Zoroastrian roots'.[57] This was a remarkable statement for a Muslim cleric to make, and its impact on his audience should not be underestimated.

Khatami's agenda at home and his ability to communicate his ideas effectively abroad made him a figure of international stature in a very short space of time. This was undoubtedly in part a reflection of foreign curiosity and fascination with an articulate and apparently rational president representing a country and government few accepted as 'normal'. But it also indicated the genuine interest in his significance as a reformer and his cultural sensitivity, as well as his ability to communicate with those groups who could best mediate his message: intellectuals and the media. While in Damascus, he chose to address the students at the University of Damascus in Arabic, a feat which won him many plaudits and admirers in the Arab world. He was treated with enormous respect in Saudi Arabia – much better, his supporters discreetly argued, than ex-president Rafsanjani when he spent nearly two weeks in the kingdom in early 1998. His trip to Italy, the first such visit by an Iranian leader since the revolution, was similarly marked with a speech at the University of Florence, where Khatami quoted from European philosophers. This was followed by a visit to the Pope, complete with photo opportunity and a request by Khatami for the Pope to pray for him. Nothing symbolized Khatami's desire for a 'dialogue of civilizations' better; and indeed, he had successfully, and to some acclaim, succeeded in getting the UN to declare 2001 the official year of 'Dialogue between Civilizations'. But there was more; in his trip to France the religious revolutionary paid his respects at the tomb of Jean Jacques Rousseau, while on a recent trip to Germany, he specifically requested a visit to Weimar (much to the enthusiasm of the local mayor) so that he could open a memorial to the Persian poet Hafez and the German poet Goethe.

There were times, of course, when he miscalculated, as when he began an impromptu discussion on the problem of 'justice' at the end of a press conference, which undoubtedly left his audience bewildered.[58] However, on the whole Khatami succeeded in transforming the international perception of Iran from a 'rogue nation', an anomaly rejecting the perceived norms of international behaviour, to a state struggling to reconcile itself with modernity and determined to pursue democratization. It was a remarkable transformation, which forced the international community to take him and his project seriously and, crucially, began a process of

---

[57] Khatami, *Hezareh-ye goftegu va tafahom*, p. 79.
[58] BBC SWB ME/3344 MED/16, 29 Sept. 1998; Iranian TV, 26 Sept. 1998.

reintegration in which Iran was no longer perceived as an antagonist. Just as the reformists sought an inclusive approach to politics in Iran, so too they sought to project this strategy in their foreign policy. The aim was to provide Iran with strategic depth cushioned through ideological integration which would provide stability and security and, above all, attract foreign investment. Thus the development of relations with Saudi Arabia effectively nullified the Abu Musa dispute with the United Arab Emirates,[59] while the breakthrough in September 1998 on the Salman Rushdie affair inaugurated a new era in relations with the European Union. This last development was indicative of the changed climate, in so far as Khatami was offering little in addition to what Rafsanjani had been saying for years – that the Iranian government would not seek to implement the *fatwa*; but while Khatami had dissociated the government from the bounty offered on Rushdie's head, the chief difference was that he had carefully prepared the ground, so that his protagonists would be willing to listen.

These successes abroad undoubtedly strengthened Khatami's popular position at home, and his supporters sought to make the most of Iran's gradual reintegration and Khatami's statesmanlike role in achieving this.[60] Iranians felt good about themselves (assisted no doubt by their World Cup victory over the United States), and Iranians abroad recognized in Khatami a president with whom they could empathize and who appeared to raise Iran's prestige on the international stage. Conservative opponents (and the opposition abroad) were not so enamoured with the apparent detente and looked to exact a heavy price from the president. Not only was Khatami's appeal for better understanding and investment a threat to their commercial and political interests but they recognized that his ability to convince foreign investors was predicated on his ability to deliver at home. This reality was not lost on the president. When asked about the internal situation by a Western journalist, Khatami responded emphatically: 'I'm determined and will do my utmost to ensure that, God willing, every group, every institution and every person in the country acts within the framework of the law.'[61]

[59] 'Saudis and Iran reject UAE complaint', BBC online, Monday, 7 June 1999 – *http://news.bbc.c.uk/ hi/english.world/middle_east/newsid_362000/362985.stm#top*
[60] Publications were regularly issued including speeches and itineraries. See e.g. B. Dad, *Khatami dar Italia* (Khatami in Italy) (Tehran: Sahafi, 1378/1998–9).
[61] BBC SWB ME/3344 MED/13, 29 Sept. 1998; Iranian TV, 26 Sept. 1998.

7 The Dialectics of Reform

As important as foreign policy has been to the Khatami presidency, it is the sphere of domestic political and economic development which has dominated the agenda, with the former predominating over the latter, for the simple reason that politics is regarded as the cradle for sustainable and secure economic growth. Furthermore, the reformists have been keen to change the relations of domination which grew up during Rafsanjani's mercantile bourgeois republic, and to ensure that any economic growth does not accentuate the disparity of wealth between social groups. The economic and political contexts are therefore intricately linked, and while the apparent focus of the reformists has been on political and social change, the economic ramifications and implications should not be under-estimated. Certainly the connection is not lost on those vested interests under challenge from the social momentum of change, who recognize that their economic power rests very firmly on political domination. The result has been an attempt to slow down this momentum, if not halt it altogether, through a process of attrition which, it is argued, will make the cost of change too high a burden for society to bear. The social and historical momentum for change, however, remains powerful and, it is argued, largely unaffected by the opposing pressure applied to it. Indeed, it gains in momentum every day that it is not quelled, and thus has effectively trans-formed itself from a social movement to a social revolution. While 'thesis' might be opposed by 'antithesis', the resultant 'synthesis' increasingly bears more of the hallmarks of the original thesis, such has been the growing domination of the reformist agenda. This process of change, which has gained considerable momentum during the Khatami presidency, while undoubtedly subject to many frustrations when viewed in detail, comes into sharper focus when viewed through the lens of broader historical patterns. Such has been the accelerating pace of change during the first Khatami administration that the most suitable and productive analysis is one in which the broad trends are delineated and highlighted. To do otherwise is to risk being overwhelmed by the minutiae of events and to fail to see the wood for the trees.

The politics of managing change

During his discussion with Western journalists in New York in September 1998, President Khatami was asked when political parties would be formed in Iran. His lengthy response to this question is worth quoting in full:

> Right now. Unfortunately, it is not up to the government to establish parties; the people must do this themselves. The experience of civil society is a new one for us. Although we embarked on this a hundred years ago, we did not succeed in practice. The constitutional system was a system that could have formed the basis of an acceptable civil society for our culture and nation. Unfortunately, internal disputes and intervention by foreigners meant that an oppressive dictatorship emerged from the heart of our constitutional system. After World War II ... again there was a good opportunity for freedom. In view of the lack of maturity of our domestic forces, we turned on each other with such ferocity that we failed to institutionalise this freedom in the country. With the coup d'état of 28th Mordad [19 August 1953], that period also came to an end.
>
> The Islamic Revolution, too, started with freedom, not with fighting and weapons ... at the start of the revolution freedom stood side by side with anarchy. Unfortunately, some groups and grouplets, which had come into being under [the shah's] regime and which patronizingly claimed the right to speak on behalf of the people abused this freedom too, transforming it into terrorist conflicts, street clashes and killings. We must learn to use freedom in practice and on the basis of experience. The state must refrain from dictatorial behaviour. The people, for their part, must learn to defend their freedoms. One of the main ways to do this is precisely through the formation of parties, groups and civil associations, civil institutions in society.
>
> One of the problems of our society now is that [...] parties as such have not been established yet. Therefore, in the conflicts that occur between groups and institutions, one does not know who one is being confronted by. So, in reply to your question as to when will it be time for parties to be established, I say to you: it was 70 years ago, but unfortunately it did not come about.[1]

---

[1] BBC SWB ME/3344 MED/14, 29 Sept. 1998; Iranian TV, 26 Sept. 1998. See also *Entekhab*, 23 Azar 1378/14 Dec. 1999, p. 2, which emphasizes the historical nature of the reformist agenda.

This rather protracted response reveals both Khatami's historical understanding of political development in Iran during the twentieth century, and his acknowledgment that the outcomes hitherto have been less than satisfactory. This failure to develop politically can be ascribed to political and social weaknesses: a failure properly to *manage change*, which has resulted in democratic and popular experiments descending into anarchy and providing a 'stepping stone' for the (re-)establishment of dictatorship, matched by a social immaturity which has facilitated autocracy through an inability to harness 'freedom' and/or an over-eagerness to delegate power to the state.[2]

There is therefore a reciprocal dialectic at work: not only must the state be virtuous, but society must be politically mature and responsible. For political development to proceed, these two facets of political life must be harmonious and complementary. The disjunction between them has been the fundamental cause of political underdevelopment, and a reciprocal development, with state and society operating in conjunction, is the optimum structure for sustainable progress. In an ideal world, such a development would happen organically, with the minimum friction or social conflict; a situation some Iranians – adopting effectively an idealized 'Whig' interpretation of English social and political development – consider occurred in England. In Iran, as in many other developing states, such an option is no longer regarded as realistic, and while organic social changes clearly do occur, overall development must be carefully managed if tensions are to be contained and the recurring cycle of social anarchy and autocracy is to be successfully transcended and transformed. For many reformists the key to this transformation lies in the alteration of ideological and cultural norms; they note that while many of the structures of democracy are in place, they clearly lack the ideological and cultural basis for their effective operation. Thus Khatami's statement: 'We must learn to use freedom in practice and on the basis of experience. The state must refrain from dictatorial behaviour.' In short, what is needed is a paradigmatic break with the past. This once again emphasizes the *hegemonic* nature of the contest currently unfolding in Iran, and that 'progress' cannot always be assessed in material terms.[3] The strategy adopted has been one of inclusivity, so that the material repercussions and any consequent 'friction'

---

[2] This theme of the potential tensions between 'tradition' and 'progress' was also articulated by Khatami in a German magazine; see *Tous*, 24 Mordad 1377/15 Aug. 1998, p. 1. For a similar argument see A. Ganji, *Tarik-khaneh-ye ashbah* (The dark house of phantoms) (Tehran: Tar-e No, 1378/1999–2000), p. 11.

[3] It is important to bear in mind that in Iran the term *hegemonic* is often used as a substitute for *totalitarian*, which is not the meaning implied here.

are minimized. It is worth noting that the reformists are less interested in a consensus *per se*, and more in ideological assimilation and inclusion.

The parameters of 'civil society'

A regular criticism of the reformist project advanced by conservatives both within and outside Iran is that they indulge in idle sloganeering intent on mobilizing the masses but have little idea about their aims, ambitions and implications. For conservatives within Iran, the concept of civil society is at once viewed both as an empty gesture and as potentially a very real threat to their political and economic status, for it seems to imply a decentralization of power, not only geographically but also politically. According to their new-found patrician self-perception,[4] such a development is undesirable, not least because it allows the 'oppressed' to hold the elites accountable and to exercise power themselves. The growth of civil society therefore poses a challenge to elite domination, and some ideologues of the right have articulated this fear in no uncertain terms, talking of a 'them and us' divide in society, between those who are arguably true Muslims and adhere to the particular relation of domination, and the rest (the vast majority) who do not. Ayatollah Misbah-Yazdi made this point explicitly in the run-up to the Sixth Majlis elections, arguing that there was indeed a stark social and political division within society. The implications of this sort of thinking soon became apparent during 1998, when the conservative elites retreated into what was rapidly criticized as a state within a state, from which they would occasionally launch violent sorties into the emergent civil society in a blatant attempt to destabilize it.[5] In the event, such attempts, either through the courts or by the use of vigilantes, tended only to strengthen the movement, in large part because, contrary to the claims of such critics, there was a relatively wide and profound understanding of the necessity, aims and function of a civil society. Thus, as the Persian newspaper *Hamshahri* articulated:

> Civil society, for its part, consists of the forces and institutions which exist in the space between the two main elements of society, that is, the rulers and the ruled. The main purposes of the institutions of civil

---

[4] See e.g. *Tous*, 15 Mordad 1377/6 Aug. 1998, where Khatami argues that according to religion people do not need guardians, quoting directly from Ayatollah Khomeini; see A. Nuri, *Shokoran-e Eslah* (Hemlock of Reform) (Tehran: Tar-e No, 1378/1999–2000), p. 118.

[5] See e.g. *Arya*, 17 Mordad 1378/8 Aug. 1999, p. 1; also *Sobh Emrooz*, 17 Mordad 1378/8 Aug. 1999, p. 1.

society (parties, groups), unions, private economic and non-economic institutes, religious entities, charitable organisations, the press and so on is for them to convey the demands of the ruled to the rulers. In addition to conveying demands, some of these institutions, that is, parties and groups, can act as citizens' levers as well. That is to say, if the government disregards their demands, the citizen can exercise an informed choice to select future rulers from party candidates, removing from the political stage parties that they consider undesirable. The constitution of the Islamic Republic of Iran provides for the activities of civil institutions.[6]

Another criticism which is occasionally levelled from abroad is that Khatami, in discussing 'Islamic' civil society, is in fact talking about something wholly different from its Western counterpart. As a consequence, what is developing and being encouraged in Iran is *not* civil society as the West would understand it. This is a fallacious argument intended to demean and ridicule the reformist agenda, and it has been challenged by senior administration officials such as Seyyid Hadi Khamene'i, one of Khatami's vice presidents and staunchest supporters.[7] It pays little attention to the detail of the discussion, which, as proper attention to Khatami's words shows, while intended to situate and contextualize the concept of civil society within an Islamic intellectual framework, nevertheless addresses many of the issues of human rights and accountability with which citizens of Western democracies would be familiar. Khatami's most comprehensive and concise articulation of his views was presented at the Islamic Conference Organization in December 1997, and it is worth quoting this section of his speech in full:

The civil society which we seek to establish in our country – and would also like to recommend to other Muslim countries – is fundamentally different to the civil society born out of Greek classical philosophy and the Roman Empire's political heritage; that is to say a civil society which has passed through the Middle Ages and has now gained its special identity in the modern world. However, the two concepts of civil society should not necessarily contradict each other as far as their manifestations and outcomes are concerned. For this reason, we should never downplay the importance of learning – without imitating and copying – from the positive achievements of Western civil society.

In its historical and theoretical aspects, Western civil society was primarily inspired by the Greek city states, and subsequently, by the

---

[6] BBC SWB ME/3274 MED/2, 9 July 1998; *Hamshahri*, 7 July 1998.
[7] *Jame'eh*, 17 Khordad 1377/7 June 1998, p. 1.

Roman political system. On the other hand, the historical and theoretical essence of the civil society that we have in mind is rooted in the esteemed Prophet's Medina. Changing the name of the city from Yathrib to Medina was not merely a change of titles, in the same way that changing the era of Jahiliya [the term given the age of 'ignorance' before the advent of Islam] to the Day of Allah is also not merely a change of names and title. Medina is not merely a land or territory, just as the Day of Allah is not merely a specific unit of time ...

Islamic thought and culture are the pivots of the civil society we have in mind and there should be no sign in that society of individual and group despotism or even dictatorship of the majority and efforts to destroy the minority. In such a society, humans and their rights are respected and revered. The citizens of Islamic civil society have the right to determine their destiny, supervise the implementation of their affairs and question their rulers and statesmen. Furthermore, in such a society, the state is the people's servant not their patron, and, as such, it is at all times accountable to the people upon whom God has bestowed the right of self-determination.

Our civil society is not a society in which only Muslims are the only true citizens and enjoy all the rights. Rather, it is a society in which any human treading the path of law and order has rights, the defence of which is one of the most important obligations of the state. Respecting human rights and observing its limits and boundaries is not something which we utter simply as a matter of political expediency in order to join some universal chorus. Instead, what we say is the natural outcome of our religious principles and learnings. After all, we have learnt that the Commander of the Faithful, His Holiness Ali – peace be upon him – once instructed one of his provincial governors to ensure that justice applies to all his people not only Muslims.

Our civil society is neither domineering nor submissive. It fully recognises the rights of the people to determine their destinies and enjoy access to the means and resources they need for a dignified life. This society, furthermore, does not succumb to the will of any bully. In its bid to stand on its own two feet, it obeys the words of the Holy Koran and considers it as an obligation to provide all the requirements and necessities for material, economic and technological progress. Rejecting and negating both domination and submission also means repelling and shunning coercion and deceit in relations with other countries, and replacing these with logic and the principle of mutual respect.

The civil society which we intend to establish will be based on our collective identity, for the achievement of which there is a need for the continuous movement and endeavours of thinkers and scholars. This is not a treasure to be acquired overnight. It is, rather, an eternal spring of life and spirituality whose waters we have to keep drinking to quench our thirst. Its benefits are therefore gradual and depend on the care taken to recognise the heritage and traditions of the beliefs and thoughts of Muslims, on the one hand, and the exact and profound scientific and philosophical understanding of the contemporary world on the other. For this very reason, the pivot and axis of this movement are the scholars and thinkers of the community and our success in continuing to move along this path will depend upon the belief that politics should serve scholarliness and thought and not bind thinkers and scholars into a tight framework.[8]

Not only does Khatami emphasize in this speech that this civil society *is not a treasure to be acquired overnight*, he also stresses the importance of thinkers and scholars to the fulfilment of this project. It is the function of scholars to disseminate this message and educate the general public through the vehicle afforded by a larger and more dynamic press. In the first year of the Khatami administration the Ministry of Culture gave licences to 200 new publications, increasing the total number of publications to some 800. Moreover, much to the irritation of the conservatives, the press were given considerable leeway to print exactly what they wanted, including probing investigations and critical questions as well as discussions of the wider implications of civil society. Thus articles appeared on the necessity for pluralism within an Iranian context in which the authors acknowledged the religious foundations of Iranian society but stressed nonetheless that society must be tolerant and inclusive if it hopes to remain strong and stable.[9] Well-known thinkers such as Abdolkarim Soroush were afforded particular prominence, with lengthy discussions and interviews on the nature of popular rights, the implications for religion in society and, most pointedly, criticism of the selective manner in which the conservatives applied the law. Indeed, Soroush's argument that the people did in fact enjoy 'human rights' was given considerable prominence, as was Khatami's insistence on the defence of such rights.[10]

---

[8] BBC SWB ME/3099 S1/4–9, 11 Dec. 1997; Iranian TV, 9 Dec. 1997.
[9] *Tous*, 7 Shahrivar 1377/29 Aug. 1998, p. 6.
[10] See e.g. *Jame'eh*, 7 Tir 1377/28 June 1998, p. 6; 8 Tir 1377/29 June 1998, p. 6; 9 Tir 1377/30 June 1998, p. 6. See also A. K. Soroush and M. Kadivar, *Manazere dar bare-ye pluralism dini* (A debate on religious pluralism) (Tehran: Salaam, 1378/1999–2000); occasional translations of relevant foreign articles were also included, e.g. S. Fairbanks, 'Religious Government and Democracy', first published in the *Middle East Journal*, vol. 52, Winter 1998, in *Tous*, 4 Mordad 1377/26 July 1998, p. 6.

At the same time, the impression should not be given that the vast majority of the people possessed an ideological commitment to civil society and political participation. This was quite certainly not the case, and an understanding of the term and its political implications remained very much the preserve of a tightly focused, if expanding, intellectual elite. There is little doubt that the term 'civil society' and associated concepts have become pervasive in Iranian popular discourse, largely as a result of the energy of the press, but its social penetration is undoubtedly uneven, and interpretations of it differ. Many people may well consider it to be a 'good' thing, but for varying reasons; some undoubtedly regard civil society and political pluralism as fundamental for the security of religion and the perpetuation of the Islamic Republic. Soroush and Khatami would both consider this a major reason for supporting such development. Such arguments are also useful political tools in the attempt to persuade opponents to join the cause. In a similar vein, it was emphasized that political development and plurality were essential for economic development, and that the two strands of development could not be viewed in isolation from each other. Indeed, it was even argued that the security of being able to think freely was an essential prerequisite for investment.[11] Such plurality was given practical expression by the continued existence of a number of hardline conservative papers, despite the fact that sales were declining. Indeed, many of these papers could now only survive through state support, and it was often joked that sales levels were only maintained because so many free copies were left in public offices – useful, people retorted, for wrapping parcels. Nevertheless, it is a sign of the growing importance of the press to the political struggle that even the notorious vigilante group Ansar-e Hezbollah saw fit to produce its own publication, *Jebheh* (Front), a title which ironically lends weight to the argument that many hardliners are still fighting the Iran–Iraq War.[12]

Constitutionalism and historical appropriation

A central facet of the discussion of civil society was the debate on constitutionalism and the need to implement the constitution. As noted above, one of Khatami's strengths was his argument that he simply sought to

[11] *Aftab Emrooz*, 14 Shahrivar 1378/5 Sept. 1999, p. 6.
[12] Something of the public antipathy towards these papers can be garnered from the response I received from a passer-by on attempting to buy a copy of *Jebheh*. He simply told me not to waste my money on such rubbish!

implement the constitution which was agreed in 1979 with the full approval of Ayatollah Khomeini. The constitution, it was noted, contained many of the guarantees of civil and political rights which the reformists wished to pursue, and the debate surrounding it extended to a vigorous discussion of the historical significance of constitutionalism in which both sides sought to legitimize their arguments by appropriating the historical record. For the conservatives, the essence of constitutionalism was anathema to Islam, and if this proved a difficult argument to pursue in the light of Khomeini's obvious support for the 1979 constitution, they turned to the Constitutional Revolution to emphasize their point, arguing that what people had in fact wanted was *Mashru'eh* (the Sharia) not *Mashru'teh* (constitutionalism); the extra 't', it was insisted, had been inserted by unscrupulous British diplomats. For the reformists, this was blatant nonsense. On the contrary, the march of democracy, heralded by the press, was a natural course of historical development which had taken effect not only in the West but in most of the Third World.[13] Iran's experiment, it was argued, had in fact begun in the Constitutional Revolution;[14] and, as Khatami outlined, it was continued during the period leading up to the coup of 1953. In a radio phone-in Khatami was explicit about this continuous (reformist) narrative:

> Of course, you know that the first charter of the civil society was written by a great religious scholar, the late Na'ini, during the Constitutional Revolution, which has recognised the right of the people; the right of the people to vote; the responsibility of the government to the people and the right of the people to question the government. It has been defined. Constitutionalism means that power is subject to the will of the people and the supervision of the people.[15]

It soon became apparent that the entire history of twentieth-century Iran could be judged on the reformist credentials (or otherwise) of the participants. Thus the constitutionalists failed because they weren't reformist

[13] H. Bashariyeh, 'Iran and the Critical Passage to Democracy', *Aftab Emrooz*, 1 Shahrivar 1378/23 Aug. 1999, p. 7.
[14] For a lengthy article on the semantics of 'constitution' and the importance of the Constitutional Revolution in initiating political development in twentieth-century Iran, see H. Nozari, 'The Place and Importance of Constitutionalism in Contemporary History', *Iran*, 19 Mordad 1378/10 Aug. 1999, p. 10; see also 'One Hundred Years Struggle for a House of Justice', *Tous*, 14 Mordad 1377/5 Aug. 1998, p. 6; 'The Role of the Press in the Constitutional Revolution', *Tous*, 13 Mordad 1377/4 Aug. 1998, p. 6. By the following year, writers were more critical in their comparisons; see *Khordad*, 18 Mordad 1378/9 Aug. 1999, p. 6; *Iran*, 19 Mordad 1378/10 Aug. 1999, p. 10; *Sobh Emrooz*, 23 Mordad 1378/14 Aug. 1999, p. 6.
[15] BBC SWB ME/3318 MED/17, 29 Aug. 1998; IRIB radio, 27 Aug. 1998.

enough, or were not in harmony with social attitudes, or alternatively because society was not ready for what they had to offer.[16] The Pahlavis, on the other hand, indicated by the coup against Mosaddeq that they were emphatically against any sort of change.[17] Indeed, as Khoeniha argues, it was not only the Pahlavis who were anti-reform, but their American backers too.[18] The implication of this sort of argumentation is clear: reform has historical roots and is a process which has been continuing for some time. Those who oppose reform inevitably fail. Iranian history, and to some extent the world in general, is divided between reformists and reactionaries, modernizers and conservatives, and it is the former who are marching with the tide of history.[19]

Reform and reaction

As noted above, the reformist movement very soon began to dominate the map of political discourse, defining its terms and injecting new debate into the nature and structure of the Islamic Republic. The ideological contest was soon accompanied by an attempt to challenge the institutional strength of the conservatives, a task entrusted in the first instance to the minister of culture, Ata'ollah Mohajerani, and the minister of the interior, Abdullah Nuri. The former was to challenge cultural norms and perceptions through the expansion of the press and publishing in general, while Nuri sought to begin the restructuring of the administration. These two overtly political projects would underpin the subsequent economic reforms, which everyone expected but also recognized would be the most difficult aspect of the reform process. This was so for two salient reasons. First, the economic restructuring the reformists wished to implement entailed a criticism of the activities of the previous administration, in short of Rafsanjani, and such a

[16] See e.g. the interview with M. Turkman, *Khordad*, 18 Mordad 1378/9 Aug. 1999, p. 6. Other articles attempted explicitly to accommodate Fazlollah Nuri, the firebrand opponent of the Constitutional Revolution; see *Sobh Emrooz*, 23 Mordad 1378/14 Aug. 1999, p. 6; 2 Shahrivar 1378/24 Aug. 1999, p. 6.

[17] Dr Mosaddeq is then conversely elevated into a pro-reform hero; indeed, his political resurrection as an icon of the reformists has been remarkable. See e.g. *Tous*, 28 Mordad 1377/19 Aug. 1998, p. 6; 28 Mordad 1377/19 Aug. 1998, p. 5; *Sobh Emrooz*, 28 Mordad 1378/19 Aug. 1999, p. 6; *Neshat*, 28 Mordad 1378/19 Aug. 1999, p. 8, which prints a half-page picture of a dejected Mossadeq with the headline '28 Mordad: sunset of the national government'; and for added interest see *Khordad*, 28 Mordad 1378/19 Aug. 1999, p. 6, in which the coup is analysed using Marx's '18 Brumaire'.

[18] Seyyid Mohammad Mousavi Khoeniha, interviewed in *Time* Europe, 10 July 2000; see also M. Kadivar, *Baha'ye Azadi: defa'at Mohsen Kadivar* (The Price of Freedom: the defence of Mohsen Kadivar) (Tehran: Ghazal, 1378/1999–2000), p. 151.

[19] The parallel with current British politics is striking.

direct assault on his legacy was deemed impolitic by the new administration while it was still finding its feet and needed the support of bureaucrats who still retained strong ties of affection to the former president. More crucially, however, it was recognized that economic restructuring would ultimately undermine the commercial and financial foundations of conservative power and as such would be resisted vehemently.[20] Better, then, to consolidate power and dominate the ideological terrain before moving on to more difficult pastures. It can be argued that Khatami sought to win the battle before it was fought by neutering the more extreme opposition to his plans and assimilating those willing to be persuaded.

The room for manoeuvre with respect to assimilation is not as limited as some observers believe, for the simple reason that the conservatives do not represent a monolithic block. They are divided not only according to economic status – the wealthy are on the whole less determined to destabilize the government than their acolytes because they fear the personal consequences of social and political disorder – but also in generational terms. Khatami plays on both these facets to great effect, arguing that his reforms are the only guarantee against political upheaval and the exaction of popular revenge, and also appealing to the younger generations among, for example, the *bazaaris*, often considered a bastion of conservatism. The new generation in the bazaar are no less enthused about the prospect of global integration, and the more open markets promised thereby, than their student brethren. Moreover, as soon became apparent, many erstwhile conservatives were making very public moves towards the reformist camp; notable among these was the former head of the Revolutionary Guards, Mohsen Rezai.[21]

Among the more significant practical measures taken by the Khatami administration during its first year in office, outside the sphere of cultural liberalization, were changes in administrative personnel and the financial patronage available to Majlis deputies. Interior minister Nuri soon gained a notoriety equal to if not greater than that of Mohajerani in the eyes of the conservatives, not only for his enthusiasm in defending the right of students to free speech, but also for his zeal to restructure and decentralize power.[22]

---

[20] The bazaar had proved during Rafsanjani's administration how intransigent it could be in defence of its interests.

[21] See e.g. *Jame'eh*, 30 Tir 1377/21 July 1998, p. 1. It was around this time that Rezai's son 'defected' to the United States, a curious episode which Rezai not surprisingly explained away as a US conspiracy against him; see *Jame'eh*, 29 Tir 1377/20 July 1998, p. 1; see also BBC SWB ME/3279 MED/13, 15 July 1998; IRNA news agency, 13 July 1998.

[22] See e.g. *Salaam*, 14 Esfand 1376/5 March 1998, p. 1. It is interesting that the Persian press, and the conservative press in particular, has adopted the English word 'meeting' to denote any student political gathering. See e.g. *Jame'eh*, 26 Khordad 1377/16 June 1998, p. 4.

Indeed, such was conservative suspicion of Nuri that Khamene'i did not delegate responsibility for the Law Enforcement Forces to him, largely, it seems, because many conservatives feared the changes he might impose.[23] Majlis deputies viewed with growing concern not only his replacement of provincial governors, a significant move in light of their influential role in the administration of elections, but, more crucially, his attempts to curtail their powers of patronage by removing their rights to dispense government funds. Some deputies protested that this was a step too far; Nuri justified it by arguing that these monies, far from being spent on the constituents, were being abused for overtly political motives. Coming on top of his other changes, it was this policy, which offended deputies from all camps, that proved the catalyst for his impeachment, although the stated reason was his apparent liberalism and the threat this apparently posed to national security.[24] Deputies nevertheless remained sensitive enough to his popularity, especially among students, to schedule his impeachment to fall during the World Cup contest in France, when popular attention was elsewhere.[25] Khatami was explicit in his support for his ousted interior minister, not only openly backing him but subsequently, and much to the fury of deputies, appointing him vice president with very much the same area of responsibility.[26] This somewhat confounded the conservatives' argument that they had impeached Nuri because he had failed the president, and that his impeachment was concluded as an effort to assist the president.[27] Nuri, for his part, pointed out that 'ministerial responsibility was impeached, not my ideas', noting somewhat mischievously that 'some people are still upset by 2 Khordad'. Others emphasized that the impeachment would make no difference to Khatami's domestic policy.[28] Far more effective was the argument that the deputies had exercised their legal rights and used legal avenues of protest.[29] Thus, while the move remained unpopular, it was based on an argument and strategy which the administration could not fault, given their own emphasis on the rule of law, and Khatami

[23] See Nuri's interview in *Tous*, 10 Shahrivar 1377/1 Sept. 1998, p. 6, where he argues that there was little point in being given responsibility for the Law Enforcement Forces if one could not be in control of them.

[24] For Nuri's defence see BBC SWB ME/3260 MED/2, 23 June 1998; IRNA news agency, 21 June 1998.

[25] The impeachment actually took place on the day of US–Iran encounter in the World Cup. Of the 265 deputies present, 137 voted for impeachment and 117 against, and 11 abstained.

[26] *Jame'eh*, 21 Khordad 1377/11 June 1998, p. 1; 1 Tir 1377/22 June 1998, p. 1. He was in fact charged with 'developmental affairs'.

[27] See e.g. Nateq Nuri's explanation of the impeachment in BBC SWB ME/3260 MED/1, 23 June 1998; Iranian TV, 21 June 1998.

[28] *Tous*, 7 Shahrivar 1377/29 Aug. 1998, p. 2; 27 Mordad 1377/18 Aug. 1998, p. 6; *Jame'eh*, 1 Tir 1377/22 June 1998, p. 1.

[29] *Jame'eh*, 27 Khordad 1377/17 June 1998, pp. 1–2.

conceded that 'Impeachment is among the rights of the Majlis and, in any case, we respect the decision of the honourable Majlis deputies.'[30]

At the same time, so forceful and socially relevant were the arguments propounded by the reformists that conservatives found themselves consistently confounded by their continued and rising popularity. Every time, it appeared, the reformists were assailed, their stature in the popular imagination grew simply because they had been successfully identified with notions of freedom, plurality and dialogue, positive attributes contrasted favourably with the dogmatism, avarice and apparent totalitarianism of the conservatives. Moreover, for all their numerical superiority, the reformists were perceived as the valiant David battling a resilient and unmerciful Goliath. Nowhere was this perception more obviously seen than in the arrest and trial of the mayor of Tehran, Gholamhussein Karbaschi, whom the conservatives blamed for their election defeat in 1997. While Karbaschi did indeed play a vital role in Khatami's election, especially in Tehran, it reveals much about the conservatives' strategy that they constantly pursued individuals in the expectation that the incarceration of a few key figures would deprive the reformist movement of leadership, which as a result would wilt and die. Karbaschi's trial should have been sufficient to indicate that this would not be the case and that, on the contrary, such persecution of popular individuals would only elevate them further in public esteem.

Karbaschi had been unpopular with the Tehran *bazaaris* for a number of years, in particular for his unorthodox methods of tax collection and his occasional circumvention of the law in his ambitious bid to make Tehran not only the finest Islamic capital but self-financing as well. Nevertheless, his popularity with the municipality workers and the young, and his closeness to then President Rafsanjani, made him by and large untouchable. It is certainly true that during his tenure Tehran experienced none of the social unrest which afflicted other major cities during the 1990s, and there is little doubt that Rafsanjani appreciated this valuable political service. With the election of Khatami, the somewhat dejected conservatives began looking for a scapegoat, and determined to secure the conviction of Karbaschi on charges of embezzlement and fraud. Few were convinced that the charges would stand up, and while there was some acknowledgment that not all his business practices were perfect, the general consensus was that here was an effective manager being persecuted by a vindictive clique. Others argued that the real reason Karbaschi had been pursued was because he made no secret of his intention to break up the

---

[30] BBC SWB ME/3260 MED/3, 23 June 1998; IRNA news agency, 21 June 1998

commercial power of the bazaar, citing as evidence of this overall strategy his reorganization of some food sectors.[31] It is certainly true that the conservatives and their allies in the judiciary were eager to make life as difficult as possible for the mayor, and it was only Khamene'i's timely intervention which ensured his release on bail, fearing that his continued incarceration would only incite the Tehran crowd. On his return home, crowds greeted him with the chant '*Karbaschi, Karbaschi, Amir Kabir-e Iran*', in an allusion to the tragic nineteenth-century modernizing prime minister, executed by an ungrateful (reactionary) monarch. It was an association which said much for Karbaschi's popularity but also undoubtedly irritated his former patron Rafsanjani, who was a great admirer of Amir Kabir, on whom he had apparently modelled himself. That his protégé should 'usurp' this epithet cannot have pleased Rafsanjani, whose silence on the issue of the trial proved to be his first serious political mistake.

Karbaschi, for his part, provided a bravura display during his trial, ensuring it was televised and performing enthusiastically for his nation-wide audience, many of whom stayed up late into the night to catch the latest instalment. A poll conducted after the trial estimated that some 91.5% of the population watched the trial on television, with 22% watching the entire proceedings and 37% watching at least three sessions. Only 1.1% claimed not to have watched it at all.[32] As an event, it further assisted in the politicization of the public, and it also proved to be a turning point in public perception of the judiciary and the Law Enforcement Forces, notably as a result of the manner in which Karbaschi objected to their behaviour and performance. In defending his lieutenants, who had also been arrested, Karbaschi showed himself to be staunchly loyal towards his employees, as well as principled in his arguments. His original training as a *mullah* gave him access to theological discourse and arguments, which he used effectively against the judge-prosecutor, and in general his articulate, intelligent and robust defence confounded and confused his prosecutors, whose only response was to become more extreme in their determination to convict him.[33] The public became enthralled with his verbal jousts with the prosecutor, and his implicit and occasionally explicit ridiculing of the *ulema*.

---

[31] Karbaschi had been pivotal during Rafsanjani's presidency in setting up a chain of supermarkets (*Refah*) under the rubric of modernization, with the obvious implication that these new stores would challenge the cartel posed by the bazaar. Fierce resistance ensured that this 'chain' never really took off. Sources indicate that Karbaschi was determined not to be deflected so easily.

[32] See *Tous*, 5 Mordad 1377/27 July 1998, p. 1. It was claimed at the time that the trial was the most watched and heard programme on radio and television since the revolution; see *Jame'eh*, 22 Tir 1377/ 13 July 1998, p. 1.

[33] See e.g. BBC SWB ME/3272 MED/10, 7 July 1998; IRNA news agency, 5 July 1998.

All this, of course, not only enhanced Karbaschi's personal popularity among the populace at large but also won him new admirers, many of whom were bureaucrats and administrators like himself, moving from sympathy towards commitment to the reformist cause. Many felt the impending conviction to be harsh and unjust, while those who had looked to Rafsanjani realized with some disappointment that he had failed to protect *his* mayor. The pro-Khatami Majma Rohaniyun Mobarez went so far as to issue a statement calling the attack on the municipality a 'political calamity'.[34] The entire episode was extensively covered in the country's press, which stressed the unjustness of the attack against him, and also resulted in a best-selling book, again much to the irritation of the conservatives.[35] Somewhat belatedly, Ayatollah Yazdi, the head of the judiciary, sought to publish his version of the trial, calling it the untold story; but owing to poor sales, it remained largely untold.[36]

More shocking for many people than the attacks on Karbaschi were the allegations of torture made by municipality officials against the judiciary, Law Enforcement Forces and prison officials.[37] While no one doubted that the head of the prison service, Ladjevardi, was partial to the use of torture, it came as a considerable shock that it should be used against municipality officials, and moreover that they should so effectively raise a hue and cry about it.[38] Their protest marked the beginning of a major assault on the conservative grip on the forces of coercion.[39] In the meantime, Karbaschi was able to turn even his impending imprisonment to good use. While the judge graciously acknowledged that the defendant's previous services would be taken into account when sentence was passed, Karbaschi basked in the widespread support he had garnered, to the extent that some offered to pay his fine.[40] Most moving, however, was the revelation that a young girl had sent him a gold coin for his defence fund. A tearful Karbaschi wept in court as the letter from the girl was read out, and he urged her to reclaim her gift because he could not possibly accept it. He added: 'I was detained

---

[34] *Tous*, 8 Mordad 1377/30 July 1998, p. 1.

[35] E.g. *Jame'eh*, 18 Khordad 1377/8 June 1998, p. 1; 19 Khordad 1377/9 June 1998, p. 1; also, e.g., *Jame'eh*, 24 Tir 1377/15 July 1998, p. 1, where it is recounted that a 'tearful' Karbaschi thanks citizens for their support. The book is G. Karbaschi, *Mohakemeh va Defa* (Trial and Defence) (Tehran: Gostar, 1377/1998–9).

[36] See e.g. *Neshat*, 8 Shahrivar 1378/30 Aug. 1999, p. 1.

[37] *Tous*, 7 Shahrivar 1377/29 Aug. 1998, p. 4; for the police response see *Tous*, 14 Shahrivar 1377/5 Sept. 1998, p. 1, in which the municipality officials are accused of lying.

[38] The police chief responsible, Gholamreza Naqdi, was later convicted, although his prison sentence was light; see BBC SWB ME/3584 MED/5, 12 July 1999; IRNA news agency, 10 July 1999.

[39] See e.g. the subsequent press enquiries about illicit detention centres: BBC SWB ME/3308 MED/14, 18 Aug. 1998; Iranian TV, 15 Aug. 1998.

[40] *Tous*, 15 Mordad 1377/6 Aug. 1998, p. 1; see also *Jame'eh*, 13 Mordad 1377/4 Aug. 1998, p. 1.

in the Shah's prisons, mostly in solitary confinement, for more than three years. All over the period I did not cry at all, but I cried all the 11 nights which I spent in the prison of the Islamic Republic.'[41]

It proved to be a perfect end to a triumphant piece of political theatre which had captivated audiences and facilitated the further politicization of society, and which in its widespread appeal had reinvigorated and expanded the basis of the social revolution taking place. Along with Nuri's impeachment, it showed in stark terms the gulf between conservative perceptions and the social reality on the ground. As Behzad Nabavi, a leading member of the Organization of the Mujahideen of the Islamic Revolution (OMIR; not to be confused with the Mujahideen-e Khalq Organization, MKO) argued, the conservative position was simply not convincing:

> How can impeaching the most prominent member of the Khatami cabinet for the sake of implementing his elections slogans, mean supporting him? ... The reason that these opponents ... are guilty, is that they do not believe in the votes of 20 million people and they consider them to be the uninformed and disloyal majority; and they only consider the 7 million who voted for their candidate as the 'pure republicans' and the outstanding citizens who have the right to have a say, albeit in a limited fashion, in the fate of the country and the system.[42]

Indeed, far from being cowed, the reformists took the battle to the masses, raising the tempo each time in response to what was regarded as conservative provocation, continually strengthened by their conviction of the righteousness of their cause and the inevitability of its victory. Nuri, for example, told students at a meeting organized in his honour by the Office for the Fostering of Unity (Daftar-e Tahkim Vahdat) at Tehran University that 'we should not be concerned with the outcome of the impeachment', adding for good measure the acute observation of Ayatollah Motahhari,[43] who had been keen to refute suggestions that Islam was spread by the sword, that 'if anyone were to be beaten up for saying "I don't believe in God" at the advent of Islam, Islam would not have existed today.' Noting that Islam was for freedom, Nuri argued that Islam would be dealt a heavy blow if it were characterized as 'the religion of strangulation and tyranny', and added that the defence of freedom required resistance and occasionally sacrifice. This last comment, which sounded like an incitement to revolt, infuriated the conservatives almost as much as the student chants against

[41] BBC SWB ME/3277 MED/3, 13 July 1998; IRNA news agency, 11 July 1998.
[42] BBC SWB ME/3259 MED/3, 22 June 1998; IRNA news agency, 19 June 1998.
[43] One of the chief ideologues of the Islamic Revolution, assassinated in 1979.

the Voice and Vision of the Islamic Republic (respectively state radio and television, widely regarded as 'his master's voice') and, most controversially, calls for the dissolution of the Majlis.[44] Majlis Speaker Nateq Nuri felt compelled to answer his critics, both on the issue of the impeachment, with which he dealt in some detail, and on the broader criticisms of the Majlis, an institution which he described evocatively as 'the manifestation of the independence of the country and the embodiment of the republican nature of the political system'. This high-minded opening was, however, followed by a descent into conspiratorial politics which denied the social reality of the political grievances, blaming instead 'foreign elements ... for instigating all these recent events and incidents, manipulating the events without the knowledge of local people and being aided by a number of local individuals. Why else would the BBC conduct an interview on the issue of dissolving the Majlis in Iran?'[45]

Not only did such an analysis insult the intelligence of ordinary Iranians, who were increasingly irritated by the unwillingness of the conservatives to accept that the people might have genuine grievances, but his long-winded attempt to explain the impeachment process seemed to most people to be a confession rather than a clarification. Indeed, despite all their attempts to appear reasonable, the conservatives compounded their credibility problems by continuing to denounce 'reactionary intellectuals' and the threat of 'cultural onslaught'[46] and by passing laws whose ambiguous wording provided the authorities with enormous scope to restrict press freedom and women's rights. One such law, for example, prohibited the use of exploitative images of women and men,[47] a move which was regarded by many journalists as an initial attempt to censor the press – a perspective endorsed by some conservative deputies, who argued that the press needed to be constrained since they were abusing the favourable climate following Khatami's election. Hasan Kamran Dastejerdi, a conservative deputy from Isfahan, noted that 'Some of the photographs that are published in magazines are such that they propagate the culture of the West and Majlis deputies, especially women, were unable to remain silent about this.' Other

---

[44] BBC SWB ME/3268 MED/7–8, 2 July 1998; IRIB radio, 1 July 1998; IRNA news agency, 30 June 1998.

[45] BBC SWB ME/3272 MED/13, 7 July 1998; IRIB radio, 5 July 1998; it would of course be an altogether different story some two years later when the Majlis was dominated by reformists.

[46] BBC SWB ME/3226 MED/9, 14 May 1998; Iranian TV, 12 May 1998; see also Nateq Nuri's condemnation of 'sick intellectuals', *Tous*, 7 Shahrivar 1377/29 Aug. 1998, p. 1; and the allegation by the commander of the Revolutionary Guards, Rahim Safavi, that 'intellectuals' were paid from abroad, *Tous*, 19 Shahrivar 1377/10 Sept. 1998, p. 2. See Khamene'i's comments in *Jame'eh*, 23 Khordad 1377/13 June 1998, p. 1.

[47] BBC SWB ME/3305 MED/12, 14 Aug. 1998; Iranian TV, 12 Aug. 1998.

deputies were less convinced of the altruistic motives of the conservatives, and decided in any event to argue against the bill on the grounds that it was a badly thought-out and constructed law which would be open to abuse by the judiciary. According to Majid Ansari:

As a clergyman, I agree with the principle of safeguarding society from degeneration, corruption and immorality, and I declare my support for any measure aimed at preventing ethical and religious problems; however, the people who drew up this bill have not confined the question of the exploitative use of women and men to the issue of vulgarity, but have framed it in an absolute way … According to the bill ambiguous cases are viewed as offences and a sentence of flogging has been foreseen for them, something which can lead to conflict and chaos in the judicial process.[48]

In contrast, the new interior minister, Abdolvahed Musavi-Lari, was unequivocal in stating the government's support for women and the proactive role they should be playing in society: 'In a society that is giving priority to deserving and capable individuals, there is no difference between men and women and in our opinion, gender is not important. What is important is humanitarianism and the required level of intellectual and managerial competence.'[49]

Some commentators argued that there was no reason why women could not become members of the Guardian Council, and asked why, given the availability of highly educated women, there were not any women ministers.[50] The seemingly pedantic narrow-mindedness of the conservatives was each time matched with a more open, inclusive response by the reformists. President Khatami, for instance, emphasized the importance of constructive criticism to the proper functioning of a state, stressing the importance of freedom to the foundations of religion. Attacking the exclusivity of the conservatives, Khatami emphasized that Iran belonged to all Muslims who favoured the dignity of Islam,[51] and argued that no one group should impose its ideas on society and seek to use religion to legitimize its political positions. He also pointedly referred to the growing gulf between the conservatives and the rest of society by urging the clergy to make contact with the people and not 'stand on ceremony' with them.[52] In a speech to the Revolutionary Guards, he argued that they should avoid

---

[48] BBC SWB ME/3309 MED/11, 19 Aug. 1998, from *Tous* website, 16 Aug. 1998.
[49] BBC SWB ME/3316 MED/17, 27 Aug. 1998; IRNA news agency, 25 Aug. 1998.
[50] *Jame'eh*, 16 Tir 1377/7 July 1998, p. 4; 28 Tir 1377/19 July 1998, p. 6. The implication was that the conservative Majlis would never approve them.
[51] BBC SWB ME/3316 MED/17, 27 Aug. 1998; IRNA news agency, 25 Aug. 1998.
[52] BBC SWB ME/3272 MED/11, 7 July 1998; IRIB radio, 5 July 1998.

aggressive and narrow-minded approaches which would alienate young people, and his minister of the interior stressed that officials should not interfere in the private lives of individuals.[53] Similarly, while the conservatives clearly missed the point by criticizing the celebrations surrounding the Iranian victory over the United States at football in the World Cup, characterizing the win as a victory against global arrogance, Khatami urged the population to learn from the team spirit and sporting rivalry of the Iranian national side. While Ayatollah Yazdi, the head of the judiciary, dismissed the idea of football diplomacy as 'childish' and unbecoming of 'grown-ups', Khatami saw it as an opportunity to extend his dialogue of civilizations, a position supported by the reformist press.[54]

Where the conservatives ridiculed and dismissed the intelligence of the masses, Khatami pointedly tackled the issue of social and political elitism by arguing that the real heroes were the people themselves and those who were a manifestation of their will.[55] Indeed, the reformists actively encouraged popular participation in an effort to ensure that the groundswell of opinion which had thrust Khatami into office would be consolidated and extended. Elaborate preparations were made, for instance, to commemorate the first anniversary of Khatami's election victory with the avowed intention of institutionalizing '2 Khordad' as a momentous event in Iranian history, a turning point which should be consolidated and built on.[56] Characteristically, student leaders were central to the organization of events throughout the country, stressing that 2 Khordad marked a moment of national uprising against violence. They also took the opportunity to chant slogans against the state television and radio and the judiciary and Law Enforcement Forces, which was duly noted by the reporters from state television who were present.[57] Such gatherings were becoming increasingly frequent events, indicative of the growing militancy of the student body throughout Iran and its irritation at the failure of the conservatives to appreciate the depth of feeling in the country. In a student demonstration in Mashhad, for instance, organized in conjunction with the local *basijis* (Islamic militia), a petition was handed in praising Karbaschi, calling for

---

[53] *Jame'eh*, 3 Tir 1377/24 June 1998, p. 1; *Tous*, 19 Shahrivar 1377/10 Sept. 1998, p. 4.

[54] BBC SWB ME/3260 MED/5, 23 June 1998; IRNA news agency, 22 June 1998; BBC SWB ME/3260 MED/4, 23 June 1998; Iranian TV, 21 June 1998; BBC SWB ME/3271 MED/4, 6 July 1998; Iranian TV, 4 July 1998. See also Khatami's comments, BBC SWB ME/3260 MED/5, 23 June 1998; Iranian TV, 21 June 1998; BBC SWB ME/3271 MED/3, 6 July 1998; IRIB radio, 3 July 1998; *Jame'eh*, 31 Khordad 1377/21 June 1998, p. 1.

[55] BBC SWB ME/3305 MED/11, 14 Aug. 1998; IRIB radio, 12 Aug. 1998.

[56] See e.g. *Salaam*, 30 Ordibehesht 1377/20 May 1998, p. 1; 31 Ordibehesht/21 May 1998, p. 1; 2 Khordad 1377/23 May 1998, p. 1; 2 Khordad 1377/23 May 1998, p. 1.

[57] BBC SWB ME/3235 MED/1, 25 May 1995; IRNA news agency, 23 May 1998; Iranian TV, 23 May 1998.

his acquittal and asking why the conservatives had not fallen in line with the 'turbulent wave' of the nation. They were particularly incensed by the regular use of violence against newspaper offices and students, and demanded to know from the judiciary

> why no decision has been taken regarding the case referred [to it] by the president concerning offences committed by the judiciary and the counter-intelligence unit of the Law Enforcement Force in the course of the investigations into the Tehran municipality case – which has been prepared by two people endorsed by and involved in the judiciary and which includes instances of psychological and physical torture and forced confessions from [Tehran's district] mayors, and which had a direct bearing on the case of the Tehran mayor.[58]

Such comments infuriated the conservative establishment, who viewed them as essentially treacherous. But their responses were limited and somewhat shallow, rarely addressing the issue at hand – Nateq Nuri tended to be the occasional exception which proved the rule, although, as noted above, his answers were poorly articulated – and instead condemning what they viewed as the growth of political and social anarchy, disunity and 'liberalism'.[59] Attempts to identify the reform process with sexual promiscuity by Ayatollah Misbah Yazdi, fast becoming the chief ideologue of the right, elicited a harsh response from Karrubi, the secretary general of the Majma, who pointed out that 'the main purpose of the Islamic Revolution in Iran was to develop the country politically', stressing that Ayatollah Khomeini himself had 'emphasized the necessity of cultural and ideological revolution, and the struggle against repression and dictatorship'. Noting the importance of freedom within the law, Karrubi then tackled Misbah Yazdi's criticisms directly: 'Freedom does not mean idleness, sex and promiscuity. What kind of things are these to say? Why should we compel a learned man who has a respectable personality to say, during the Friday prayers, that defenders of freedom in this country are under sexual pressure and that, to them, freedom means sexual promiscuity?'

Equally ridiculous, as Karrubi pointed out, was the claim that protests had occurred in Qom following news that students had clapped and whistled at the celebrations held for the anniversary of Khatami's election victory. The absurdity of this charge was beyond belief, retorted Karrubi, who also noted that there had been copycat incidents in other parts of the

---

[58] BBC SWB ME/3309 MED/10, 19 Aug. 1998, from *Hamshahri* website, 17 Aug. 1998.
[59] See Khatami's response to the charge of fostering disunity, BBC SWB ME/3279 MED12, 15 July 1998; Iranian TV, 13 July 1998.

country, where people, obviously fed up with the pedantry of the conservatives, had also clapped and whistled in support of Khatami. 'We should deal with people in a rational, and sincere and reasonable manner, and we should not deal with issues in an abnormal way ... We should remind people of their mistakes instead of exaggerating issues. Whistling and clapping are not banned in Islam and at the time of the victory of the Islamic Revolution many people clapped in the presence of Imam Khomeini, may God be satisfied with him.'[60]

As Khatami himself was to point out later, 'Those who are against legitimate and legal freedoms have nothing to say.'[61] The ideological bankruptcy of the conservatives was clear and damning, and while they continued to use the courts to try to impose their will, their frustration led to a series of violent attacks on their opponents, in an effort to beat them into submission. Something of this frustration can be gauged by the treatment they received from an increasingly vociferous and combative press. The harassment of journalists and newspaper offices was proving an increasingly regular occurrence; but many journalists began to relish the antagonism, which merely cemented their convictions. The ridicule they heaped on the conservatives, and the often farcical nature of the contest, were best witnessed in the summer of 1998 in attempts to close down the reformist newspaper *Jame'eh*, whose editorial staff not only organized public rallies (chiefly of students) and very publicly fought attempts to have them banned but immediately re-opened under a new name, *Tous*, with a headline which was calculated to aggravate, proclaiming boldly: '*Tous* in the service of society [*jame'eh*]', a move which raised cheers and righteous indignation in equal measure.[62] The judiciary was furious at what it considered the irresponsible behaviour of the minister of culture, Ata'ollah Mohajerani, who was fast becoming the *bête noire* of the conservatives.[63] Indeed, as early as August 1998 conservative deputies initiated proceedings to impeach Mohajerani, revealing that they had yet to learn the lessons of their recent experiences and remained wedded to the idea that political pressure exercised through the courts and on the streets would result in a restoration of political quiescence.[64]

---

[60] BBC SWB ME/3278 MED/11, 14 July 1998; IRNA news agency, 11 July 1998.

[61] BBC SWB ME/3316 MED/16, 27 Aug. 1998; Iranian TV, 25 Aug. 1998.

[62] *Jame'eh*, 10 Tir 1377/1 July 1998, p. 1; 19 Khordad 1377/9 June 1998, p. 1. The paper even published comments in the Arab press about the impending closure; see *Jame'eh*, 13 Tir 1377/4 July 1998, p. 1; *Tous*, 3 Mordad 1377/25 July 1998, p. 1. To stress the continuity for those that had missed the point, the cover of the last issue of *Jame'eh* was printed, while the masthead noted that this was a 'new beginning' (*dore-ye jadid*). See also *Tous*, 4 Mordad 1377/26 July 1998, p. 1.

[63] *Tous*, 10 Mordad 1377/1 Aug. 1998, p. 4; see also Mohajerani's comments in *Salaam*, 13 Esfand 1376/4 March 1998, p. 1.

[64] *Tous*, 19 Mordad 1377/10 Aug. 1998, p. 1.

The conservatives recognized that their grip on the forces of coercion, in particular the armed forces (including the rank and file of the revolutionary guards and to some extent the *basijis*), was not a foregone conclusion, but they had extensively penetrated both the Law Enforcement Forces and judiciary, and they also controlled the Ansar-e Hezbollah and associated vigilante groups. The Ansar, whose numbers remained limited and probably did not exceed a few thousand core members throughout the country, were committed to an authoritarian interpretation of Islam, and had no time for liberal experiments and political pluralism.[65] On a more practical level, they were financed, fed and housed by key members of the conservative faction, and thus had sound economic reasons to pursue their ideological convictions. Their activities in the run-up to and during the 1997 presidential election campaign were immensely counterproductive to the conservative cause and, as noted above, effectively facilitated Khatami's victory. Their main tactic was to scour the main cities (chiefly Tehran) on their motorbikes looking for signs of 'decadence', and they were known regularly to harass young people for a range of sins, from conversing with the opposite sex to wearing the wrong shirt (normally a Western brand).[66] In an effort to give them an appearance of legitimacy, their leader, Allakaram, would organize protest marches, one of the most curious being against 'rap music'. Needless to say, these marches rarely attracted widespread support, although many people attended out of curiosity. In another misplaced attempt to appear 'normal' they acquired the epithet 'pressure group' (*goroh-e feshar*); and indeed, one commentator was emphatic that all democracies needed pressure groups and that these were Iran's, although he was less able to explain away the more violent aspect of their activities.[67]

With the judiciary and the Law Enforcement Forces under effective conservative control, the Ansar were periodically unleashed upon the unsuspecting masses, principally students, in an effort to quell their zeal and quite literally put the 'fear of God' into the increasingly disrespectful masses. While the mercantile bourgeoisie were shameless in using religion as a tool of political control, the Ansar represented the sharp end of this opiate for the masses; a gentle reminder of the social and political reality, as the conservatives understood it.[68] It was not, however, as is often stated, an exercise of strength, but one of weakness; an increasingly frustrated reaction to the events on the streets and in the media which the conservative

---

[65] Their numbers are debatable and, demonstrations aside, they have rarely fielded more than fifty members at any one time, which suggests a much lower core membership.

[66] See e.g. *Jame'eh*, 5 Mordad 1377/27 July 1998, p. 2.

[67] Interview with author.

[68] Members of the Ansar understood 'democracy' to be weighted according to the level of force

establishment found difficult to comprehend, let alone contain. Students and the press, as well as anything that could remotely be regarded as liberal (bookshops, cultural centres), were regular targets,[69] but in September 1998 tensions increased sharply when Mohajerani and Nuri (along with his son) were attacked and beaten during Friday prayers in Tehran, and Nuri's turban was thrown off in a calculated insult which shocked most Iranians.[70] In assaulting a cleric so overtly, the conservatives had broken a cardinal rule in the Islamic Republic according to which the *ulema*, whatever their differences and often violent disagreements, remained respectful to their profession. In a similar vein, many were astonished that two members of the government could be attacked with such impunity. The nearest the Ansar had previously come to such acts had been the heckling of public officials and (often violent) disruption of events, both during the election campaign and subsequently during Friday prayer sermons and speeches they disapproved of. This had been tolerated, although their typically harsh and vindictive language was condemned.[71] In this case, however, the Ansar's behaviour was difficult to tolerate and easy to condemn: few conservatives were comfortable with what had been done in their name, and some were undoubtedly aware how self-defeating the whole exercise had been.[72] The reformist press capitalized on the incident, arguing that the right wing were deliberately seeking to cultivate an atmosphere of fear, which had to be combated.[73] Khatami himself was furious, and his anger was sensed and appreciated by a reformist movement which occasionally wondered what it might take to shake his normally calm demeanour.[74]

available and applied. Thus, if one could beat up ten people, one's importance in voting terms equalled that of ten men. This was generally known as *demokrasi-ye chomaghi* (cudgel democracy).
[69] See e.g. *Salaam*, 12 Esfand 1376/3 March 1998, p. 1; also *Aftab Emrooz*, 11 Mordad 1377/2 Aug. 1998, p. 1; *Tous*, 20 Mordad 1377/11 Aug. 1998, p. 2.
[70] *Tous*, 14 Shahrivar 1377/5 Sept. 1998, p. 1.
[71] *Salaam*, 29 Ordibehesht 1377/19 May 1998, p. 1. Nuri's speech in Mashhad was disrupted a week earlier, with Ansar members calling for his execution; see *Tous*, 9 Shahrivar 1377/31 Aug. 1998, p. 2. Khatami was also a frequent target, and while he argued for tolerance, he was eventually drawn to the courts after some hardline papers proved particularly slanderous. Even then he tended towards leniency; see BBC SWB ME/3321 MED/9, 2 Sept. 1998; Iranian TV, 31 Aug. 1998.
[72] Some groups were anxious to dissociate themselves from the *Ansar*; see *Tous*, 24 Shahrivar 1377/14 Sept. 1998, p. 1.
[73] See e.g. *Tous*, 16 Shahrivar 1377/7 Sept. 1998, p. 1; 18 Shahrivar 1377/9 Sept. 1998, p. 1; 19 Shahrivar 1377/10 Sept. 1998, p. 1. With typical enthusiasm for political theory, *Tous* also decided that it was now opportune to publish an article entitled 'John Locke and the Idea of Tolerance'; see *Tous*, 21 Shahrivar 1377/12 Sept. 1998, p. 6. This reflected a growing trend among reformist commentators to identify themselves with Protestants (and pluralists), while the conservatives were identified with Catholics (and absolutists). See esp. discussions of the life of Martin Luther in *Jame'eh*, 27 Tir 1377/18 July 1998, p. 6; 29 Tir 1377/20 July 1998, p. 6. Such notions of course have a pedigree stretching back to Jamal al Din al Afghani. Another figure who features prominently is Ayatollah Taleqani, the left-leaning cleric who died in 1979; see e.g. *Tous*, 18 Shahrivar 1377/9 Sept. 1998, p. 7.
[74] *Tous*, 15 Shahrivar 1377/6 Sept. 1998, p. 2.

Then, as if to emphasize that violence was no longer the prerogative of the conservatives, there occurred the sudden and unexpected assassination of the former head of the prison service, Asadollah Ladjevardi, and an attempt on the life of Mohsen Rafiqdoust, head of the Foundation of the Oppressed. Ladjevardi was notorious throughout Iran for his administration of torture and his maltreatment of prisoners, and his demise was applauded by many intellectuals, some of whom criticized Khatami's public offer of condolences. The president, of course, had very little choice but to condemn such acts of violence, although there is little doubt that he harboured no affection for the man, and in fact was instrumental in his removal from office. The assassination was blamed on and claimed by the Mujahideen-e Khalq Organization, although this has never been verified.[75]

Rafiqdoust emerged unharmed after a sniper attack in his office; but one suspects that there was little rejoicing at his escape among either the reformists or many other Iranians, who saw in Rafiqdoust the worst excesses of the bourgeois republic. With customary audacity and no hint of irony, Rafiqdoust shrugged off the incident as an act of terrorism against democracy.[76] Significantly, the authorities did not automatically blame the Mujahideen-e Khalq for this incident, as if to emphasize that more local grievances were involved. As it turned out, the would-be assassin was a disaffected war veteran, angry that his monthly pension from the Foundation (about 30,000 rials) was so ridiculously low, though this was not a view the authorities thought prudent to disseminate.[77] It was yet another sign that social dissatisfaction had reached critical mass. But for all the increase in social tension, Khatami was adamant that the reformist cause would retain the moral high ground and credibility given by operating within the law, even if its current terms and application left much to be desired. He was also acutely aware, as were many of his supporters, that the destabilization of the government and social anarchy would be just the excuse conservatives were looking for to restore autocracy. The spectre of Mosaddeq and the *coup d'état* which toppled him was never far from the mind of either camp.

For Khatami, the real, durable vehicle for change would be the electoral procedure established in the constitution but yet to gain widespread credibility in society. It was true that the Islamic Republic had administered comparatively more elections than any other political order in Iranian history; but, owing to the restrictions imposed on candidates, there was a clear crisis of confidence among voters, and – Khatami's election

---

[75] BBC SWB ME/3318 MED/18, 29 Aug. 1998; IRNA news agency, 27 Aug. 1998.
[76] *Tous*, 24 Shahrivar 1377/14 Sept. 1998, p. 2.
[77] BBC SWB ME/3344 MED/11, 29 Sept. 1998; *Jumhuri-ye Islami*, 27 Sept. 1998.

excepted – few voters took the process seriously. Even his own election was viewed by a cynical public as an accident the establishment would never repeat. For Khatami, however, short of violent revolutionary change, the only other realistic option was change through the ballot box, and the Iranian public had to be educated in its use and to trust in its effectiveness. Furthermore, it was important that the social energy being unleashed should be channelled, organized and disciplined so that the democratic impulse could be programmatic and constructive rather than simply a reaction to events. In other words, political parties had to become a reality. Rafsanjani had spoken in favour of parties several times, but there had been no developments, and even Nateq Nuri was partial to the occasional favourable comment, if for no other reason than to show his commitment to democratic norms.[78]

Political parties had been guaranteed under the constitution but were subsequently restricted during the war, and their birth was much overdue. Khatami recognized that the creation of successful political parties required a social impetus and political maturity which had to be nurtured, and he feared that the hasty introduction of political parties would only lead to personality-led and -dominated organizations which would merely reinforce the traditional attitudes he sought to change. Hence, in the initial stages a series of trade associations and professional organizations were approved by the interior ministry.[79] The student organization, the Office for the Fostering of Unity, with its transparent procedures, democratic systems and horizontal structures, has proved an excellent example of such an association at work; it also trains the next generation of political leaders in the normative practices of democratic government. Sceptical observers were persuaded to accept the idea of political parties when it was emphasized that these provided the only viable means to channel the political tensions being generated. In other words, the conservatives saw in the foundation of parties the merit of control, while the reformists recognized the merits of pluralism.[80] Many had considered that the Servants of Construction would rapidly convert into a fully-fledged party, but Karbaschi's trial and imprisonment hindered any further development in that direction, since only he had sufficient drive and administrative ability. In fact, in the general political turmoil of the first full year of Khatami's

[78] BBC SWB ME/3141 MED/15, 3 Feb. 1998; IRIB radio, 1 Feb. 1998.
[79] E.g. the Society of Kermanshahi Students and Alumni, the Yazd Almohsenin, the Islamic Centre of Teachers of the Town of Borujen, the Association of Industrial and Economic Specialists and Managers and the Society of Legal Experts Defending Human Rights. See BBC SWB ME/3271 MED/4, 6 July 1998; IRNA news agency, 4 July 1998.
[80] See e.g. interior ministry comments: BBC SWB ME/3146 MED/13, 9 Feb. 1998; IRNA news agency, 7 Feb. 1998.

presidency, few people noticed the foundation of Iran's first genuine political organization since 1979; but without any fanfare and most inconspicuously, at the end of January 1998 the Islamic Iran Solidarity Party, complete with constitution and manifesto, was formed.[81]

There was one election in 1998 which offered an opportunity to extend the process of socialization, but its administration also revealed the extent to which the conservatives would still seek to manipulate and control the electoral process. In retrospect, the election for the Assembly of Experts in October 1998 has paled into insignificance when contrasted with the subsequent local council and Majlis elections. Yet it was an important event in that it signposted the competing strategies of the two camps. The Assembly of Experts was the constitutional body of some eighty-three jurists whose task it was to elect the Leader. It was elected every eight years, with the election of 1998 proving the third such exercise, and met twice a year, producing a resolution which was rarely significant and largely irrelevant to the lives of Iranians. Indeed, few people could be sure of the exact role of this august body of conservative clerics, except occasionally to pontificate on matters of metaphysical significance. Then, at some stage in the build-up to the elections, some reformists noticed that the constitutional function of the Assembly was not simply one of election but also, if need arose, impeachment. The notion that the Leader could be impeached was one which had gained currency as that of the 'absolute' *velayat-e faqih* had declined, being the logical extension of the argument that the Leader was subject to the law like everyone else.[82] This, of course, raised the question of what measures could be taken if the Leader contradicted laws, in particular the Shari'a. And, it transpired, just as it was the Assembly whose task it was to monitor the activities of the leadership, so theirs too was the responsibility for the removal of the leader.[83]

This revelation turned the electoral contest into anything but a formality, and reformists swung enthusiastically into action in an attempt to galvanize the population into voting for reformist candidates. Faezeh Hashemi, Rafsanjani's energetic daughter, for instance, loudly called for qualified women to stand for election, since women represented half the population.[84] Not surprisingly, the conservatives were horrified at the prospect of losing control of the Assembly and by extension the Leadership, which

---

[81] BBC SWB ME/3141 MED/15, 3 Feb. 1998, from *Tehran Times* website, 1 Feb. 1998. In the event it did not begin activities for some six months; see BBC SWB ME/3275 MED/7, 10 July 1998; IRNA news agency, 8 July 1998.

[82] See Articles 111 and 112 of the constitution.

[83] See in particular Nuri's extended explanation of the duties of the Leader and of the Assembly, *Tous*, 28 Mordad 1377/19 Aug. 1998, p. 2.

[84] BBC SWB ME/3308 MED/16, 18 Aug. 1998; IRNA news agency, 16 Aug. 1998.

many considered the linchpin of the mercantile bourgeois oligarchy. At first they sought a political alliance in the interests of 'unity', but this was swiftly rebuffed by a reformist movement sensing blood:

The faction defeated in the 2 Khordad 1376 presidential election is nowadays clutching at straws in order to save itself from drowning and being eliminated from the political arena by the people's vote and final judgement ... They are ostensibly raising this slogan with the aim of unifying and elevating the forces within the system, something which experience has shown these gentlemen do not believe in ... They are overlooking the fact that in the years when they held the reins of power they never let anyone else in their ranks and proclaimed themselves to be the owners of the revolution, the country and its management. And now that they have been eliminated and wish to enter a system which they beat, battered and crushed for years, and which has come into power thanks to their narrow-mindedness, monopolism and totalitarian-ism, they say we are your brothers.[85]

In the attempt to prevent any outcome which would harm their interests, the conservatives mobilized their institutional powers in the Majlis and Guardian Council, raising the electoral age from fifteen to sixteen,[86] rigor-ously vetoing candidates they disliked and in general reducing the electoral process to the level of farce.[87] Indeed, at one stage, candidates had to be 'shipped in' to ensure that some constituencies were actually contested. The turnout was unsurprisingly low, despite official proclamations and exhortations to the contrary,[88] and the whole affair concluded as a somewhat anti-climatic non-event, making the point that spontaneous enthusiasm was no substitute for good organization and preparation. The full institu-tional might of the conservative establishment was brought to bear on a reformist vanguard which had failed to enthuse the general population, with the consequence that while the conservatives had suffered yet another public relations fiasco and concomitant loss of credibility, they had in practical terms retained control of an important constitutional instrument.[89]

---

[85] BBC SWB ME/3304 MED/12, 13 Aug. 1998; *Salaam*, 6 Aug. 1998.

[86] *Tous*, 8 Shahrivar 1377/30 Aug. 1998, p. 1; in contrast, of course, the administration praised the merits of youth.

[87] Out of 396 hopefuls, 149 were approved; see BBC SWB ME/3344 MED/11, 29 Sept. 1998; IRNA news agency, 26 Sept. 1998.

[88] See e.g. BBC SWB ME/3275 MED/7, 10 July 1998; IRNA news agency, 8 July 1998; BBC SWB ME/3368 MED/22, 27 Oct. 1998; IRNA news agency, 25, 26 Oct. 1998.

[89] For the full results see BBC SWB ME/3368 MED/21, 27 Oct. 1998; IRIB radio and Iranian TV, 25 Oct. 1998.

In political terms, it can be argued that the result was a draw, and the press succeeded in raising questions about the role of *velayat-e faqih* within the political system which had hitherto been the province of student groups and intellectuals. But the reformists were reminded that victory was not a foregone conclusion, and there was considerable criticism within the reformist movement about the speed and pace of reform, and the need to remain connected to society at large. It was, in short, a valuable lesson.

The politics of economic reform

Khatami had been elected on a platform of social justice, and while many of his constituents were intent on securing political development, many others were similarly anxious for some alleviation of the economic hardships they had been suffering. The disparity in wealth which had emerged during the Rafsanjani presidency had been growing at an alarming rate, and while many of the new economic elite tended to enjoy their position with discretion, there were also growing signs of confidence and opulence. In the Caspian littoral for instance, magnificent villas were being built with every conceivable amenity, which at best are occupied for ten weekends in a year. These stood side by side with the markedly less salubrious dwellings occupied by the majority of the people. Moreover, unemployment was high, particularly among the young, and inflation on many key goods appeared to rise in leaps and bounds – often, it seemed, in relation to the hard currency exchange rate. It was difficult to convince an average Iranian that his grocery bill had risen because the rial had devalued against the dollar; yet the reality that Iran, as an oil producer, was essentially dependent on the value of the dollar (officials had indeed argued that Iran was effectively a dollar economy) meant that there were stark differences in the standards of living between those with access to hard currency and those whose income was denominated in rials. Every time the rial was devalued, the cost of living for most Iranians rose just as dramatically as it fell for those with foreign bank accounts.

Khatami was anxious to deal with these problems and recognized the need to address the issue publicly,[90] but he was also acutely aware that economic policy could not be developed and implemented in the absence of an overall political strategy because politics and economics were intimately and explicitly related. Conversely, while the emphasis may have been on political development, the economic implications have never been

[90] *Salaam*, 16 Esfand 1376/7 March 1998, p. 1.

out of sight, and it is erroneous to argue that Khatami does not have an economic policy. Rather, Khatami and his supporters realize that economic reform in the absence of political development will at worst be illusory and unsustainable, and at best serve the political and economic interests of those very groups who are antithetical to his project. The current relations of domination, established under Rafsanjani, are not conducive to sustainable, investment-orientated economic development which will benefit the majority of the Iranian population. Rather, any immediate economic growth will simply enhance the wealth and power of the mercantile bourgeoisie, which is why they are so enthusiastic about economic development and have consistently argued that political development should be shelved. Because serious economic development requires political as well as economic restructuring, emphasis has been given to preparing the political ground, because the economy is quintessentially a political problem. To put it another way, as Khatami has said, in order for the economy to grow, one needs a sound investment strategy and an environment which is attractive and secure for potential investors who will be willing to invest in the economy for the long term. Such an environment requires a rationalization of the political system, an erosion of arbitrariness and informality in negotiations (the hallmark of the mercantile mentality) and a legal framework which is transparent and accountable. To take one example, few Iranian companies until the mid-1990s ever possessed accounts of any worth, and while Rafsanjani encouraged the development of proper accounting procedures, it is a safe bet that such practices never penetrated the economic system to a significant extent. Yet foreign companies seeking partnerships and joint investment invariably demand to see accounts, and the necessary mental and practical transformation will have to take place if the economy is to develop.

Khatami argued that political pluralism was the handmaiden of economic liberalization and that one fed into the other.[91] For the economy to grow, it had to be freed, not only from government restrictions (as the conservatives demanded) but from the vagaries of the mercantile bourgeoisie (a reality they obviously rejected). A free market was therefore defined not simply in relation to the government but also, crucially, in relation to the commercial groups which had come to dominate the economy and influence its practices. If the economy was to grow, it needed to diversify, decentralize and effectively privatize. For new entrepreneurs to be successfully nurtured, there had to be political and legal security, with a framework

[91] See e.g. Alviri's comments in *Tous*, 15 Shahrivar 1377/6 Sept. 1998, p. 6; see also 'Amniat, shart asly sarmayegozari toleedi' (Security, the first prerequisite of productive investment), *Iran-e Farda*, vol. 8, no. 57, Shahrivar 1378/Aug.–Sept. 1999, pp. 2–4.

for commercial arbitration. For taxation to increase as a proportion of government revenue, methods of collection had to be streamlined; and, importantly, people had to be willing to pay. For a population to be willing to pay taxes, its relationship with the state had to be transformed and integrated, such that the government served its citizens and was seen to do so. If the people 'owned' their government they would be less reluctant to submit to a tax culture. There had to be a new bond of trust between government and people in which the people were not only represented but empowered. Economic necessity can therefore be seen to have driven political changes; but it is important to recognize that the relationship is reciprocal and not a question of economic determinism. The reformists recognized that the overall development of the country – the transition from traditionalism to modernity – required a transformation of economic relations, a thrust from mercantile to industrial capitalism which, given the urgency of development, required a political impetus.[92] In other words, for all the persuasive economic logic, there had to be political will.

At the same time as underlying economic determinants, such as population growth, the fall in government revenue and the impact of globalization, were clearly directing the economy towards the destination aspired to by the reformists – encouraging a belief in the inevitability of success – there was also a prevailing view that the transition needed to be managed effectively and that unfettered industrial capitalism could be as damaging to the nation as its mercantile precursor. Furthermore, it is worth remembering the limits of this ambition, and that what is at issue is a *process* of transition which many accept will clearly take some time to complete. For all the enthusiasm for economic diversification, Iran is likely to remain an oil-centred economy for at least another generation, and as a result the state will continue to play a pivotal role in the management of the economy. Privatization remains, as a consequence, a goal within the limits of this structural reality. Yet transformation even within these limited bounds would yield valuable economic and political results. Put simply, Iran is not a poor country – recent studies have shown, for instance, that despite the apparent fall in per capita income, if assessed according to a food basket calculated at local prices, standards of living remain comparable to those in Turkey. Considering the damage done to the economy over the past twenty years, this is a clear indication of the

---

[92] An interesting factor was the high rate of consumption: 'The president compared the per capita consumption per head of goods with those in other countries, saying that the country's consumption rate was too high. He stressed: "We need production and investment."' See BBC SWB MEW/0566 WME/3, 1 Dec. 1998; IRIB radio, 24 Nov. 1998. High consumption is considered by some economic historians to be a prerequisite for industrialization.

underlying wealth of the nation. Unlocking this wealth involves the dismantling of the mercantile bourgeois hegemony.

In a long-awaited speech in August 1998, President Khatami finally gave his verdict on the Iranian economy, effectively implicating the Rafsanjani administration in wilful economic mismanagement through a preoccupation with style rather than substance. He also began to direct attention towards the main target of reformist economic plans, the largely unaccountable and opaque Foundation of the Oppressed, the quintessential symbol of all that was wrong with the Iranian economy. This televised address outlined Khatami's views on the economy, the fundamental problems of unemployment, inflation, red tape and monopolies, and his blueprint for its reform and restructuring, and as such it is worth quoting in some detail:

I have said in another place that our economy is diseased, and that it is a chronic disease. It has existed for some decades in this country. Naturally, such a disease cannot be cured easily, unless we carry out a proper spring cleaning and a fundamental change and uproot the disease. Unfortunately, even in spite of the invaluable efforts and achievements – such as those before and during the construction era [i.e. under the Rafsanjani administration] which are all invaluable – you will see that there are still many economic problems, because the foundation of our economy is diseased. And fundamental work, that is bringing about a fundamental change in the economic structure of society, in terms of economic changes and management, requires initiative, patience, tolerance and time. One cannot bring about such an upheaval overnight and society could not tolerate it either; however, it is a fundamental duty to strive for that change ...

... in formulating our policies we have prioritized ... However, we believe that economic issues and human issues, in general, and the solutions to them are not inseparable. In fact they are related to one another. Therefore in considering such issues, we must see everything as a whole. Therefore, the prioritization is relative.

... The first point we looked at is the socio-economic viewpoint regarding economic issues ... Although we attach importance to science and scientific theories, we must not forget that the economy is subject to a variety of cultural, social, political, climatic and geographical conditions, and we must approach economic problems with a socio-economic outlook ... Bearing in mind the position of youth and women in economic development, especially in view of the youngness of our society, and in view of the fact that, thanks to the Islamic Revolution, women entered into life's arenas, we cannot ignore the concerns of youth and women or their presence and participation in the process of improving our economy. The other point that we must bear in mind when thinking about economic improvement ... is to respect the need to protect the environment in its capacity as a guarantor of healthy social life today and in the future for the generations to come.

... Our second policy is to give priority to social justice ... The aim of humanity and Islam is to establish justice. The aim of the Islamic Revolution was to establish social justice ... However when we say that social justice is more important it means [that if] under certain conditions there is a contradiction between economic growth and social justice, then the policy of the government is to favour social justice even at the cost of slowing down economic growth...

... One of our important policies is job creation. As one of our problems has been employment and unemployment, creating jobs is one of the important priorities and major policies of the government. In order to achieve that, first we have to utilise fully the existing production capacities. Secondly we must eliminate complicated and unnecessary regulations in order to facilitate investment, job creation and so forth.

... we must try so that government resources are more efficient; the current situation is unacceptable. Secondly, we must gain the trust of the private sector for cooperation and investment. That is an important task. Thirdly we must reduce and eliminate monopolies, both in goods manufacturing and distribution stages. We must provide facilities for investment ... we must bring about confidence for investment and prevent trespasses on investments and profits gained from lawful activities. This, in itself, can assist the participation of the private sector. And finally, we must attract foreign resources and capital, including the capital belonging to dear Iranians residing abroad or non-Iranians wishing to invest in Iran. Where it is necessary and where, in our view, priority should be given, and in order to complement our domestic investments, we must try to utilise foreign capital, both Iranian and non-Iranian.

... as far as the monopolies stipulated in the constitution are concerned, whilst maintaining government ownership or government custodianship over these affairs, we must enact laws and regulations which allow the competitive use of these monopolised resources. As for monopolies which have been created because of various circumstances, bearing in mind the alleviation of those needs and the change in circumstances, we must try to eliminate these monopolies, reduce them at the first opportunity. And in the third case, monopolies that have been created as a result of relationships, we must pursue this task [removing monopolies] with greater determination.[93]

In addition, Khatami outlined the need to cultivate a tax culture,[94] encourage the private sector and foster greater competition among banks. He also argued that the government would provide mechanisms by which foreign currency accounts could be held in Iran on which interest would be paid, according to international rates. While the speech was criticized for being big on ideas but less clear on detail of implementation – a reality of which Khatami was himself aware – it did nevertheless lay down the main parameters of government policy and reveal to the Iranian public how serious was the task ahead of them. It was calculated that the economy would have to grow by some 6.7 per cent annually if the estimated 15 million jobs needed were to be created, and this, Khatami estimated, would require a doubling of the ratio of investment to GDP from 16 per cent to 30 per cent.[95] This in turn represented a doubling of the Iranian job market, and presented a huge task for any government, along with a serious strategy for the attraction of investment. Indeed, so far from painting a rosy picture of a growing economy with regularly balanced budgets, Khatami's administration revealed what many foreign economists had argued: that Rafsanjani had been running regular deficits in which shortfalls in revenue were made up by the issue of more rials, leading to further devaluation and inflation. This practice, imposed on the central bank by the former government, was no longer an option, not least because Nurbakhsh, the central bank governor, was more anxious than ever to assert the independence of the central bank and gain for it responsibility for monetary policy, a situation which has evolved in practice if not in theory. Indeed, Khatami has been largely happy to let the central bank run the day-to-day economy while the government focuses on macroeconomic policy.

Khatami did not inherit a healthy economy, despite the protestations of Rafsanjani, who had been cultivating an image as the *sardar-e sazandegi* (general of construction).[96] Inflation was high, unemployment was growing

---

[93] For the full text see BBC SWB ME/3298 MED/4–11, 6 Aug. 1998; Iranian TV, 2 Aug. 1998. The programme was subsequently approved by Khamene'i; see BBC SWB ME/3297 MED/5, 5 Aug. 1998; Iranian TV, 3 Aug. 1998.

[94] See also comments by Hoseyn Namazi, the minister of economics and finance, on the importance of tax reform: BBC SWB MEW/0551 WME/1, 18 Aug. 1998; Iranian TV, 11 Aug. 1998. See also BBC SWB MEW/0521 WME/4, 20 Jan. 1998; Iranian TV, 11 Jan. 1998.

[95] BBC SWB ME/3274 MED/3, 9 July 1998; Iranian TV, 7 July 1998; see also BBC SWB MEW/ 0567 WME/6, 8 Dec. 1998; Iranian TV, 29 Nov. 1998.

[96] See comments by Nurbaksh: BBC SWB ME/3226 MED/10, 14 May 1998; Iranian TV, 12 May 1998.

and investment and privatization had yet to take off.[97] While there was no doubt that Rafsanjani had overseen several significant infrastructural projects, it was also now revealed that a substantial number of industrial projects – some 11,500 – had been left uncompleted owing to poor management and lack of funds.[98] On top of this, the oil price had plummeted, thereby constraining government options and forcing the imposition of an austerity programme.

Khatami's assessment of the economy and the criticism of Rafsanjani implicit in it effectively completed the political break between Rafsanjani and the reformists which had emerged in the run-up to the presidential elections. Rafsanjani grew increasingly irritated at the criticism launched against him, particularly by the reformist press and enthusiastic journalists eager for transparency and an assessment of Rafsanjani's wealth, and it is certainly true that, unlike Khatami himself, many of the president's supporters were less than diplomatic and occasionally unfair. But it remained a salient fact that Rafsanjani and his constituents had amassed vast fortunes on very dubious grounds, and the media wolf pack had been unleashed.[99] It was this particular facet of the reform programme, more than any other, that began to polarize and entrench opinions, and that first forced the conservatives to reflect seriously on the consequences of the reform agenda. It was also the area in which they thought Khatami to be vulnerable; but while they initially assumed the government's demise would simply be a matter of time, as Khatami's first year came to a close it dawned on the conservative establishment that far from blaming the president for their economic woes, the people were blaming the mercantile bourgeoisie, and Rafsanjani in particular. Indeed, Khatami remained overwhelmingly popular and, much to conservative consternation, his poll ratings actually went up.[100] One reason for this was his limited room for manoeuvre, given that he had to adhere to the five-year development plans drawn up by the plan and budget organization and ratified by the Majlis. Another reason was undoubtedly the fact that the conservatives had failed, and continued to fail, to produce an alternative and credible economic

[97] For detailed inflation figures for 1991–6, see BBC SWB MEW/0534 WME/3, 21 April 1998; Iranian TV, 15 April 1998. Inflation in 1997 was calculated at 16.9%, which is generally conceded as too low; see BBC SWB MEW/0521 WME/4, 20 Jan. 1998; IRIB radio, 10 Jan. 1998. In 1998 it was revealed that private investment stood at 15% of GDP, which represented a 30% decline as compared to other developing countries; see BBC SWB MEW/0535 WME/3, 28 April 1998; IRNA news agency, 22 April 1998. Unemployment is officially stated to be around 10%, though many accept it to be higher; see BBC SWB MEW/0535 WME/4, 28 April 1998; IRNA news agency, 20 April 1998.
[98] BBC SWB MEW/0543 WME/5, 23 June 1998; Iranian TV, 18 June 1998.
[99] See e.g. *Tous*, 25 Mordad 1377/16 Aug. 1998, p. 1; 4 Shahrivar 1377/26 Aug. 1998, p. 1, where the paper demands to know the whereabouts of some 35 billion rials.
[100] BBC SWB ME/3306 MED/4, 15 Aug. 1998; *Kar va Kargar*, 5 Aug. 1998.

policy. Indeed, the two camps seemed indistinguishable in terms of economic policy, and while some businessmen lamented the loss of Rafsanjani the mercantile president, for the majority of Iranians at least, Khatami appeared honest and sincere, with the guiding principle of social justice at the centre of his government. There was little if any debate on the values of privatization or the need for foreign investment, and Khatami with his policy of detente seemed to be more adept at securing international participation than his predecessor. The conservatives might pour scorn on relations with the West, and the United States in particular, but few believed that given the chance, they would be pursuing a different policy, and many privately noted that conservative politicians would be the first to rush to Washington had they been in power. Larijani's escapades in London prior to the presidential elections were regularly used as a classic example of conservative duplicity.

For Khatami, however, constructive foreign relations were a vital component of his economic policy, and foreign investment was recognized as essential. Some had argued that domestic investment would be sufficient, but after some discussion it was soon acknowledged that the oil sector would require financial and technical investment that only the West could supply. The key, as far as Iran was concerned, was to diversify its foreign sources and not be dependent on one major trading partner; and if the United States was to be included among a number of investors, then this was by and large welcomed by the reformists.[101] National interest, it was argued, had to be the predominant guiding principle.[102]

---

[101] See e.g. *Rabeteh?!* (Relations?!) (Tehran: Salaam, 1378). By the summer of 1998, it had escaped few people's attention that Iran's interests in the region had curiously coincided with those of the United States, in particular with respect to Afghanistan.

[102] *Tous*, 6 Tir 1377/27 June 1998, p. 1; BBC SWB ME/3309 MED/11, 19 Aug. 1998, from *Tous* website, 16 Aug. 1998.

8 The Tide of Reform

Few incidents better exemplify the dialectical nature of the reform process in Iran than the revelations in November 1998 of the 'chain murders', and the manner in which Khatami was able to turn a highly tense situation to advantage and catapult the reform process forward with a speed and intensity which astonished his opponents. While few recognized it at the time, the announcement that rogue elements in the intelligence ministry had been behind the assassination of prominent dissidents was to prove a watershed event in Iranian political life. This was not so much because they had occurred (such events have, sadly, not been unusual in the political history of Iran) as because of the nature of the social response, which reflected the growing maturity of political consciousness in the country. Whereas during the first decade of the revolution society had been willing to tolerate a degree of state repression in the interests of stability and security, viewing such events as a necessary evil (particularly during the conduct of a war), the popular reaction on this occasion reflected the social and cultural changes which had taken place during the 1990s, along with the explosion in media coverage which had occurred since 1997. Those elements of the conservative establishment who had supported the actions soon found themselves under embarrassing scrutiny, while a new breed of investigative journalist, with access to intelligence ministry sources, exposed the profound nature of the conspiracy. Indeed, so aggressive were the media and so voracious was the public's appetite for information and justice that the subsequent revelations threatened completely to undermine the relations of domination characterized as the mercantile bourgeoisie, and by extension the entire character of the Islamic Republic. This, of course, was exactly what the reformists sought to do and precisely what the conservative establishment was struggling to prevent. The result was the accentuation of tension throughout 1999 and towards the Sixth Majlis elections, which arguably has yet to subside. In Nateq Nuri's words, the two sides were now at war.[1]

---

[1] *Salaam*, 9/4/1378 (1999), quoted in A. Ganji, *Tarik-khaneh-ye ashbah* (The cellar of phantoms) (Tehran: Tar-e No, 1378/1999), p. 280.

The chain murders

In late November 1998, a series of particularly brutal murders of political dissidents and writers transformed the political atmosphere in Iran. The noted nationalist politician Dariush Foruhar and his wife Parvaneh, who had apparently accidentally come upon her husband's assailants, were stabbed up to twenty-five times.[2] The bodies of two writers were discovered later. The intellectual community was shocked by these events and speculation immediately turned to the motive for the killings, with suspicions rapidly coming to rest on various government organizations, in particular the Revolutionary Guards and the Ministry of Intelligence. Commentators noted with disdain that the Law Enforcement Forces were uncharacteristically slow in pursuing leads, in stark contrast to the manhunt for the assassins of the former prison chief, Ladjevardi.[3] The perpetrators may have congratulated themselves on work well done, since their main aim had been to terrorize the intellectual community and the ideological pillars of the reformist movement, which by all accounts they appeared to have done. Soon, for instance, it was being argued that a list of potential victims had been collated.[4] However, they fatally miscalculated on a number of counts, principally in underestimating the determination of President Khatami and the government to apprehend the culprits, and the sheer audacity of the liberalized press in speculating, analysing and pointing the finger.[5] Not only had they misread the changes that had occurred within Iranian society but, crucially, they had failed to recognize the divisions within the establishment which turned an attempted surgical strike into a political crisis of the first magnitude. It should not be forgotten that the main sources for the revelations which were to follow came from within the Ministry of Intelligence itself, principally from a former deputy minister of intelligence, Saeed Hajarian,[6] who, along with other insider informers, fed information to the press, and in particular to a vigorous and articulate writer (and former Revolutionary Guard), Akbar Ganji. As such, the murders revealed less of a division between the institutions of the Islamic Republic and more of the growing rift within them. It is also undoubtedly

[2] H. Kaviani, *Dar jostejoye mohafal jenayatkaran* (Investigating the murderous associations) (Tehran: Negah-ye Emruz, 1378/1999), p. 30.
[3] Ibid., p. 35.
[4] Ibid., p. 38.
[5] Ganji, *Tarik-khaneh-ye ashbah*, p. 17.
[6] See e.g. Hajarian's comments to the seventh annual conference of the Office for Fostering Unity, in which he talks of groups operating within the Ministry of Intelligence: M. A. Zekryai, *Hijdahom Tir Mah 78 beh raviat jenahaye siyasi* (The 18 Tir 78, from the perspective of political factions) (Tehran: Kavir, 1378/1999–2000), p. 58.

true that Khatami and his government, while resolved to pursue the matter, could not have been so emphatic and comprehensive in this pursuit had Ayatollah Khamene'i not been convinced of its necessity.

It is quite clear that many 'establishment conservatives' had themselves been shocked, in particular by the brutality of the murders, and concerned at the potential consequences. Nevertheless, their protestations of outrage that such events could take place in the Islamic Republic of Iran fell on somewhat deaf ears, given that many people considered them culpable for having engineered an atmosphere of hate in which such attacks could take place.[7] The question of culpability came into sharper focus when the government confirmed, as many had suspected, that agents from the Ministry of Intelligence had been responsible for the deaths. Denunciations and denials became louder and louder as the reformists sought to probe deeper into the web of conspiracy, while conservatives attempted a rapid process of damage limitation by isolating the mastermind of the murders – one Saeed Emami, known also as Eslami – as a rogue agent, somewhat unconvincingly said to be planted by foreign powers bent on destroying the reputation of the Islamic Republic. It was pointed out that Emami had been a student in the United States (apparently at the University of Oklahoma) and had been recruited on his return to Iran in the early 1980s, when his 'enthusiasm' for the cause was noted as both a positive advantage and something of a handicap. One official is said to have noted on his file that he should never be given any position of senior responsibility.[8] Why then, asked persistent journalists, had he been appointed to probably the most sensitive senior post of all, that of deputy minister for security, by the former minister Ali Fallahian? Was Fallahian not responsible for his choices?[9] More investigations revealed that Emami had been connected to a number of conservative groups, had lectured on the evils of a Khatami administration to a group of clerics, and was closely associated with the editorial board of the hardline newspaper *Keyhan*.[10] Khatami himself was in no doubt that Emami represented the sharp end of hardline conservatism, and while many senior conservatives sought to distance themselves from him and emphasize his distinctiveness, few were convinced, and the president was not among them. Indeed, in one meeting with students, Khatami, giving vent to a rare display of frustrated anger, described the hardliners as 'fascists'. The students were impressed by the

---

[7] Ganji, for instance, ridiculed the notion of Israeli complicity; see *Tarik-khaneh-ye ashbah*, p. 259.

[8] Kaviani, *Dar jostejoye mohafal jenayatkaran*, pp. 149–53. According to a report in *Salaam*, Emami was actually recruited by Fallahian during a trip to the United States.

[9] Ibid., p. 122, and pp. 235–48; see also *Khordad*, 18 Mordad 1378/9 Aug. 1999, p. 3.

[10] Ganji, *Tarik-khaneh-ye ashbah*, pp. 183–5, and also pp. 325–39.

righteous ire expressed by their president, the conservatives unsurprisingly outraged by the characterization. It marked yet another escalation in the continuing contest.

As the conservatives attempted to extract themselves from a compromising situation, denying links between themselves and the murderers and ensuring that the judiciary and Law Enforcement Forces were slow if not inept in their investigations, the reformists fought their battle in the pages of the press, mixing speculation with allegation in a potent cocktail calculated to discredit and enrage the pillars of the conservative establishment. In a sign that the conflict was once again shifting gear, one of the principal targets became former president Hashemi Rafsanjani, who now found himself the target of accusations from the pen of Akbar Ganji, who alleged that the murders recently discovered were but the tip of an iceberg which extended far back into the Rafsanjani presidency.[11] In a series of highly articulate articles, Ganji systematically destroyed Rafsanjani's political credibility, benefiting from sources from within the administration who helped to underpin his speculations with a strong dose of plausible evidence.[12] Some of Ganji's articles are so politically sophisticated that it is doubtful he wrote them all on his own. Particularly interesting is his application of Arendt's ideas of 'Eichmann in Jerusalem' and the 'banality of evil' to the case.[13] Ganji argued that Rafsanjani had sanctioned (or in the very least turned a blind eye to) a policy of state terror designed to cow recalcitrant dissidents into submission, a policy which had emerged through Rafsanjani's focus on economic development and relative uninterest in political matters.[14] Rafsanjani's indignant denials were to no avail, as 'sources' within the ministry revealed a string of unreported murders and attempted murders. Fallahian had, after all, appointed Emami, and it was simply not possible that Rafsanjani would not have been aware of what had been going on. He was, it was alleged, at the very least guilty of wilful neglect.[15]

---

[11] Ibid., p. 395.

[12] In reviewing the Karbaschi conviction, for instance, Ganji quotes an unnamed *marja-e taqlid* (Source of Emulation) in Qom (possibly Montazeri) as saying that Rafsanjani is unreliable and disloyal: ibid., p. 198.

[13] Ganji, for example, discusses the concept of ideology and quotes liberally from Foucault, Popper, Strauss, Marx (including the *Communist Manifesto*), Weber and Tilly in pursuit of his arguments; see *Tarik-khaneh-ye ashbah*, pp. 22, 37, 47, 68, 78, 107, 286, 448. It should be remembered that these are *newspaper* articles intended for a general readership, the intention clearly being not only to inform but to *educate* civil society. On Arendt, see ibid., pp. 26–8.

[14] Ibid., p. 16.

[15] One argument suggests that Rafsanjani had successfully curtailed such activities abroad, particularly after the Mykonos affair, since he recognized their negative effects on commercial relations, but had allowed something of a free hand at home – so long, of course, as his hegemony was not threatened.

When Nateq Nuri protested that these speculations and allegations were an affront to Islam and the Imam, Ganji defiantly retorted that such investigations were necessary to uncover the lies at the heart of the system, quoting Ayatollah Motahhari to point out that in Islam the end never justifies the means.[16] When Mohammad Hashemi alleged that Ganji's posting to Turkey had made him vulnerable to the Israeli secret service Mossad, Ganji retorted that by the same token Hashemi's own residence in the United States prior to the revolution made him vulnerable to the CIA![17]

Emami, meanwhile, was blamed for a host of sins, including an attempted murder of numerous writers on a bus trip to a conference in Armenia and the production of the notorious television programme *Hoviat* (Identity), which claimed to expose the traitorous activities of intellectuals – and which had been broadcast during the Rafsanjani presidency.[18] Ganji even argued that Emami was behind the mysterious witness 'C', who had implicated the Iranian leadership in the Mykonos trial in Berlin,[19] suggesting that Emami had masterminded the assassination in order to destroy any hopes of a European–Iranian detente.[20] Article after article sought to expose the web of deceit and conspiracy at the heart of the Islamic Republic, the state within a state, where dubious ayatollahs issued equally dubious *fatwas* condemning dissident thinkers and writers to death.[21] These were, argued Ganji, the forces of tradition, antagonistic to the modern age and comparable to the Taleban in Afghanistan or the Algerian extremists.[22] In short, the conservatives were being characterized as the rotten core of a corrupt and disreputable system, and the Iranian public, who had never seen quite the like of this before, lapped it all up.

Emami's sudden death through suicide in Evin prison only fuelled conspiracy theories, Ganji noting from his own experience in Evin that 'suicide' was not normally an option in the maximum-security gaol.[23] Finding themselves continually wrongfooted by the media, some conservatives injudiciously decided to defend Emami, not in what he had done, which of course remained reprehensible, but in the causes of his actions: he may have been misguided, it was argued, but his intentions were decent.[24]

---

[16] *Tarik-khaneh-ye ashbah*, pp. 186–7. Ayatollah Motahhari, one of the chief ideologues of the Islamic Revolution and a close companion of Ayatollah Khomeini, was assassinated in 1979.

[17] *Sobh Emrooz*, vol. 2, no. 341.

[18] Kaviani, *Dar jostejoye mohafal jenayatkaran*, p. 65; Ganji, *Tarik-khaneh-ye ashbah*, p. 318.

[19] A number of Kurdish dissidents were assassinated in the Mykonos restaurant in Berlin in 1992.

[20] Ganji, *Tarik-khaneh-ye ashbah*, p. 267.

[21] See e.g. *Ba Tasveer (Saeed Emami)* (With picture [Saeed Emami]), *Adineh*, 139, Mordad 1378/ Aug. 1999, p. 9.

[22] Ganji, *Tarik-khaneh-ye ashbah*, p. 34.

[23] Ibid., p. 250.

[24] See in particular an interview with Massoud Dehnamaki, one of the leaders of the Ansar-e Hezbollah, in *Neshat*, 18 Mordad 1378/9 Aug. 1999, p. 8.

Reformists retorted that his intentions were nothing less than the fall of the Khatami government and the destruction of civil society.[25] Realizing this, their determination was renewed and the momentum of the reform movement redoubled – much to the consternation of the conservatives, who, far from having terrorized their opponents, had simply intensified their earnest desire for change. To paraphrase Talleyrand, the murders proved worse than a crime, they were a mistake.

The imprisonment of Kadivar

The tragedy of the murders, far from undermining Khatami, served on the contrary to strengthen him, as supporters acknowledged his determination and respected his bravery in having stood up to the hardline conservative establishment. Not only were those (immediately) responsible arrested, but such activities were roundly condemned, and the minister of intelligence, Dori Najaf-abadi, was replaced by a man widely respected for his genuine humanitarian integrity, Ali Yunesi.[26] For a brief moment, it seemed that a corner had been turned, and the ministry was no longer a haven for conservative hardliners. Over the next year, the ministry of intelligence announced that it would desist from any economic or commercial activities, which had begun during Rafsanjani's administration, and Yunesi sought to reassure an uncertain public about the security activities of the ministry.[27] Ironically, however, as an indication of its radical reformation, it gradually became apparent that its access to various sensitive areas, in particular information about the murders, was being restricted. Thus by the following year a hapless Ali Yunesi announced that he had no further information on the murders.[28] The ministry may have been purged, but as a result it was also rendered impotent in matters of crucial importance.

It was quite clear that a huge practical task lay ahead, and while social attitudes had clearly shifted, few considered that the root causes of the Emami fiasco had been dealt with, or the real culprits apprehended. There was, for instance, continued concern at how some members of the conservative established had 'mourned' Emami's death and effectively eulogized

---

[25] See e.g. *Sobh Emrooz*, 1 Shahrivar 1378/23 Aug. 1999, p. 1.

[26] Kaviani, *Dar jostejoye mohafal jenayatkaran*, p. 134.

[27] *Arya*, 2 Shahrivar 1378/24 Aug. 1999, p. 1; *Iran*, 2 Shahrivar 1378/24 Aug. 1999, p. 1; *Sobh Emrooz*, 28 Azar 1378/19 Dec. 1999, p. 12. The ministry took the opportunity to criticize the 'pressure groups'; see *Sobh Emrooz*, 6 Shahrivar 1378/28 Aug. 1999, p. 1.

[28] *Fath*, 25 Azar 1378/16 Dec. 1999, p. 3. In a curious reversal, the ministry was finding itself attacked by hardline newspapers such as *Keyhan*; see *Arya*, 30 Azar 1378/21 Dec. 1999, p. 2.

him.[29] Fallahian had been elected to the Assembly of Experts,[30] and Rafsanjani, now increasingly characterized as *ali-jenab sorkh poosht* (His Red Eminence – an allusion to Cardinal Richelieu), may have been wounded and politically discredited but he nevertheless remained, in practical terms, untouched.[31] Indeed, arguably his public humiliation only bred resentment and a desire for revenge.

Feeling increasingly vulnerable and persecuted by the continuing press attacks, which sought to expose the 'hollow authority' of the conservative establishment and the mercantile bourgeois republic in general, the conservatives increasingly identified themselves with the leadership and argued that an attack on one was an unforgivable assault on the other. By emphasizing this connection the conservatives sought not only to shore up their authority among ordinary devout Iranians but also to facilitate charges of treason and anti-Islamic behaviour against their opponents; and these efforts were regarded as particularly urgent, because reformist investigations were reaching the conclusion that conservative criminals were hiding behind the leadership, and their criticism of the latter's authoritarian style, which had been a running motif of the reformist political campaign, was now losing much of its diplomatic veneer. Some writers were going so far as to allege that the Islamic Republic had failed in its primary mission to provide freedom, and that for the majority of people there seemed to be little practical difference between the monarchy which had been overthrown and the Islamic Republic which had replaced it. This is in fact exactly what a hitherto little-known cleric, Mohsen Kadivar, had argued in an interview with the newspaper *Khordad*. That his sister was married to the hated minister of culture, Ataollah Mohajerani, and that the interview had been conducted in Abdullah Nuri's newspaper only intensified the conservatives' irritation and convinced them that a malevolent 'clique' was seeking to destabilize their comfortable commercial hegemony.

Mohsen Kadivar was not a politically active *mullah*; he had spent much of his time lecturing to students on the political philosophy of Islam, in particular developments in Shi'a political thought and the concept of the *velayat-e faqih*, which he explored and explained in a thorough, comprehensive and scholarly manner devoid of the theological hyperbole occasionally bestowed on Khomeini's innovative concept. The subsequently published versions of his lectures very rapidly became best-sellers,

---

[29] Ganji, *Tarik-khaneh-ye ashbah*, pp. 315–17; see also 'Editor of Keyhan defends Emami', *Neshat*, 20 Mordad 1378/11 Aug. 1999, p. 3.

[30] Ganji, *Tarik-khaneh-ye ashbah*, pp. 381–83; Ganji of course did not relent in his criticism of Fallahian; see ibid., pp. 408–10, also in *Sobh Emrooz* 4/7/1378 (1999).

[31] Others were termed *ali-jenab khakestari* (His Grey Eminence): Ganji, *Tarik-khaneh-ye ashbah*, p. 394.

and he was generally recognized in intellectual and student circles as an innovative thinker willing to speak his mind.[32] For much of his career he had been left to his own devices, and as a *mullah* he had not been subjected to the levels of harassment suffered by lay thinkers such as Soroush. In the aftermath of the murders, however, he felt compelled to speak out against what he perceived to be the failures of the Islamic Republic, and to highlight his understanding of the popular mood. He was taken to task by the conservative (mercantile) establishment for two particular expositions: one in the interview noted above in the pages of the newspaper *Khordad*, and the other during a lecture given at a mosque in Isfahan which was followed by questions from the audience. He was specifically criticized for drawing unfavourable comparisons between the monarchy and trends within the Islamic Republic; for alleging a poor record on the application of freedom; and for drawing attention to the inherent illegality of secretive *fatwas* issued against dissidents. His discussions, however, covered a great deal more ground, especially pertaining to the character and nature of the *velayat-e faqih*, for which, it must be noted, he was significantly *not* summoned to court, reflecting perhaps the strength of his case and the reality that the source for much of his analysis remained Ayatollah Khomeini himself.[33]

In his interview with *Khordad*, Kadivar emphasized the popular and populist nature of Khomeini's governance, noting that he was socially aware and connected to the people. Indeed, he argued that the secret of Khomeini's political success was in large measure the fact that his ideas resonated in society. He added that Khomeini was emphatic about the republican nature of the government and the necessity to implement the rule of law, based on the popular will. There was no room in the new order for 'absolute' power, and rights and powers were clearly delimited by the law. This point, argued Kadivar, was also emphasized by Ayatollah Motahhari, the chief clerical ideologue of the Islamic Revolution.[34] Such arguments were undoubtedly controversial as far as the conservative authoritarians were concerned, though, as noted above, the court summons did not accuse Kadivar of undermining the notion of the 'absolute' *velayat-e faqih*, a concept which the conservatives were keen to encourage but

---

[32] See e.g. M. Kadivar, *Nazriyeh-haye dowlat dar fiqheh Shieh* (The views of the state on Shia jurisprudence) (Tehran: Ghazal, 1378/1999–2000) and *Hokumat-e Velaye* (The government of guardianship) (Tehran: Ghazal, 1378/1999–2000).

[33] Kadivar also drew from the constitution and from other religious thinkers such as Naini (in the Constitutional Revolution), Motahhari, Taleqani and Montazeri. See M. Kadivar, *Baha'ye Azadi: defa'at Mohsen Kadivar* (The price of freedom: the defence of Mohsen Kadivar) (Tehran: Ghazal, 1378/1999–2000), p. 167.

[34] Kadivar, *Baha'ye Azadi*, pp. 149, 152.

often failed to support with any evidence. Indeed, it is remarkable how much evidence the reformists drew from Khomeini to support their own understanding of the *velayat-i faqih*. For Kadivar the notion of the 'absolute' *vali-e faqih* had been perverted and taken out of context.[35] There was no intention to imply 'absoluteness' beyond the law. On the contrary, Ayatollah Khomeini had repeatedly emphasized the importance of the law, by which, as a Muslim, he was in any case bound. As in the seventeenth-century theories of absolute monarchy advanced by such as Jean Bodin, the ruler was absolute *within* the law. Arguably, the notion of 'absoluteness' was more a conceptual designation intended to distinguish Khomeini's *faqih* from its precursors and to give it a singular authority in spiritual matters, not by extension the law.[36] It was in this sense directed at his fellow *ulema*, who, as noted in earlier chapters, Khomeini often found restrictive, orthodox and dogmatic. While the *vali-e faqih* would function as the final arbiter and authority, it was an altogether different interpretation and emphasis to argue for arbitrary power devoid of legal restrictions and responsibilities. If this was indeed Khomeini's intention, then why, it could be asked, had he decided to establish institutions such as the Expediency Council to resolve disputes, rather than simply intervening himself?

This authoritarian interpretation, argued Kadivar, was in fact a reinvention of the monarchical and despotic system which the revolution had overthrown; regrettably, it seemed as if only the superficial elements of the monarchical system had been eliminated and that the fundamental framework had survived and was now resurfacing. This was likewise true, he argued, of the Islamization of society, which may have been achieved on the surface, but had not resulted in a genuine spiritual renaissance. On the contrary, the revolution's achievements were limited and incomplete, and instead of politics becoming religious (ethical), religion had unfortunately become political. As if this were not enough to draw the wrath of his opponents, Kadivar continued that in the eyes of many people who had fought in the revolution for the right to make their own decisions and control their own destinies, there was little difference in their experience of the monarchical regime and of that of the Islamic Republic. It was, he noted, 'as if it were an Islamic monarchy!' A system of government in which the ruler was divinely ordained and in which free speech was of only cosmetic importance could not be considered *fiqhi* or described as Islamic Republican. If the *vali-e faqih* is not subjected to the law, then the state can no longer be considered an Islamic Republic. He roundly condemned conservative arguments that the people were like 'orphans' who needed

[35] See his discussion of the two strands of thought in ibid., p. 200.
[36] See his answer on this matter to a member of the audience in Isfahan in ibid., pp. 202–3.

decisions made for them, and pointed out that if these views had been expressed at the beginning of the revolution, then people would not have supported it. It was not acceptable, argued Kadivar, to establish an Islamic Republic and then impose a piecemeal and gradual reduction of people's rights. On the contrary, people had rights which must be upheld.[37]

More damningly, and again to the irritation of the conservatives, Kadivar, in his address in the mosque in Isfahan, condemned the abuse of the law which some clerics practised, especially in the issue of *fatwas* which, he argued, were applied with no recourse to traditional jurisprudence. Not even the Prophet, he argued, would have issued a secret *fatwa* in which the accused was not allowed a defence. Quoting Imam Ali, he criticized the tendency to terrorize people and carry out clandestine attacks.[38] Here, interestingly, Kadivar was asked by one person in the audience how he viewed the assassination of one of Mohammad Reza Shah's prime ministers, Ali Mansur, following the issue of a *fatwa*. Kadivar responded by arguing that such a *fatwa* was legitimate, not because the government was un-Islamic but because effectively a state of war existed between the state and the religious establishment. This, he said, legitimized such attacks; but he also pointed out that Ayatollah Borujerdi was not always satisfied with the activities of the Fedayin-e Islam.[39]

Another interesting aspect of the discussions was Kadivar's articulation of 'religious nationalism', the inclusive ideology underpinning much reformist thinking and reflecting the emerging synthesis of ideas which for much of the twentieth century had been distinct and separate. While 'nationalism' had been condemned by strict Islamists as an invention of the West and a tool of imperial control, it had now clearly re-emerged as a legitimate strand of political thought, albeit with a religious hue, in a development which signified a return to pre-Pahlavi conceptions of national identity. That is not to say that nationalism and Iranian identity had been unimportant or had disappeared from Iranian political life (the 'Gulf', after all, has remained 'Persian'); but while in the early days of the revolution it had been disguised under multiple layers of religious clothing and effectively subsumed, now, after years of cautious cultivation by Rafsanjani (who urged Iranians never to forsake their identity), it was making a forceful return to the political stage. Thus Kadivar could argue that there was no contradiction between religion and patriotism, pointing

[37] Ibid., pp. 153, 156, 167, 157, 159, 160.
[38] Ibid., pp. 183, 188.
[39] See ibid., pp. 201–2. Ali Mansur was assassinated in 1965 following the ratification of legislation providing American 'government' employees with extraterritorial rights. Ayatollah Borujerdi was the senior ayatollah until his death in 1961 and was widely respected by all parties. The Fedayin-e Islam were a politico-religious group which used assassination to get their message across.

out that great religious leaders, including Ayatollah Borujerdi, could not be considered unpatriotic, nor could national leaders be considered irreligious. More interestingly, Kadivar argued that the most significant personage prior to the revolution, Dr Mohammad Mosaddeq, was a religious man, whose piety was acknowledged by Khomeini. In an intensely nationalistic narrative, which echoed Soroush, Kadivar then argued that Iran was an ancient land with a sophisticated culture rich in religion. Iranians, he argued, were religious before Islam and after the arrival of Islam. They were the heirs of a profound religious and national tradition, and had to appropriate that which was good and useful from the West, which was at present the repository of human wisdom. It was important to come to terms with 'modernity' and not to use religion as an excuse to set aside reason.[40]

Kadivar's defence in court was not as exuberant as that of Karbaschi, relying instead on constitutional and legal precedents and quoting extensively and wherever possible from prominent religious thinkers. He questioned the legality of the Special Clerical Court but, unsurprisingly, to no avail. His conviction and sentence were effectively foregone conclusions aimed at sending a warning shot across reformist bows. Nevertheless, the proceedings, and the conviction, did not go unremarked. Students were acutely aware of the signal being sent, while the prolific Ganji penned a number of articles criticizing the court and proudly announcing that if Kadivar was guilty, then so was he because he held the same views. To emphasize this he also condemned the views expressed by Ayatollahs Khazali and Jannati, who sat on the Guardian Council, to the effect that the people were orphans who needed guidance, and that the *velayat-i faqih* was a divinely ordained institution with no responsibility to the people, quoting Khomeini in support of his criticisms. With characteristic bite he also ridiculed Khazali's more esoteric suggestion that the Guardian Council had a duty to ensure the young did not go to hell, which, Ganji argued, implied that somehow they had acquired the keys to heaven! In sum, argued Ganji, Saeed Emami was still alive and with us.[41]

The student riots

The conservatives had served notice that they would use their influence and control over the judiciary to re-establish and reinforce their authority. Yet, much to their irritation, their exercise of power more often than not

---

[40] Kadivar, *Baha'ye Azadi*, pp. 163, 164.
[41] Ganji, *Tarik-khaneh-ye ashbah*, pp. 78–9, 212–13, 239, 276.

resulted in a marked reduction of their authority, with the consequence that social challenges and protest increased. This in turn resulted in their own supporters calling for a more forceful show and exercise of power, when paradoxically the reverse strategy would have been more beneficial for them. The cycle of repression and protest which emerged thus facilitated a reduction in social authority, which encouraged a greater use of force, leading to even less authority, a greater sense of vulnerability and an intensely cohesive (if brittle) siege mentality. The closure of the magazine *Zan* (Woman), owned by Rafsanjani's daughter Faezeh Hashemi, was a case in point. While her arguments in favour of the Servants of Construction and her family's importance irritated politicians on both left and right of the political spectrum, it was her vitriolic attack on the head of the judiciary which shocked many conservatives (and arguably damaged her father's standing). *Zan* had been banned because of its decision to print a New Year message from the former empress Farah Diba, although there were additional concerns about Faezeh Hashemi's apparent attempts to cultivate links with the former royal family (she had been planning a trip to the United States), and some people pointedly referred to her impromptu visit to the tomb of the former shah while on a trip to Cairo.[42] While apologizing for the publication of the New Year message, Faezeh Hashemi used the platform of the Majlis to launch a bitter attack on Ayatollah Yazdi:

I am addressing people such as His Excellency Mr Yazdi and people who carry the pompous title of the representative of the supreme jurisconsult. They have not put in one thousandth of the effort the Hashemi family has put in to ensure the success of the revolution. They accepted willingly the oppressive acts of the Pahlavi family. Undoubtedly, supporters of the revolution will find it hard to accept those people's belief that the revolution and revolutionary families owe them something.

Your excellency Mr Yazdi, as the head of the Judiciary you are supposed to be the symbol of justice. It was particularly unexpected of you to point the finger and raise such serious charges against me – a member of a well known family – so easily ... Does the country not have laws? So why do you try and establish justice through demagoguery? Are there no limits to what one does to acquire power and hang on to one's position? Is any kind of behaviour justifiable?

Your Excellency, Mr Yazdi, as the Head of the Judiciary, you will not do badly if you take the law seriously at least once in your life. You can at least go over it. Take a look at Article 168 of the Constitution, the

---

[42] BBC SWB ME/3507 MED/2, 13 April 1999, from *Keyhan* website, 8 April 1999.

> press law and the law on the Revolutionary Court ... Do you not know what legal procedure should be followed?[43]

While few reformists appreciated the pointed references to the Rafsanjani family and its apparent importance to the revolution, there was some acknowledgment that in this case the judiciary was once again indulging in double standards;[44] but aside from some newspaper commentary, there was little reaction to these developments. Encouraged, the judiciary then took aim at the flagship newspaper of the reformist cause, and a favourite among students, *Salaam*. This newspaper, whose staff were well connected with the student body, had taken note of the Majlis' moves to clamp down on the press through the ratification of a new press law and had printed a letter purporting to be from Saeed Emami, advising on tighter press laws.[45] The suggestion, or indeed revelation, that the new law was part of a calculated policy of political destabilization aimed specifically at the Khatami government prompted a swift response: the paper's owner, Hojjat-ol Islam Khoeniha, was summoned to the Special Clerical Court, while the newspaper was suspended to pre-empt an outright ban.[46]

A number of groups protested at the closure of this flagship paper and at the treatment of Khoeniha, with some papers noting the contrast with the treatment of Emami. Students at the University of Tehran, outraged at the decision, decided to hold a small demonstration to express their opposition to the measures.[47] Students had regularly held demonstrations before, but not all of them had been licensed by the Ministry of the Interior, and on this occasion no permit had been secured. Conservative hardliners decided that this time something had to be done, and after having liaised with the local police forces and ensured that they would politely look the other way, they sent in groups of Islamic vigilantes, generally thought to be members of the Ansar-e Hezbollah. The resulting assault on the student dormitories, in which at least one person (an off-duty soldier) was killed and a number injured, sparked the most serious riots in the twenty years of the Islamic Republic, completely disorientating the conservatives and effectively shattering their apparent and certainly no longer real monopoly of street violence.

---

[43] BBC SWB ME/3508 MED/2 14 April 1999, from *Iran* website, 12 April 1999.

[44] Ganji, *Tarik-khaneh-ye ashbah*, p. 181.

[45] See Kaviani, *Dar jostejoye mohafal jenayatkaran*, p. 163.

[46] Khoeniha had a close relationship with student bodies which stretched back to the early days of the revolution, when he liaised between Ayatollah Khomeini and the students who had seized the US embassy. Technically he decided to close the paper before a formal ban could be imposed; see BBC SWB ME 3595 MED/3, 24 July 1999, from *Tehran Times* website, 22 July 1999.

[47] *Neshat*, 23 Mordad 1378/14 Aug. 1999, p. 2; *Iran*, 18 Mordad, 1378/9 Aug. 1999, p. 1; *Khordad*, 18 Mordad 1378/9 Aug. 1999, p. 5; BBC SWB ME/3584 MED/1, 12 July 1999; IRNA news agency, 9 July 1999.

In three days of demonstrations which occasionally turned to rioting, the student movement, and many other disaffected elements in society, turned their ferocity on the conservative establishment and made plain the strength of the social revolution which had taken place. This was a coordinated show of strength in which student organizations throughout the country operated in broad harmony and sent shock waves through the conservative establishment, which probably for the first time sensed real fear.[48]

Both the minister of higher education and chancellor of Tehran University protested; the former resigned in disgust at the assault, which was compared with the shah's dispatch of paratroops on to the campus in 1962, while Khatami called for calm. From the main conservative leaders came only an unusual and deafening silence, which encouraged some critics, such as Mehdi Karrubi, to ask whether the conservatives were indeed supporting these 'pressure groups'.[49] Nateq Nuri failed to make any initial comment, telling reporters that he thought it prudent to wait and see how things would turn out before commenting. Ayatollah Khamene'i, meanwhile, who found himself subjected to the most vicious slogans, including ones which accused him of protecting the murderers of Foruhar and calling for his death, first responded by turning the other cheek. He condemned the attack on the students in no uncertain terms and urged people, even those who ostensibly supported him, not to resort to violence, even if provoked:

> Let us say, for the sake of argument, that they insulted the leader. You should still be patient and remain silent. Even if they burn and tear up my photograph, you should remain silent and preserve your strength for the day when the country needs it ... [Crowd weeps] ... Now, let us say that a young person or a deceived student said or did something. It does not matter. I do not mind [crowd weeps].[50]

His performance in the first four days of the demonstrations was highly ineffectual and immensely damaging to his prestige, as protestors mocked and conservatives recoiled at the thought of an indecisive Leader.[51]

[48] BBC SWB ME/3586 MED/1, 14 July 1999; IRNA news agency, 12 July 1999; BBC SWB ME/3585 MED/4, 13 July 1999; IRNA news agency, 11 July 1999. In a sign of the times the authorities switched off mobile phone networks to prevent coordination. For a list of the cooperating student groups, see Zekryai, *Hijdahom Tir Mah 78 beh raviat jenahaye siyasi*, pp. 453–4.

[49] BBC SWB ME/3586 MED/8, 14 July 1999; IRNA news agency, 12 July 1999; BBC SWB ME/3586 MED/6, 14 July 1999; Iranian TV, 12 July 1999; Zekryai, *Hijdahom Tir Mah 78 beh raviat jenahaye siyasi*, p. 33.

[50] BBC SWB ME/3586 MED/5, 14 July 1999; Iranian TV, 12 July 1999.

[51] Conservatives were concerned that the institution of the *velayat-e faqih* was being undermined; see *Sobh Emrooz*, 17 Shahrivar 1378/8 Sept. 1999, p. 1.

Eventually, under some pressure from conservative advisers who cautioned him against prevaricating like the shah (with all the associated implications), he changed his tone and, while careful not to condemn the students, called on the government forces to 'terrify and crush down the wicked enemies'.[52] However, the gradual subsidence of the demonstrations probably had less to do with the Leader's remonstrations and more to do with the self-discipline of the student movement, aware that the demonstrations were descending into rioting which was damaging to the cause and which many suspected had been encouraged by *agents provocateurs*.[53] Word rapidly spread that conservative strategy was aimed at encouraging social anarchy in order to facilitate a coup and the restoration of (authoritarian) order. Even Khatami warned against a descent into anarchy.[54] The spectre of Mosaddeq loomed large in people's minds, and the student activities petered out, to be replaced by a somewhat lacklustre demonstration by 'pro-government' supporters.[55]

While the establishment was eager to stage a show of strength,[56] if for no other reason than to restore its own confidence, there was also widespread condemnation of the initial attack, and Khatami ordered an immediate investigation.[57] Some 1,500 students were arrested, but at least 113 police officers found themselves in similar circumstances, although unofficial figures were much higher – nearer 400. In addition, some senior officers, including the commander of the Law Enforcement Forces in Tehran, Brigadier Nazari, were dismissed and arrested.[58] The result was that, far from the students being demoralized – although they were forced to regroup

---

[52] BBC SWB ME/3587 MED/1, 15 July 1999; IRNA news agency, 14 July 1999; see also the comments of the Supreme National Security Council, BBC SWB ME/3588 MED/1, 16 July 1999; Iranian TV, 14 July 1999.

[53] BBC SWB ME/3586 MED/3, 14 July 1999; IRIB radio, 13 July 1999; see also the interview with students in BBC SWB ME/3587, 15 July 1999; Iranian TV, 13 July 1999. See also comments by Reza Hojati in *Entekhab*, repr. in Zekryai, *Hijdahom Tir Mah 78 beh raviat jenahaye siyasi*, pp. 326–7.

[54] See Ganji's comments published in *Sobh Emrooz*, repr. in Ganji, *Tarik-khaneh-ye ashbah*, pp. 302–14; BBC SWB ME/3587 MED/1, 15 July 1999; Iranian TV, 13 July 1999.

[55] BBC SWB ME/3587 MED/3, 15 July 1999; Iranian TV, 13 July 1999. The other analogy, of course, was that of Bani Sadr; see Zekryai, *Hijdahom Tir Mah 78 beh raviat jenahaye siyasi*, p. 183, in which Ibrahim Yazdi, the leader of the Freedom Movement, points out that Khatami is no Bani Sadr.

[56] It is worth bearing in mind that it was in July that thirteen Jews, along with a number of Muslims, were arrested in Shiraz on charges of espionage; see BBC SWB ME/3584 MED/6, 12 July 1999, from *Al Quds* website, 7 July 1999. This move was, incidentally, criticized by Ganji; see *Tarik-khaneh-ye ashbah*, pp. 391–93.

[57] BBC SWB ME/3584 MED/2–5, 12 July 1999. See also comments by the interior ministry, BBC SWB ME/3585 MED/2, 13 July 1999; IRNA news agency, 12 July 1999.

[58] *Neshat*, 20 Mordad 1378/11 Aug. 1999, p. 3; see also *Aftab Emrooz*, 3 Shahrivar 1378/25 Aug. 1999, p. 3; *Arya*, 3 Shahrivar 1378/25 Aug. 1999, p. 1.

and rethink – it was the law enforcement forces that found themselves recoiling from an unexpected setback. Having previously been virtually immune from legal retribution, many found themselves not only publicly condemned and disowned but under arrest.[59]

These events had divided the conservatives, with the wealthy establishment shocked at the prospect of political upheaval and potentially severe consequences for its status in society. While some pointed out that Khomeini would have condemned any such attack on the young,[60] financial rather than ideological considerations seemed to be uppermost in conservative minds. It became rudely apparent that as an 'establishment' it had the most to lose. Massoud Dehnamaki, one of the leaders of the Ansar-e Hezbollah, made plain his bitterness when he exclaimed that his 'patrons' had effectively abandoned him. Student leaders meanwhile were more resolute in their attitude, protesting at the arrest of their colleagues and issuing a list of demands (including the dismissal of police chief Lotfian and the reopening of *Salaam*);[61] and while recognizing that such an exaggerated response from the authorities was regrettably to have been expected, they were in no doubt where the blame lay.[62] Their sense of historical mission was also clear in the official statement issued by the Office for Fostering Unity, in which it was noted that students had always been in the forefront of the fight for freedom and against dictatorship – and had suffered for it.[63]

Although they supported the student leader and journalist Tabarzadi, many students considered the officially denounced student instigator, Manoucher Mohammadi, to be a stooge. Mohammadi, who received considerable attention in the Western media because of the high profile afforded to him by the Iranian authorities, was a peculiar character. His student record was poor, and technically he had long since completed his studies.[64] Yet he had been regularly invited, and allowed, to travel abroad and attend conferences, particularly in the United States, where he met and was interviewed by a wide range of Iranian opposition groups. There Mohammadi commented, in a rather stilted and rehearsed manner, on the need for democracy and civil society and on the importance of the student

---

[59] See SNSC (Supreme National Security Council) announcement, BBC SWB ME/3585 MED/6, 13 July 1999; Iranian TV, 11 July 1999; also *Iran*, 24 Mordad 1378/15 Aug. 1999, p. 1.

[60] Zekryai, *Hijdahom Tir Mah 78 beh raviat jenahaye siyasi*, p. 35.

[61] BBC SWB ME/3587 MED/6, 15 July 1999; IRNA news agency, 14 July 1999.

[62] Announcement no. 8 laid the blame on the judiciary, the LEF and 'pressure groups'; Zekryai, *Hijdahom Tir Mah 78 beh raviat jenahaye siyasi*, pp. 442–3. This view was echoed by Karrubi in ibid., p. 31.

[63] Statement repr. in Zekryai, *Hijdahom Tir Mah 78 beh raviat jenahaye siyasi*, pp. 303–4.

[64] See E. Sahabi's comments, ibid., pp. 202–3.

movement. For most Iranian students, who knew how difficult it was to secure visas to the West, Mohammadi's regular trips were a cause more for suspicion than for envy, and many concluded that he had been recruited by the intelligence ministry. It seems more likely that Mohammadi was a political simpleton who revelled in the limelight afforded to him and began to aspire to a political role well beyond his means and abilities. When he was arrested, it dawned on him in no uncertain terms that his political influence among the students extended little further than his imagination.

The clampdown nevertheless reinvigorated elements among the conservatives, who began to believe that a more forceful approach to politics was the only realistic way forward. Far from reflecting on recent events, more hardline adherents, especially in the Revolutionary Guards, decided that now was the time to send the president a warning. Khatami's handling of the demonstrations had been viewed with ambivalence by many people, who felt that he should have intervened more energetically in support of the students, especially when a number were sentenced to death.[65] But in retrospect many of his supporters accepted that his actions in demanding an end to the demonstrations were in actual fact prudent, especially when it became apparent that some hardliners were seeking to exploit the unrest.[66] Initially, however, Khatami's popular authority seemed to have been damaged, and in light of this suggestion of weakness several conservative newspapers 'leaked' a letter from Guard commanders (though not the overall commander Safavi) warning the president that their patience was running thin and all but proclaiming the intention to launch a coup.

This explicit threat once again resulted in a reduction of the conservative establishment's popular authority, as many people, though eager for the restoration of order and even critical of the students, were aghast at the audacity and illegality of the Guard's action. Not only did it confirm what many reformists had been arguing since the scandal over Emami first came to light, that the conservatives were seeking to overthrow the government, it rallied the reformist cause and extended its popularity.[67] The pro-Khatami *Majma* issued its own stern warning to the Revolutionary Guards, noting that the durability of the *velayat-e faqih* did not depend on the use of

---

[65] Students often served notice that they would repay like with like, and lists of potential targets were issued which ensured that their colleagues were unlikely to have such sentences fulfilled. The politics of fear clearly worked both ways. The sentences were later commuted; BBC SWB ME/3829 MED/1, 2 May 2000; IRNA news agency, 30 April 2000.

[66] See E. Sahabi's acute analysis in the newspaper *Akhbar-e Eqtesad*, repr. in Zekryai, *Hijdahom Tir Mah 78 beh raviat jenahaye siyasi*, pp. 200–2.

[67] See Majid Ansari's comments, ibid., p. 45; see also the comments of the Islamic Revolution Mujahideen Organization, ibid., pp. 156–7. Such views were echoed later in the year; see *Sobh Emrooz*, 6 Shahrivar 1378/28 Aug. 1999, p. 1; 17 Shahrivar 1378/8 Sept. 1999, p. 1.

arms and force.[68] Indeed, even conservatives who detested Khatami were divided over the merits of military intervention and the consequences this would have for the character of the Islamic Republic. Khatami himself dealt with the approach in a dismissive manner which enhanced his stature and humiliated the Guard commanders, insisting on a letter of clarification from Safavi himself. Quoting from Khomeini's last will and testament, he simply pointed out that the Imam had insisted the armed forces stay emphatically out of politics. The Guard commanders, whose authority over their own men in these matters was always in doubt, were effectively neutered.[69]

The student demonstrations had once again raised the level of the political contest, as the revelations over the dissident murders had done. Commentators noted wryly that the election campaign for the Sixth Majlis, to be held in February 2000, had already begun in earnest, as Khatami urged his followers to achieve their aims through the proper legal channels. Indeed, as the political environment began to settle once again in the summer of 1999, it was apparent that the surface calm was disguising a brewing storm. Many papers criticized, not for the first time, the inherent bias of state television in seeking to withhold news of the demonstrations,[70] while vigorous discussions continued with respect to the uses and abuses of violence within Islam as Soroush and Musavi-Tabrizi challenged the chief proponent of violent action, Ayatollah Misbah-Yazdi, to a public debate.[71] Misbah-Yazdi was coming under increasing criticism, even from other *mullahs* (including, significantly, Ayatollah Montazeri, the marginalized former heir to Khomeini and the man seen as the most obvious challenge to the authority of Ayatollah Khamene'i), for what they considered to be his misinterpretation of Islam and incitement to violence.[72]

---

[68] Zekryai, *Hijdahom Tir Mah 78 beh raviat jenahaye siyasi*, pp. 25–30; see also the comments of the Islamic Iran Participation Front in ibid., pp. 50–5, and the Islamic Revolution Mujahideen Organization in ibid., pp. 113–16.

[69] See Mohajerani's condemnation of the leaking of the letter; *Iran*, 24 Mordad 1378/15 Aug. 1999, p. 1.

[70] BBC SWB ME/3585 MED/7, 13 July 1999, from *Iran News* website, 11 July 1999. See e.g. *Arya*, 25 Mordad 1378/16 Aug. 1999, p. 3; *Iran*, 2 Shahrivar 1378/24 Aug. 1999, p. 10; *Khordad*, 3 Shahrivar 1378/25 Aug. 1999, p. 1; *Sobh Emrooz*, 3 Shahrivar 1378/24 Aug. 1999, p. 6; *Neshat*, 18 Mordad 1378/9 Aug. 1999, p. 1; *Iran*, 18 Mordad, 1378/9 Aug. 1999, p. 1; 19 Mordad 1378 /10 Aug. 1999, p. 2.

[71] See for example, *Arya*, 25 Mordad 1378/16 Aug. 1999, p. 3; *Iran*, 2 Shahrivar 1378/24 Aug. 1999, p. 10; *Khordad*, 3 Shahrivar 1378/25 Aug. 1999, p. 1; *Sobh Emrooz*, 3 Shahrivar 1378/24 Aug. 1999, p. 6; *Neshat*, 18 Mordad 1378/9 Aug. 1999, p. 1; *Iran*, 18 Mordad, 1378/9 Aug. 1999, p. 1; *Iran*, 19 Mordad 1378 /10 Aug. 1999, p. 2; *Arya*, 31 Mordad 1378/22 Aug. 1999, p. 1; also *Neshat*, 23 Mordad 1378/14 Aug. 1999, p. 2.

[72] See also Kermani's letter in *Fath*, 26 Bahman 1378/15 Feb. 2000, pp. 7–8; also *Fath*, 1 Esfand 1378/20 Feb. 2000, pp. 6–7.

Lotfian too was repeatedly criticized, especially after he declared that if his forces adhered to the law, the country would be plunged into crisis.[73] Mohammad Salamati, the head of the Islamic Revolution Mujahideen Organization, went further than many others when he argued that 'pressure groups' seemed to have their roots outside the country, thereby turning a traditional conservative argument on its head, but also publicly voicing what many had noticed, that *all* conservatives, inside and outside the country, had a vested interest in the failure of the reformist project.[74]

On a broader level, commentators noted the significance of the student movement, and in a comparative assessment of democratization compared it to similar protest movements abroad,[75] as well as to previous student movements in Iran,[76] while conservative pundits lamented the 'failure of authority'.[77] Nobody defended the assault (there was much concern that the youth had been 'lost'[78]), although again Massoud Dehnamaki argued that the initial student demonstration was itself illegal and provocative.[79] His protestations, however, proved somewhat self-defeating as reporters contrasted his claimed 'first-hand' information from the scene with the denials that the Ansar-e Hezbollah had been in any way involved.[80] Indeed, despite the repeated condemnations of the assault, it was increasingly clear that many conservatives had not fully appreciated the reasons behind the students' anger, seeking as they did to explain it away in terms which absolved them of guilt.[81] This was particularly apparent when Ansar-e

[73] His answers to the Majlis were more evasive; see *Entekhab*, 2 Mordad 1378/11 Aug. 1999, p. 2. Lotfian was finally replaced (although not held to account) in June 2000; see AFP, 'Police chief gets top military post', 29 June 2000.

[74] Zekryai, *Hijdahom Tir Mah 78 beh raviat jenahaye siyasi*, p. 140; see also Hajarian's interview in *Sobh Emrooz*, 25 Mordad 1378/16 Aug. 1999, p. 8.

[75] Ganji, *Tarik-khaneh-ye ashbah*, pp. 291–301; parallels with apartheid South Africa were increasingly drawn.

[76] See E. Sahabi's analysis, quoted in Zekryai, *Hijdahom Tir Mah 78 beh raviat jenahaye siyasi*, pp. 188–98; see also 'Havadess Koye daneshgah tajli cheh bood?' (What do the events of the University dormitory represent?), *Iran-e Farda*, special issue, vol . 8, no. 55, Tir 1378 (1999–2000), pp. 2-4; 'Parandeh sar bar balaye koye daneshgah' (A flight over the university dormitory), ibid., pp. 5–6; 'Panj roozi keh Iran ra takan dad' (Five days which shook Iran), *Adineh*, 139, Mordad 1378/Aug. 1999, pp. 10–14.

[77] See the contrasting views of *Iran News* and *Keyhan International*: BBC SWB ME/3688 MED/6, 16 July 1999; IRNA news agency, 14 July 1999.

[78] See Abdi's comments, quoted in Zekryai, *Hijdahom Tir Mah 78 beh raviat jenahaye siyasi*, p. 68. Faezeh Hashemi also made a much-publicized visit to the students, with mixed results; see ibid., pp. 100–102.

[79] *Jebheh*, 16 Mordad 1378/7 Aug. 1999, p. 5; see also the comments of the conservative political group Jame'eh Ruhaniyat Mobarez in Zekryai, *Hijdahom Tir Mah 78 beh raviat jenahaye siyasi*, p. 15.

[80] See his interview with *Sobh Emrooz*, reprinted in Zekryai, *Hijdahom Tir Mah 78 beh raviat jenahaye siyasi*, pp. 369–71; see also the official Ansar-e Hezbollah denials in ibid., pp. 391, 401–2.

[81] See e.g. the aggressive interview conducted by the conservative newspaper *Resalat*, which sought to blame students for initiating the problem; reprinted in Zekryai, *Hijdahom Tir Mah 78 beh raviat jenahaye siyasi*, pp. 317–20. Student organizations frequently protested against such coverage, *Keyhan* being a popular target; see ibid., p. 331.

Hezbollah demanded that it should be armed, notwithstanding the chorus of voices repudiating violence.[82] It was as if the two discourses, left and right, had become so divided as to lose any interconnection.[83]

Even as Ayatollah Yazdi, the head of the judiciary, announced that justice would be swiftly meted out for the perpetrators of the dormitory assault,[84] his conservative-dominated judiciary continued to target journalists and students, clearly intent on engineering the results to the forthcoming Majlis elections.[85] Khatami, meanwhile, took pains to ensure that the investigation into the assault was as objective as possible, and much to everyone's surprise, the public was not faced with a whitewash: the report proceeded to dismiss notions that the student demonstrations were anything but a spontaneous reaction to the unprecedented assault, confirming police culpability and questioning the presence of members of 'known pressure groups'.[86] Reinforced in his position by Khamene'i's public endorsement of his presidency,[87] Khatami also took steps to replace key personnel, including the head of the Foundation of the Oppressed, Mohsen Rafiqdoust, and Ayatollah Yazdi. The new judiciary chief, Ayatollah Hashemi Shahroudi, was known to have conservative leanings but was also respected as fair-minded,[88] although Abbas Abdi warned people not to have exaggerated expectations as to what he might be able to achieve.

As time went on, the extent of the judiciary's partisan leanings became increasingly apparent, and the sense that reform was urgent was matched by a recognition of the magnitude of the task ahead. Calls for a 'neutral judiciary' which would be a source of national pride rapidly came to sound like wishful thinking.[89] While some editors asked whether Shahroudi would become another Khatami,[90] it was soon apparent that conservative judges were intent on going out with a bang rather than a whimper. Shahroudi himself indicated his preference for press affairs not to reach the courts, but many of his judges had different ideas.[91] In fact, so persistent was their pursuit of reformist publications that editors simply opined that

[82] See Zekryai, *Hijdahom Tir Mah 78 beh raviat jenahaye siyasi*, pp. 394–6.

[83] *Sobh Emrooz*, 1 Shahrivar 1378/23 Aug. 1999, p. 3.

[84] BBC SWB ME/3585 MED/6, 13 July 1999; Iranian TV, 11 July 1999.

[85] *Aftab Emrooz*, 11 Mordad 1377/2 Aug. 1998, p. 1; see also the letter of the Freedom Movement to Khatami criticizing the inconsistent performance and biased approach of the LEF in Zekryai, *Hijdahom Tir Mah 78 beh raviat jenahaye siyasi*, p. 176.

[86] For the complete text of the report see *Entekhab*, 25 Mordad 1378/16 Aug. 1999, p. 6; for the Tehran Council's report, see *Aftab Emrooz*, 3 Shahrivar 1378/25 Aug. 1999, p. 2.

[87] *Aftab Emrooz*, 3 Shahrivar 1378/25 Aug. 1999, p. 3.

[88] *Arya*, 20 Mordad 1378/11 Aug. 1999, p. 3.

[89] *Iran*, 24 Mordad 1378/15 Aug. 1999, p. 3.

[90] *Aftab Emrooz*, 30 Mordad 1378/21 Aug. 1999, p. 6.

[91] *Sobh Emrooz*, 25 Azar 1378/16 Dec. 1999, p. 1.

things could have been much worse if Yazdi had stayed, leading some to consider whether the crisis that had afflicted the Ministry of Intelligence would next strike the judiciary.[92]

There ensued a series of jousts with the press, according to the conservatives the principal cause of all the political turmoil and agitation, in which the editors would seek to extend the limits of debate under the protection of the minister of culture, who, having survived an impeachment motion with some flair earlier in the year, was proving increasingly robust in his defence of the press;[93] for its part, the judiciary would take every opportunity to suppress, restrict and if possible impose an immediate ban on publication. One of the most interesting examples was the closure of *Neshat* following an opinion piece condemning the continuation of execution under Islamic criminal law, which it argued was simply a form of state-inflicted violence.[94] Its closure became a *cause célèbre* which naturally was widely and very publicly condemned as yet another act of counterproductive intolerance.[95]

The campaign for the Sixth Majlis and the arrest of Nuri

President Khatami was convinced that if change were to be sustainable it had to be effected through legal channels with the minimum dislocation and disruption to the order of the state. While this was always an idealized aspiration in the face of continuous conservative resistance, he was able to convince his supporters that they should channel their anger and frustration towards a coherent campaign to secure the Sixth Majlis.[96] Evidence that this was achievable had been offered by the first local council elections held in 1999, which represented the first serious attempt at decentralization and empowerment of the population. The Guardian Council had viewed this process with suspicion and had sought to hinder its completion, but despite the limited remit bestowed on councillors, people were enthused by the prospect of taking back power, and Khatami was personally decisive in ensuring

---

[92] *Fath*, 24 Azar 1378/15 Dec. 1999, p. 5.

[93] During the impeachment process conservative deputies were shown to be extremely ill-prepared and ignorant of global realities, as when one deputy criticized Mohajerani for 'allowing' such critical texts as Huntington's *Clash of Civilizations* to be published. Mohajerani retorted that unfortunately his remit did not extend to the United States!

[94] See Emadaldin Baghi's commentary on the article, which appeared in *Neshat*, 8 Shahrivar 1378/30 Aug. 1999, p. 1.

[95] *Arya*, 16 Shahrivar 1378/7 Sept. 1999, pp. 1–2; *Sobh Emrooz*, 15 Shahrivar 1378/6 Sept. 1999, p. 1; *Iran*, 15 Sharivar 1378/6 Sept. 1999, p. 14.

[96] *Sobh Emrooz*, 6 Shahrivar 1378/28 Aug. 1999, p. 1.

that this modest exercise in popular democracy would work. Nevertheless, though important, activity at this level paled into relative significance when compared to the prospect of control of the Majlis.

This was the next great target and, Khatami argued, a goal of which reformists should not lose sight. Achievement of control of the Majlis was important for two salient reasons: not only would it confirm the popular nature of the reformist movement and the undiminished stature of Khatami, it would also enable the reformists to seize the initiative with respect to the legislative agenda. If the law against the press was harsh, for example, it could be reformed through the parliament. The conservatives, who had always believed that the reformist movement was a fleeting affair and that Khatami would prove to be a transient and ineffectual president, gradually came to the conclusion that the loss of the Majlis would not only extend the duration of this temporary phenomenon but effectively confirm and consolidate it. This realization was slow in coming; it was the end of summer 1999 before some conservatives began to appreciate the depth and profundity of the continuing social revolution that was taking place and openly argued that they must adapt to the reality of changed circumstances. As one conservative commented, they must persuade the people through logical argument. Shaken by events over the summer, the conservatives were less confident than they had been about the use of raw force and sought to re-emphasize the importance of economic over political issues;[97] but at the same time they sought to hedge their bets by various attempts at election manipulation, using their strength in the judiciary to close down papers and imprison key opponents and that in the Guardian Council to vet potential candidates.

In many ways the conservatives' fundamental strategy remained unchanged. They still believed that a strategy of elite containment would work best, shielding the naïve public from the demagoguery of the reformists, who would naturally 'return' to the straight and true path. But the mode and tone of its application had shifted, tending to be more selective and subtle. While this worked to some extent with the vetting of the Guardian Council, which resulted in some 10 per cent of candidates being designated unsuitable, it backfired disastrously with the trial of vice president Abdullah Nuri, whom the conservatives were determined to prevent from standing for election and possibly becoming Speaker of the new Majlis.

The reformists were more sanguine about their chances. For them the strategy was simple: flood the market with so many candidates in a sort of political human wave assault that sufficient candidates were bound to get

---

[97] See e.g. Khamene'i's comments; *Khordad*, 3 Shahrivar 1378/25 Aug. 1999, p. 1.

through. As one student commented, the establishment might vet the 'big names' but there were plenty of replacements in the wings. Indeed, the coordination of the campaign among the various reformist groups, collectively known as the 2 Khordad Front[98] (some eighteen groups in all, led by the Islamic Iran Participation Front), was impressive and confounded the conservatives, who had privately believed that the size of the movement would inevitably lead to division and a dilution of the vote. On the contrary, candidates negotiated constituencies, with some withdrawing where they felt the reformist vote would be harmed by their standing.

Much of this coordination (but not all: student groups and other organizations were also important) was achieved through the medium of the press. It not only listed the important candidates but also maintained the momentum of the movement through critical articles challenging the use of violence and raising the spectre of Emami,[99] with editorials praising the reformist movement and its crucial importance to the development of the country and with commentaries ridiculing the Fifth Majlis and the conservatives in general.[100] This latter tactic was exemplified by the public outrage at the Majlis' sudden and inexplicable decision to abolish the holiday commemorating the nationalization of oil under Dr Mosaddeq (29 Esfand) and replace it with another religious holiday (which would vary according to the lunar calendar). That it should fall in the run-up to the New Year (a very practical holiday whose removal would inconvenience many) was one bone of contention, but its symbolic value was probably even more important, and the fact that the Majlis could abolish it almost as an afterthought was seen as an act of immense political stupidity by many commentators. The deputies were ridiculed for their ineptitude and lack of social sensibility, while the government showed its political astuteness by immediately criticizing the move.[101] For some, who noted the coincidence of a British embassy statement in the same week supporting investment in the Iranian oil industry, this was confirmation of British links with the conservatives (suspicions of which dated back to Larijani's fateful visit to London in 1997) and was a gift by the Majlis to the resurgent British.[102] Taken aback by the fierce public response, the Majlis quickly backtracked from what was undoubtedly one of its least admirable decisions.

---

[98] The allusion and resemblance to Mosaddeq's National Front are clear.
[99] *Sobh Emrooz*, 31 Mordad 1378/22 Aug. 1999, pp. 6–7; see also *Fath*, 30 Bahman 1378/19 Feb. 2000, p. 7.
[100] See e.g. *Sobh Emrooz*, 17 Shahrivar 1378/8 Sept. 1999, p. 4; *Iran*, 8 Shahrivar 1378/30 Aug. 1999, p. 1.
[101] *Arya*, 28 Mordad 1378/19 Aug. 1999, p. 3.
[102] *Sobh Emrooz*, 1 Shahrivar 1378/23 Aug. 1999, p. 5.

Much of the media success in whipping up public enthusiasm for the Majlis election can be put down to conservative errors of judgment, the most obvious being the decision to arrest the former interior minister Abdullah Nuri. The recital of the charges against him lasted two hours and ran to more than 40 pages. They included spreading falsehoods with intent to damage the Islamic Revolution and Republic, supporting the dissident senior cleric Ayatollah Montazari and advocating relations with the United States and Israel. Nuri had remained a popular political figure and was held in particular affection by the student organizations, although some people felt he had been unnecessarily provocative in his pronouncements. Now, however, his defence, fully covered in the press (and the subsequent best-selling book *Hemlock of Reform*) thrust him into even greater public prominence.[103] His argument (widely seen as a collective effort by the reformists) pulled no punches in its criticisms of the system and the leadership, quoting extensively from Ayatollah Khomeini in the process (principally his published and widely available collected writings and sayings *Safieh-e Nur* [Pages of light]), and crucially and somewhat controversially drawing on the sayings of Ayatollah Montazeri.[104] After the customary challenge to the legitimacy of the court, which, he argued, was meant to have been a temporary expedient, not a permanent judicial fixture,[105] Nuri began a defence which resembled a stern and highly articulate lecture to his conservative persecutors. Defending his paper's right to print the interview with Kadivar, in which the latter had drawn attention to the issue of illicit *fatwas*, Nuri pointed to the fact that one member of the jury had, in a television programme, already characterized the victims of the serial murders as apostate, thereby confirming the validity of Kadivar's concerns.[106] He added that crimes were crimes, irrespective of clothing and position, in a clear assault on the continued reverence some people retained for those in clerical dress.[107] When challenged on his decision to publish the writings of Ezatollah Sahabi, Nuri defended the latter's integrity and added that it was curious that in Iran people had the right to free speech but not the right to communicate it![108]

---

[103] See e.g. *Sobh Emrooz*, 16 Aban 1378/7 Nov. 1999, pp. 2, 11; *Sobh Emrooz*, 19 Aban 1378/10 Nov. 1999, pp. 6–7. See A. Nuri, *Shokoran-e Eslah* (Hemlock of Reform) (Tehran: Tar-e No, 1378/1999–2000).

[104] *Arya*, 19 Aban 1378/10 Nov. 1999, p. 2; the judge considered discussion of Montazeri too sensitive and sought to suppress it, which of course only heightened popular interest.

[105] Nuri, *Shokoran-e Eslah*, p. 101.

[106] Ibid., p. 84.

[107] *Sobh Emrooz*, 13 Aban 1378/3 Nov. 1999, p. 1; this was carried in banner headlines.

[108] Nuri, *Shokoran-e Eslah*, p. 89.

It was in his explication of Khomeini's thought and legacy that Nuri most irritated his prosecutors and disorientated the conservative establishment. Taking the position that ideas were susceptible to interpretation, Nuri asked why, if God's religion was open to a plurality of interpretations, the Imam's thought was considered monolithic and certain? He then argued that as far as he was concerned, the most important facet of Khomeini's political philosophy was that of 'rights'; he pointed out that Khomeini, in a speech in Behesht Zahra on his arrival back in Iran in 1979, had himself emphatically stated that the destiny of every person was in their own hands, and nobody had any right to appropriate it. Khomeini, argued Nuri, had said that no one was in need of a representative and that freedom was the first right of every individual. Accordingly, 'The people who have rebelled want freedom ... these people who want freedom and independence are not animals. They are civilized. The animals are those who have taken freedom and independence from them. Freedom and independence are among the first rights of humanity.' The pertinence of Khomeini's words was not lost on anyone inside or outside the court. Nuri continued that, according to Khomeini, 'freedom' was not something *given* by others; it was provided by divine grace and enshrined in the law. As such it was not man's to give or indeed take away. He then emphasized Khomeini's respect for the people, their wishes and their foundational role in both the establishment of the Islamic Republic and the position of the Leader, who, if indirectly elected, was elected nonetheless. Nuri also quoted from Khomeini's now well-known edict that no one had the right to enter another's house or to harass people on the street without recourse to the law. Facing the court, Nuri concluded that if he was being accused of being against the murder of dissidents, the development of a police state and military intervention (i.e. by the Revolutionary Guards), then he was indeed guilty.[109]

Somewhat shaken by Nuri's extensive knowledge of Khomeini's sayings, the prosecutor decided himself to draw on Khomeini in his argument with respect to Nuri's promotion of ties with the United States, indicating Khomeini's implacable opposition – unless, of course, the United States were to change its policies. Nuri responded by arguing that one had to view Khomeini's position within the context of his own time. He pointed out that Khomeini's vehement opposition to King Fahd (whom he rated worse than Saddam Hussein) had not prevented the establishment of relations between Iran and Saudi Arabia – a move which, he added, was in fact beneficial to Iran. Moreover, contrary to his own assertions Khomeini had

---

[109] Ibid., pp. 117–21.

eventually agreed to a ceasefire with Iraq in 1988. Had Khomeini died in 1987, would we have continued fighting, asked Nuri? Turning to Islamic history, Nuri pointed out that the Prophet had continued to communicate with his enemies; did Imam Hasan not write to the Umayyad Caliph Moawiya? Nuri said that it was absurd that a country as small as Armenia lobbied in the American Congress and State Department for its interests, while Iran was seemingly prevented by domestic critics from doing the same. The reasons for engagement were sound: Iran had an economic interest which it had to pursue.[110]

If this was hard for the conservatives to take, then Nuri's advocacy of a more moderate approach to the Arab–Israeli peace process was even more shocking. Indeed, even those sympathetic to his cause found Nuri's audacious argument that Iran could not be more Palestinian than the Palestinians (or, as it was said, more Catholic than the Pope!) difficult to digest. His argument, however, remained ruthlessly logical. If Iran genuinely considered the Palestinian National Authority to be treasonous, why had it offered it diplomatic recognition, complete with an embassy in Tehran, instead of offering such recognition to Hamas or Islamic Jihad? Again, Khomeini's views had to be taken in historical context. It was unrealistic to be antagonistic to Israel when no Arab state was interested in fighting any more. The future of the Palestinians lay with them, not with anyone else. At the same time, Nuri was prudent enough to point out that at no time had his newspaper *Khordad* ever officially recognized Israel as a state, although this comment was easily lost in the bolder assertions and arguments that preceded it.[111]

Turning to more domestic matters, the court alleged that Nuri's defence of the National Front contradicted Khomeini's view that its members were irreligious and apostates. On the contrary, argued Nuri, in another clear indication of the continuing rehabilitation of the National Front, Khomeini had praised Mosaddeq as a great servant of the state. Arguing that it was unsatisfactory to be so selective in their use of Khomeini's speeches, Nuri than quoted Ayatollah Khamene'i in praise of Mosaddeq in order to emphasize his point. Far more sensitive was his defence of Ayatollah Montazeri, who, he argued, had been illegally placed under house arrest and was entitled to criticize the Leader since Khomeini had himself said that the people had the right to tell the Leader if they thought he was mistaken – even himself. If the people were so entitled, was another Source of Emulation not equally so entitled?[112] Moving to more abstract issues,

---

[110] Ibid., pp. 122–40.
[111] Ibid., pp. 141–52.
[112] Ibid., pp. 163–99.

Nuri challenged the notion that the Shari'a could be implemented in the form of a rigid system, arguing for plurality and emphasizing that the definition of what exactly constituted a Muslim was contentious and should remain inclusive rather than exclusive. He even found time to defend the use of Kant's definition of enlightenment and the independence of thought![113]

The trial effectively transformed Nuri into a popular hero – his final defence read like a political manifesto – with some youth magazines asking suggestively whether he might not be the next president after Khatami![114] Indeed, at this point Nuri's popularity seemed to exceed that of the president, whose ambiguous response to the outcome of the proceedings was widely criticized.[115] Few believed that Nuri's conviction was anything other than political, and some newspapers made this point explicitly, juxtaposing Ayatollah Yazdi's bold pronouncement that Iran had no political prisoners with a picture of Nuri.[116] Seyyid Hadi Khamene'i, the younger brother of the Leader and keen ally of Khatami, pointedly described the court as illegal and called Nuri 'a revolutionary with a brilliant record'.[117] Aware that the trial had probably elevated Nuri's stature, the head of the Special Clerical Court, Mohsen Ejei, whose credibility, like of that of the court, was now negligible, sought to dismiss public opinion as irrelevant to the judicial process and succeeded only in appearing detached and alienated from society.[118] As Nuri continued to attract extensive publicity from gaol – which undoubtedly assisted the reformist election campaign, given his insistence that he had revealed only a small amount of what he knew – there was widespread astonishment, if not bewilderment, at the conservative establishment's persecution of someone who was considered one of the 'companions' of the Imam.[119] This identification served only to increase and confirm the view that it was the conservatives, not the reformists, who were perverting Khomeini's legacy.

The excitement generated by Nuri's trial was compounded by Hashemi Rafsanjani's sudden announcement that he intended to stand for election to the Majlis.[120] It was not an entirely unexpected move, but on the back of

[113] Ibid., pp. 218, 225, 253–5. Ernest Cassirer was another proponent of freedom of thought challenged in the court: ibid., p. 235.

[114] Ibid., pp. 253–5; M. H. Abedi, 'Panj sal bad – Abdollah Nuri!' (Five years later – Abdollah Nuri!), *Iran-e Javan*, 25 Azar 1378/14 Dec. 1999, pp. 8–11.

[115] *Arya*, 25 Azar 1378/16 Dec. 1999, p. 2; *Fath*, 25 Azar 1378/16 Dec. 1999, p. 2.

[116] *Mosharekat*, 28 Bahman 1378/17 Feb. 2000, p. 8.

[117] BBC SWB ME/3737 MED/2, 14 Jan. 2000, from *Iran Daily* website, 12 Jan. 2000.

[118] *Fath*, 24 Azar 1378/15 Dec. 1999, p. 1; see also *Fath*, 24 Azar 1378/15 Dec. 1999, p. 1.

[119] *Payam-e Azadi*, 29 Azar 1378/20 Dec. 1999, p. 4; *Fath*, 29 Azar 1378/20 Dec. 1999, p. 1; see Majid Ansari's comments in *Neshat*, 18 Mordad 1378/9 Aug. 1999, p. 1.

[120] *Sobh Emrooz*, 24 Azar 1378/15 Dec. 1999, p. 1.

Nuri's conviction it was widely interpreted as opportunistic and in bad taste. Rafsanjani's transition from a moderate, centre-right politician often at odds with the conservatives into the torch-bearer of the right had, as we have seen, taken some years to materialize, although (as a manifestation of the patrimonial wing of the mercantile bourgeois republic) it was not so great an ideological transformation as some have since suggested. Rafsanjani had become increasingly bitter at the attacks launched against him and their implications for his financial security and historical legacy. He had a particular conception of himself, and it did not match that promulgated by the reformists, and by Ganji in particular. He was increasingly attracted by the idea of being the one politician who could bridge the divide between conservatives and reformists, the serious statesman at the helm, and indeed this was the scenario he had imagined for himself soon after Khatami's election. As Speaker he would restore order to the state and institute reforms with moderation.[121]

The main flaws in this plan were the utter disgust his candidacy generated among the reformists and his failure to recognize the changes which had occurred in public opinion. His memoirs, the first volume of which had been published during the summer in the form of a daily diary of each year of his political life, were poorly received and widely derided as a publishing non-event, while his tendency to call himself 'Ayatollah' was seen as presumptuous.[122] The great communicator found himself unable to communicate to the masses, now a good deal more sceptical about his ambitions and aware of his dubious past. His continued praise for the Leader and authoritative demeanour only served to alienate the electorate further,[123] and Rafsanjani soon found himself adrift and desperate to reach the shore. Aware of his poor reception among the public, he sought to reinvent himself in his own image as a man of duty, eager to be of service irrespective of public opinion.[124] Such expressions of altruism inevitably generated more questions than answers. So keen did he become to cultivate the electorate that he announced that he had sought to help Nuri and was now trying to bring about the release of Karbaschi (who eventually was released early).[125]

---

[121] *Akhbar Eqtesad*, 27 Azar 1378/18 Dec. 1999, p. 1.

[122] *Ubur az Bohran: Karnameh va khaterat-e Hashemi Rafsanjani* (Transition Through Crisis: Diary and Memoir of Hashemi Rafsanjani) (Tehran: Mo'aref Enqelab Publishing Office, 1378/1999). The memoirs were dismissively termed *Effat-nameh* after his wife, since it was argued that they dealt with little of political value and revealed more about his day-to-day family life.

[123] *Arya*, 25 Azar 1378/16 Dec. 1999, p. 2.

[124] *Sobh Emrooz*, 25 Azar 1378/16 Dec. 1999, p. 1.

[125] Attempts to get Karbaschi released were begun in December; see *Iran*, 28 Mordad 1378/19 Dec. 1999, p. 2.

Rafsanjani's entry into the fray was a huge mistake, not only in respect of his own political prestige (he would have done better to stay out; he was after all still chairman of the Expediency Council) but for the conservative campaign as a whole, since by putting himself forward he had provided his opponents with a personal target, a symbol of what the election was all about. While the reformists seemed a genuine mass movement, Rafsanjani symbolized the patrimonial autocracy of the conservatives, the personalization of the mercantile bourgeoisie. As a result he came under concerted attack, both directly and indirectly by continuous allusion to the failure of the authorities to pursue the culprits of the serial murders. Fatemeh Karroubi claimed that if she revealed what she knew it would not be good news for the Rafsanjani family, while the Majma Rohaniyun Mobarez, the reformist group chaired by her husband, refused to endorse him as a candidate.[126] By far the most serious attacks emanated from Abdi, who had once been imprisoned by Rafsanjani. In a series of talks held mainly in the universities, Abdi launched a bitter attack on Rafsanjani's record, arguing that he regarded himself as unaccountable and considered people stupid. He pointed out that it was curious, if indeed Rafsanjani was as popular as he said, that no one would come out and defend the policies of his administration.[127] More serious rumours concerned Rafsanjani's role in prolonging the war and, even more gravely, his possible involvement in what many people believed to be the murder of Ahmad Khomeini.[128]

The point was reached where reformists would judge the success or failure of the forthcoming elections on how Rafsanjani fared. Some argued that if Rafsanjani came below tenth position, this would be a sufficient humiliation, while others noted that, if the result were to be really decisive (another 2 Khordad), Rafsanjani should be elected but not nominated for Speaker. Conservatives, meanwhile, remained convinced that their man would not only win but take charge and teach the reformists a lesson. (Rafiqdoust expressed himself privately as being in no doubt that this would happen.)

In a move designed to guarantee the desired outcome, the outgoing Majlis attempted to amend the electoral law to make things more difficult for the reformists, although, as it turned out, the only serious legal amendment resulted in changes which would actually favour the reformists. Bids to ensure that only those candidates who had previously sat in the Majlis could stand again, and to prevent second-round voting, were both dismissed

---

[126] *Fath*, 30 Azar 1378/21 Dec. 1999, p. 2; *Payam Azadi*, 30 Azar 1378/21 Dec. 1999, p. 3.

[127] *Payam Azadi*, 30 Azar 1378/21 Dec. 1999, p. 2; see also *Fath*, 29 Azar 1378/20 Dec. 1999, p. 2.

[128] This was particularly serious, and while there is no evidence, many people believed that Ahmad Khomeini's sudden death was *too* sudden.

as absurd, although the Majlis did succeed in banning the use of colour pictures and placards.[129] Moreover, to universal astonishment among the reformists, the decision to ensure that any vetting was supported by documentary evidence was ratified.[130] Nevertheless, in the run-up to the campaign many reformists were seriously concerned at the political implications of vetting, since the public mood was becoming increasingly tense.[131] Concerned that voter apathy might deny them the emphatic victory they needed, reformist commentators filled the pages of the press with exhortations to vote, promising reforms and an end to 'patronising government'.[132] Responding to public despair that the political system could not be altered, Hajarian argued that the popular vote could indeed result in a change in political structures.[133] The reformists also took the opportunity to belittle their opponents, whose occasional ridiculous comments were highlighted and emphasized. A favourite target was the Friday prayer leader of Orumiyeh, Hojjat-ol-eslam Hassani, whose outbursts in support of political violence were a useful metaphor for the right in general.[134] Not surprisingly, moves continued to try to muzzle the press, or at least those elements which were considered particularly damaging. Khamene'i himself remained ambivalent, trying to be inclusive while also condemning some of their activities.[135]

Since campaigning was not officially (and legally) allowed to begin until one week before the vote, many senior reformists chose not to voice their opinions in public for fear of being accused of illegal political activity. There is little doubt, however, that intense negotiating was occurring behind the scenes to ensure as smooth an electoral process as possible, and in the event the Guardian Council was not as restrictive as many had feared.[136] Indeed, many were reassured by the Council's apparent even-handedness, although its emphasis on Tehran candidates revealed a somewhat more subtle tactic of targeting candidates in constituencies thought to

---

[129] *Sobh Emrooz*, 30 Azar 1378/21 Dec. 1999, p. 1; *Hamshahri*, 24 Azar 1378/15 Dec. 1999, p. 1. Some reformist deputies voiced their anger at such hasty and time-consuming amendments; see Nowbakht's comments in *Payam Azadi*, 30 Azar 1378/21 Dec. 1999, p. 3.

[130] *Arya*, 28 Azar 1378/19 Dec., p. 1.

[131] See BBC SWB ME/3735 MED/5, 12 Jan. 2000, from *Tehran Times* website, 10 Jan. 2000.

[132] *Sobh Emrooz*, 27 Azar 1378/18 Dec. 1999, p. 1. Significantly, Khamene'i also called for a repeat of 2 Khordad; see *Iran*, 27 Azar 1378/18 Dec. 1999, p. 1.

[133] *Fath*, 27 Azar 1378/18 Dec. 1999, p. 1.

[134] *Sobh Emrooz*, 27 Azar 1378/18 Dec. 1999, p. 12.

[135] *Fath*, 27 Azar 1378/18 Dec. 1999, p. 1.

[136] As in the Assembly of Experts elections in 1998, the conservatives offered an alliance with the left, now broadly termed 'religious nationalists'; see *Payam Azadi*, 30 Azar 1378/21 Dec. 1999, p. 1; see also *Sobh Emrooz*, 29 Azar 1378/20 Dec. 1999, p. 1. Fears of potential trouble were expressed in a number of papers, including *Arya*, 28 Azar 1378/19 Dec., p. 3, while the interior ministry emphasized that elections were competitions not battles: *Sobh Emrooz*, 24 Azar 1378/15 Dec. 1999, p. 1.

be reformist, while leaving most rural constituencies, which they felt would naturally incline towards conservatism, to their own devices. This itself was to prove a miscalculation, since the reformist movement was much more geographically integrated than the Council had realized. In total some 6,860 candidates registered for a total of 290 seats, including five allocated for the religious minorities; this represented a 30 per cent increase in candidates over previous elections.[137] Of these, some 10 per cent were disqualified by both the Ministry of the Interior and the Guardian Council, one of the most notable and symbolic being Abdullah Nuri, who had decided to register from prison.[138]

In the last week, as candidates prepared for a tense and competitive contest, the campaign machines erupted into action. It immediately became apparent that not only were the two sides' campaigns different in style and content, they were effectively addressing radically different audiences. Here were 'tradition' and 'modernity' occupying, as it were, different spaces, distinct, unrelated and utterly irrelevant to each other. While the conservatives held modest gatherings, normally in mosques and with the sexes segregated, the reformists held rallies of a kind more familiar in Western elections, complete with songs, rallying cries, leaflets and banners, despite the apparent ban on placards, colour photos and any form of scrutiny of the candidates.[139] The Islamic Iran Participation Front even adopted the intensely nationalist 'Ey Iran' as one of its anthems and proclaimed as its slogan 'Iran for all Iranians'. Indeed, much of the success of the reformists can be put down to their identification with 'religious nationalism', reflecting the resurgence of nationalism throughout society. In one rally, much to the horror of the conservatives, youths were heard chanting 'Mosaddeq, Mosaddeq, we shall continue your path.' Rather belatedly, the conservatives tried to reduce the nationalist appeal of the reformists.[140] The latter conducted a skilful campaign which bore the signs of extensive organization, and it was commented that political consultants had in fact been hired among the expatriate community. Two days before the election on 18 February 2000, some 900 candidates withdrew to ensure that the reformist vote would not be split, while a number of independent candidates heeded a call to step aside and allow candidates from the 2 Khordad Front to have a clear run.[141]

---

[137] *Fath*, 28 Azar 1378/19 Dec. 1999, p. 1.

[138] *Hamshahri*, 27 Azar 1378/18 Dec. 1999, p. 1

[139] *Arya*, 30 Azar 1378/21 Dec. 1999, p. 3. This directive seems to have been widely ignored, and as Iranian campaigns go, this was a very colourful exercise, with candidates seeking to present themselves in the most flattering light. The Rafsanjanis were no exception.

[140] BBC SWB ME/3767 MED/1, 18 Feb. 2000, from *Keyhan* website, 16 Feb. 2000. Religious nationalism marks a return to pre-Pahlavi notions of Iranian identity.

[141] BBC SWB ME/3767 MED/1, 18 Feb. 2000; IRNA news agency, 16 Feb. 2000.

With the gloves finally officially off, the reformists drafted in their senior figures to urge people to vote; among them was Ayatollah Montazeri, whose continued house arrest and media ban did not prevent him giving an interview to foreign journalists, which was subsequently reprinted, as a piece of reportage, in the Iranian media. Criticizing the Guardian Council, Montazeri endorsed the reformists and urged a high turnout,[142] as did Khatami, emphasizing that 'Our revolution belongs to young people.' In a rousing rallying cry, Khatami called on people not be apathetic to their future:

> There may be some individuals in the world today who wish to insinuate that the people of Iran do not deserve democracy, do not deserve to take charge of their own destiny and do not deserve to enjoy Shari'ah and legal freedom ... O you, the noble and generous people of Iran! O you, the religious, free and proud men and women of this country! Your involvement and your participation is a must and prerequisite to realising the lofty objectives of the revolution and the nation's historical and magnificent goals ... you must once again demonstrate your involvement and determination gloriously.[143]

Reformists hoped for the best and expected the worst; both hope and fear were ironically fulfilled.

The dialectic returns

The reformists had hoped for a stunning election victory that would set the seal on their programme and institutionalize the process of reform. Such an outcome would enable them to break free from the frenetic and frustrating contest with the conservatives which was beginning to resemble a protracted guerrilla war. The emphatic seizure of the Majlis would be a decisive victory on conservative terrain which would dispel once and for all the idea that the reform movement was a transient phenomenon. Surely then, it was argued, the conservatives would recognize the futility of their opposition and co-opt, submit or simply fade away. The reformist project was hegemonic in scope and decisive in its execution, and, ironically, in February 2000 too successful in its achievement. So dramatic was the election victory (reformists winning 189 out of the 290 seats) and so

---

[142] Montazeri issued harsh warnings against those who might manipulate the elections; see BBC SWB ME/3763 MED/13, 14 Feb. 2000, from *Emrooz* website, 12 Feb. 2000.
[143] BBC SWB ME/3763 MED/10, 14 Feb. 2000; Iranian TV, 11 Feb. 2000.

humiliating was the result for the conservatives that even pleas of caution against triumphalism could not disguise the fact that something serious and ground-breaking was under way. In many respects the result reflected a failure in the politics of managing change.

The conservatives, who had counted on maintaining a semblance of control over the legislature, now found themselves legally exposed and vulnerable. They no longer controlled either the presidency or the legislature, which was in the hands of zealous idealists intent on exposing the financial and moral corruption at the heart of the mercantile bourgeois republic. It dawned on many that the halcyon days of unaccountability were over, and, more seriously, that some of them could be asked to answer for their actions, either to the Majlis or in court. No one felt this more acutely that Ali Akbar Hashemi Rafsanjani, whose humiliation at the polls was complete. Not only did he not make it into the final list of thirty for the Tehran constituency, but obvious attempts to ensure his inclusion were greeted with derision, forcing him into a somewhat belatedly dignified withdrawal. Conservatives had counted on Rafsanjani securing the post of Speaker and thereby controlling the legislative agenda, but this was now no longer an option; not only were reformists openly boasting about their extensive legislative plans but there was also talk of the Majlis exercising its constitutional right to scrutinize state bodies. Typically, it was this challenge to the commercial power of the mercantile bourgeoisie which prompted the first serious reaction to reformist success and which has pushed the country into the grip of yet another political crisis.

The election results bore witness to the coherent and organized nature of the reformists' campaign. They won control of almost every major city, including Tehran, Mashhad, Isfahan, Tabriz and Shiraz, and also extended their dominance into the countryside, an area in which the conservatives felt they would retain control. Not only that, but many significant players in the conservative camp were denied seats, principal among them Rafsanjani, whose position in the final tally of winners for the large Tehran constituency was a matter of fierce debate. First it was argued that he had not made the final list; then it was suggested that he had indeed made the list, before a major revision of the votes saw him rise into the comfort zone. The initial reactions of the Leader and Rafsanjani himself were in fact mixtures of relief and resignation, and had Rafsanjani chosen to withdraw at this stage he would have limited the damage to his prestige. But as the implications of the defeat dawned on the conservatives a holding action was initiated which would soon be transformed into a strategy of restitution. The first indications of trouble were manifested when the acknowledged architect of the victory, Saeed Hajarian, was gunned down outside his offices on 12 March 2000. Surprisingly, he survived the assassination attempt, in what many regarded as a living metaphor for the reform movement itself.

The immediate conservative concern was that reformists would secure a two-thirds majority in the Majlis, which would allow them to vet the elected candidates for their suitability or unsuitability. According to constitutional procedure, all elected candidates had to be approved by two-thirds of their colleagues in the Majlis, and with this majority the decisions of the Guardian Council could effectively be overturned. Suddenly announcing the elections as the most problematic ever,[144] the Guardian Council delayed the ratification of the all-important Tehran results for almost three months and also selectively cancelled unfavourable election results in those provincial constituencies where it judged this would cause the least political disruption. In the event riots broke out in a number of areas, as citizens vented their rage at the arbitrary decisions of the Council; but they proved, as the Council had hoped, containable.[145] Tehran, however, was a different matter, and there were concerns about a potential popular uprising in the capital. In the event, the Guardian Council and the Ministry of the Interior locked horns in a contest which descended into legal farce as each side sought to prosecute the other.[146]

But there was a much deeper underlying fear among those hostile to reform. This revolved around the hopes and expectations the papers were generating among the people about the new regime of accountability and investigations which the Majlis would now inaugurate. Conservatives, and Rafsanjani in particular, in identifying their own interests with that of the state, argued that such a move would be detrimental and highly destructive to the structure and foundations of the Islamic Republic. Some went so far as to suggest that it could mean the end of the Islamic Republic, and indeed there was some truth in this in so far as the political destruction of Rafsanjani would in all probability result in the demise of the mercantile bourgeois republic and fundamentally alter the character of the state. Some reformists and centrist politicians were also persuaded that such a wholesale assault would be too costly a way to manage change, although more zealous partisans, including some in the press, were calling for the victory to be fully and definitively exploited. Faced with this reality, Rafsanjani as chairman of the Expediency Council suddenly announced

---

[144] BBC SWB ME/3813 MED/7, 12 April 2000; Iranian TV, 10 April 2000

[145] See e.g. BBC SWB ME/3822 MED/9, 24 April 2000; IRNA news agency, 22 April 2000; also BBC SWB ME/3823 MED/5, 25 April 2000; IRNA news agency, 23 April 2000.

[146] AFP, 'Iran's interior ministry denies vote fraud', 9 May 2000; 'Elections litigation', IRNA news agency, 23 May 2000.

that the Majlis would have no remit to investigate those bodies under the auspices of the Leader, which would have removed the Foundation of the Oppressed and the Revolutionary Guards from scrutiny. This prohibition, which was in stark contradiction to the constitution, was widely condemned as illegal and largely ignored.[147] But it did indicate the level of concern surrounding not only the reformist Majlis but also the position of the Leader, who some on the right felt could not be relied on ultimately to protect their interests; and indeed, his subsequent comments were to indicate his ambivalence towards the mercantile bourgeoisie.

In the midst of this growing tension stoked by fears of a coup or an annulment of the election results,[148] Ayatollah Khamene'i moved judiciously to stabilize the situation and ensure that the Majlis would indeed convene. Having effectively authorized the suppression of the press – a key demand of the conservatives – he then proceeded to outline his own views on two issues about which he had hitherto maintained silence: the uses and abuses of political violence and the importance of reform. Distinguishing between unlawful and legitimate violence, Khamene'i argued that there were clearly times when violence could be used but added, in a caveat that was often ignored by critics, that violence was legitimate only when prescribed by the law: 'Is violence bad or good? It is neither bad or good. Sometimes it is both bad and good. Legal violence is good. It is necessary. Unlawful violence is bad. It is ugly and it is a crime.' Moving to the question of reforms, Khamene'i made clear that reforms were 'something good':

> It is obvious that in our society there are matters which need to be corrected through reform. We need administrative reforms. We need economic reforms. We need judicial reforms. We need reforms in the structure of our security system. We need reforms in the field of laws and regulations which are uniform and which do not discriminate against anyone. If discrimination exists in our rules and regulations, it is a manifestation of corruption and must be rectified. Bribery and graft must be rooted out. If such things exist, they are manifestations of corruption and must be rectified. Methods of obtaining and acquiring wealth must be lawful and legitimate. If wealth has been acquired by some individuals through illegal means, it is corruption and must be rectified. If some individuals have taken advantage of concessions and reaped windfalls, and if they have exploited others to enrich themselves in the process, their actions constitute corruption. And corruption must be rectified. If some individuals have created monopolies in society, if not everyone has been

---

[147] BBC SWB ME/3817 MED/5, 17 April 2000; IRNA news agency, 15 April 2000.
[148] BBC SWB ME/3822 MED/6, 24 April 2000; Iranian TV, 20 April 2000.

allowed equal and fair access to existing resources, this situation amounts to corruption. And corruption must be rectified ... If there is a growing tendency towards consumerism, then this is corruption. If wheeling and dealing take the upper hand over production in economic activities, then this is corruption. All this must be reformed.[149]

There can have been few more damning indictments of the mercantile bourgeois hegemony, and there is little doubt that reformists, hearing these words, breathed a sigh of relief. Yet within a week the situation was transformed by a wholesale assault on the press following a more critical speech by Khamene'i, clearly intent on restoring some balance to the political fray.[150] This second speech was in fact more balanced than ensuing conservative actions seemed to indicate, and Khamene'i was anxious to point out that his words were not directed against the president.[151] There were several reasons for the conservative move. First, conservatives still believed that the press had dictated the agenda leading up to the elections and misled the people, and accordingly that the absence of a combative and critical press would ensure proportionally higher conservative victories in the second round of elections (held on 5 May/16 Ordibehesht 1379), thereby facilitating a better balance of deputies.[152] But there was also a sense, shared by many reformists, that the press had pushed the agenda too far too quickly and had raised expectations which might not be fulfilled. Much as in the student demonstrations a year earlier, the press corps somewhat uncharacteristically submitted to the closures, heeding the call from President Khatami among others to cool things down.[153] In the first wave some thirteen newspapers and magazines were closed down, though eventually the total would reach twenty-two.[154] The newspaper *Sobh Emrooz* survived slightly longer than many and increased its print run to one million to cope with the demand, but eventually it too was banned.

So sudden was the announcement that some suspected it was intended to compromise the position of the minister of culture and force his resignation – only the day before the first round of closures Mohajerani

---

[149] BBC SWB ME/3817 MED/3, 17 April 2000; IRIB radio, 14 April 2000. See also the subsequent speech in which he criticizes 'capitalists': BBC SWB ME/3840 MED/1–5, 15 May 2000; IRIB radio, 12 May 2000.

[150] BBC SWB ME/3822 MED/1–6, 24 April 2000; IRIB radio, 20 April 2000.

[151] BBC SWB ME/3826 MED/1, 28 April 2000; IRNA news agency, 26 April 2000.

[152] Senior police chiefs were indicating this as early as 20 February; see *Fath*, 1 Esfand 1378/20 Feb. 2000, p. 3.

[153] BBC SWB ME/3822 MED/9 24 April 2000; IRNA news agency, 22 April 2000. See the interview with Hamid Reza Jalaipour, editor of the banned *Asr-e Azadegan*, in *Time Magazine* (Europe), 2 May 2000.

[154] BBC SWB ME/3823 MED/1 25 April 2000; IRNA news agency, 23 April 2000.

had declared his intention to resign rather than shut down newspapers[155] – but in the event he remained in place. Protests did take place, especially among students,[156] but by and large they were peaceful and passed without incident, unlike the rioting which had occurred following the annulment of election results. For many, while the closure of one paper was a tragedy, the closure of the reformist press in its entirety seemed more like farce (one paper was closed after just one day in operation) and betrayed weakness rather than strength. In the absence of print journalism, people turned to the production of illicit leaflets and flyers and in some cases to the internet, while Tehran Council set up an emergency fund for the nearly 1,500 journalists left without employment.[157] As one of the surviving papers commented in its editorial, 'It bears repeating that, as history proves, closing down legitimate newspapers and magazines will only pave the way for the publication and distribution of illegal and uncontrollable nightly fliers. The Judiciary will do well to ponder this point.'[158]

Yet again, however, the conservatives decided to push their reaction one step further; and this time it definitively damaged their control over state television. A conference had been held in Berlin to discuss the election with, among others, a number of Iranian commentators, including Akbar Ganji. During this conference, several exiled Iranian opposition group members disrupted proceedings, and two in particular decided to dance in a provocative manner, probably revealing more of themselves than necessary. This minor intrusion, caught on camera, was broadcast with a public health warning on Iranian television in an effort to portray the reformists as debauched counter-revolutionaries. The head of the IRIB, Larijani, later claimed to have secured permission from the judiciary for the 'sensitive' broadcast, but this was denied by judiciary officials.[159] It was an absurd exercise in crude propaganda which outraged reformists but nevertheless led to the arrest of the Iranian participants, including Ganji, on their return.[160] For the reformists, the IRIB was yet another institution which was now beyond the pale, and it has since been banned from the Majlis.[161] Ganji, meanwhile, went to prison in good spirits, aware that incarceration

---

[155] BBC SWB ME/3823 MED/2 25 April 2000; IRNA news agency, 22 April 2000.

[156] BBC SWB ME/3825 MED/3 27 April 2000; IRNA news agency, 25 April 2000; BBC SWB ME/3826 MED/4, 28 April 2000; IRNA news agency, 27 April 2000.

[157] AFP, 'Tehran Council plans unemployment fund for journalists after press bans', 2 May 2000.

[158] BBC SWB ME/3825 MED/4, 27 April 2000, from *Iran News* website, 25 April 2000.

[159] BBC SWB ME/3822 MED/8, 24 April 2000; IRNA news agency, 22 April 2000. IRNA was beginning to relish the competition with IRIB, itself tending towards the reformist camp.

[160] Even Khatami protested at the use of this clip from the conference to arrest Ganji and others: BBC SWB ME/3822 MED/7, 24 April 2000; Iranian TV, 22 April 2000.

[161] See AFP, 'Parliament bans camera crews from legislature', 12 Aug. 2000.

was now a vital component of one's political credibility (as well as probably the safest place for him) and reassuring supporters that he would not be 'committing suicide'![162]

The conservative assault continued. Rafsanjani delivered a scathing speech which left people in no doubt that the transformation of his public persona had been completed.[163] Having silenced the press, the conservatives decided to explore the possibilities of annulling the results for Tehran, but it was an indication of the simmering social outrage that the spokesman of the Guardian Council contradicted himself several times on the issue.[164] The public were clearly suspicious of attempts to ensure Rafsanjani a seat, and while he also contradicted himself as to his intentions, students protested against the possible return of 'Akbar Shah'. Tabarzadi was particularly vocal, making it clear that students would 'definitely break their silence' if the Tehran results were annulled.[165] The interior ministry also protested, and threatened to sue Ayatollah Jannati. Following the completion of the second round, in which reformists again did well, Rafsanjani formally withdrew.[166] Finally, after much prevarication, the Sixth Majlis convened on 27 May, following a last-minute intervention by the Leader, convinced that further postponement would only lead to political turmoil.[167]

The tide stemmed?

The strength of the conservative reaction since the inauguration of the Sixth Majlis has succeeded in dampening the enthusiasm which had been mounting up to that point. The process of reform appears once again to have stalled, and some have even argued that it may be in reverse. Certainly the conservative establishment seems intent on imprisoning all its enemies. Yet, much like the suppression of the press, such crude displays of power do little to enhance either the credibility or the authority of the conservatives. In the absence of a broadly based social authority the conservatives have discovered, repeatedly, that the use of force only diminishes their standing with the people. While Ayatollah Khamene'i's

[162] BBC SWB ME/3822 MED/8, 24 April 2000; IRNA news agency, 22 April 2000.
[163] This transformation did not go unnoticed; see Iran, 11 Ordibehesht 1379/30 April 2000, p. 16; the speech is reprinted in BBC SWB ME/3828 MED/1–4, 1 May 2000; IRIB radio, 28 April 2000.
[164] See BBC SWB ME/3825 MED/1, 27 April 2000; IRNA news agency, 25 April 2000.
[165] AFP, 'Iran students warn of protest', 16 May 2000.
[166] AFP, 'Rafsanjani no longer seeking MP seat', 10 May 2000.
[167] AFP, 'Reformists on the offensive after 2 round victory', 9 May 2000.

unprecedented intervention in the legislative programme of the new Majlis (through a letter instructing its members not to discuss the legislation) may reinforce views of a conservative resurgence, such an analysis represents a superficial understanding of political and social developments in Iran and flies in the face of the material and ideological trends of the past decade. Indeed, arguably the pendulum is moving the other way already. It is quite apparent that the suppression of the print media cannot put the genie back into the bottle. The deputy head of the judiciary, Hadi Marvi, has indicated that differences of opinion exist within the judiciary as to the best way to manage the press, and it is clear that some titles will soon re-open.[168] Seyyid Hadi Khamene'i now manages two papers, *Hayat-no* and the resurrected *Jahan-e Islam*, both of which have carried provocative articles on the necessity for democratic development. Indeed, a recent editorial opined that democracy was a fundamental pillar of Islam.

While the Majlis may have been deflected from discussing an amendment to the press law, it is worth noting that this suspension is temporary, and Khamene'i, having subjected himself to public scrutiny and criticism through his overt (and unnecessary) intervention, is not one to ignore the public mood, whatever the conservative pressures. Time and again he has shown an unwillingness to operate as an extension of the conservative cause, despite repeated attempts to co-opt him. A recent poll for the Ministry of Culture has shown that the public is not happy with the recent suppression of the press and persecution of journalists and does not accept that they constitute a threat to the state. Rather, they view the recent backlash as part of a continuing factional dispute which has little to do with the interests of the state. Some 110,000 people signed a petition calling for the release of journalists.[169] It is important to recognize that society has been effectively politicized over the past few years and is unlikely to remain docile in the face of repeated provocation.[170] This is particularly true of the student movement, which continues to be active.[171] The Majlis, as an extension of society, is likewise neither submissive nor ignorant of the use of political manoeuvring. The frustration of some

[168] G. Abdo, 'At crossroads: Iran's reforms stall after a strong start', *International Herald Tribune*, 15 Aug. 2000; see also AFP, 'Courts may let some banned newspapers re-open', 14 Aug. 2000. According to IRNA, Marvi also reassured journalists that there was no 'list' of arrestees: IRNA, 14 Aug. 2000.

[169] AFP, '110,000 sign petition', 26 June 2000.

[170] A more humorous example of this was the recent riots which erupted in the town of Qir in Fars province when a judge sought to have a grocer arrested for flirting with his wife. The grocer, argued the citizenry, was cross-eyed. BBC News Online, '"Flirting" grocer's arrest triggers riots', 31 July 2000.

[171] The recent acquittal of most of the police officers involved in the dormitory assault was greeted with astonishment, though some concluded that the officers charged were merely scapegoats.

deputies at Khamene'i's intervention was barely suppressed, and they have reacted angrily at what they regard as the biased reporting of the state television and radio service, which they argue has incited and indeed organized hardline protest outside the Majlis.[172] While they have avoided directly criticizing the Leader, they have promised to continue making reforms and criticized conservative 'exploitation' of the Leader's comments.[173] Indeed, apart from any revised press law they have moved to ban police and military forces from universities, thus securing the campuses as centres of debate and repaying their debt to their other main pillar of support.[174]

One of the most interesting developments during summer 2000 was the vigorous contest between the Islamic Republic News Agency (IRNA) and the well-known bastion of the conservative press *Keyhan*, each charging the other with betrayal and treason. When *Keyhan* began accusing IRNA, along with a number of noted intellectuals – specifically, Abdolkarim Soroush and Mohsen Kadivar – of having received money from the United States, IRNA began to hit back, describing a 'media mafia' orchestrated by managers of the newspaper, whose intention was to incite violence and engender a culture of confrontation. IRNA went on to detail the paper's involvement with the various anti-intellectual programmes broadcast on national television (such as *Hoviat*) and its connections with Saeed Emami and other dubious characters linked with the Ministry of Intelligence.[175] Playing *Keyhan*'s game better than *Keyhan*, IRNA chose to reveal what it knew in a series of articles, always promising its readers more the next day. Its newspaper *Iran Daily* also joined in the fray, arguing that 'One of the biggest catastrophes facing the Islamic Revolution since its victory in 1979 is the presence of lowly dwarfs who consider themselves to be a superior race in the arenas of culture and thought.' It added: 'The fact is that since they foolishly view themselves as the descendants of prophets, their line of thought is shadowy, indeed grey', and challenged: 'Who are these traitors who shamelessly try to belittle a great revolution?'[176] With characteristic political astuteness, IRNA then dubbed the paper's staff 'Keyhanis' – much to the distress of ordinary workers at the paper, who protested that they too disagreed with the operations of their employers. In a letter to the news agency, they pleaded not be labelled Keyhanis:

> Why not conduct an unbiased survey among *Keyhan*'s employees so everyone can see that almost 95% of them are completely against the

[172] AFP, 'Fighting breaks out in parliament over press bill', 6 Aug. 2000.
[173] Reuters, 'Iran's reformers renew claim to mantle of change', 14 Aug. 2000.
[174] AFP, 'Bill before parliament would ban police and army from universities', 28 June 2000.
[175] IRNA news agency, 22 July 2000.
[176] IRNA news agency, 23 July 2000.

way the heads of the paper have been dealing with political, economic, cultural and social developments in society. *Keyhan*'s stances and accusations are damaging the pillars of the Islamic Revolution as well as its values and aspirations. We are sure that if *Keyhan* continues to follow this path, it will go bankrupt in the near future, as the paper's income from advertisements and its circulations have dramatically decreased. We face numerous taunts from people for working for the paper and we ask you not to make the situation worse for us.[177]

To rub more salt in the wound, IRNA decided to check the popular pulse by organizing a phone-in opinion poll. Of the 1,520 calls taken over a two-day period, it noted that 92 per cent supported the agency's firm stance against *Keyhan*, while 5 per cent opposed it and 3 per cent called for a truce. Before that truce was finally arranged, IRNA divulged some of the opinions about *Keyhan* it had received. It was described as 'anti-religionist', 'destructive' and – ironically, given the terms in which it liked to couch its own accusations – 'a den of Satan'. The general conclusion was that its low circulation indicated the negligible public interest in it.

What this acute dispute revealed, in the absence of other papers, was that despite all the suppression carried out, the debate, and society, remain alive. Indeed, recent moves to ban a book written by Emadeddin Baghi (former editor of *Fath*), *The Tragedy of Democracy in Iran*, which dealt with the serial murders, shows that some issues simply will not disappear.[178] 'An army may be resisted, but not an idea whose time has come.'[179]

Yet one should not underestimate the inherent strength of the mercantile bourgeoisie and the web of accumulated vested interests it represents. It is indeed testament to Rafsanjani's political astuteness and considerable skill that he was able to give shape to a political structure of considerable cohesion and internal authority, even if it did not extend further than the contracting interest group. The question remains how far this group is able to maintain its interests in the face of mounting social pressure and criticism. The reformist movement has shown considerable discipline and patience in its contest with the conservatives, but the reformers must fear that public apathy will take hold and secure the continued durability of the mercantile bourgeoisie by default. There is little doubt that the conservatives are ideologically bankrupt and have shown little skill or intellectual agility in reinventing themselves. Take, for example, Ayatollah Jannati's comment: 'You cannot save Islam with liberalism and tolerance ... I am

[177] IRNA news agency, 25 July 2000.
[178] AFP, 'Iran orders book critical of regime's democracy off the shelves', 12 Aug. 2000.
[179] Victor Hugo, *Histoire d'un crime* (1852).

announcing clearly and openly that the closure of the newspapers was the best thing the judiciary has done since the revolution.'[180] Their strategy seems to revolve around bludgeoning their opponents to a standstill. This is a dangerous game to play, and has so far encouraged the reformists to concede ground rather than force a political crisis, which would undoubtedly bring the revival of mass politics in a manner unseen since the Islamic Revolution. Yet patience is not everlasting, and both sides recognize that there is a critical juncture beyond which repression will prove catastrophically counterproductive. Khatami has consistently sought to avoid this outcome, himself fearful that, like Mosaddeq, he may be unable to control its consequences; yet he has also warned his opponents that to push things too far could prove explosive.

There is, however, another reason for Khatami's caution in the months following the inauguration of the new Majlis, and that is his preoccupation with the economy. The government has recognized that failing to address the country's serious economic problems could prove disastrous both for itself and for the state as a whole;[181] but it also holds to its conviction that economic reform in the absence of legal and political development is illusory and fragile. One must get one's house in order before spending money. Investment is vital to development programmes – domestic but also, emphatically, foreign investment, as Khatami has repeatedly stated – and there is little doubt that the new Majlis will devote considerable time to reforms intended to secure foreign investment. In many ways, the reformists consider the political battle won: the language of politics in Iran has been transformed and people talk freely about their rights. Now it is time to turn to the details of economic reform, which paradoxically will prove more damaging to the interests of the mercantile bourgeoisie than any political and social liberalization (though all are, of course, interrelated). With their ideological veneer exposed and effectively removed, the mercantile bourgeoisie are now confronted with the real challenge to their status posed by economic reform. Accountability, transparency and privatization will do more harm to their political position than any explicitly political challenge, although it is worth bearing in mind that the latter has been an important prerequisite for the former. As *Iran Daily* commented in an editorial, 'It seems that conservatives are now more worried about their own future than the future of the country and the reform movement', and it added that 'the conservatives believe the fulfilment of reforms will bring about changes in the society that will not be favourable to them.'[182]

---

[180] Quoted in Abdo, 'At crossroads'.
[181] See Majid Ansari's comments, IRNA news agency, 15 Aug. 2000.
[182] IRNA news agency, 25 July 2000.

9 Conclusion

Few observers would deny that contemporary Iran is a complex country with its own distinctive social and political characteristics. An appreciation of cultural distinctiveness, however, should not be extended to a perception that the country is somehow anomalous to 'normative' political development. At the same time, models of political development should not be so rigidly applied that the particular case study itself is forced to conform or be consigned yet again to the periphery of (social scientific) acceptability. While the historian protects the distinctiveness of his subject and rejects the application of models, so too the political scientist enthused with a universal theory seeks a broad application irrespective of particularities. This opposition may be a caricature; but in many ways it encapsulates the tensions between the two disciplines, however manufactured they may be. In the field of contemporary history, it is a tension which serves no purpose. Not only must a hypothesis exist as a framework and guide to the research to be undertaken, it must be sufficiently flexible to acknowledge distinctive traits. As an exercise in political history and development, this study has employed a tripartite approach which brings together a working hypothesis with a recognition of historical distinctiveness and empirical depth. It is only by combining these essential ingredients that one can begin properly to analyse and appreciate political developments in contemporary Iran and to provide an assessment of possible trajectories for this development.

In seeking to develop a working hypothesis, this study has first had to challenge a number of assumptions about political development, especially the view, held by many, that Islam and democracy are inherently and eternally incompatible. This, it has been argued, is a conception characteristic of orientalism, which can be challenged by reassessing the nature of secularization and the 'secularization thesis'. The aim here has not been to refute such hypotheses definitively but to indicate the ambiguity of the debate and to create intellectual space for the infusion of new ideas, as debated by Iranian thinkers such as Abdolkarim Soroush. At the same time, this study has sought to provide a theoretical framework which would not only inform the analysis, but would, in reflecting views shared by some of the leading political thinkers in Iran, also provide a platform from which intellectual and political currents in the country could be better appreciated. It can be argued that such an approach helps to mitigate the problems of cross-cultural interpretation.

The aim of this study, therefore, has been not only to provide a dynamic model of development which suggests the mechanics by which political developments proceed, in this case juxtaposing an interpretation of *patrimonialism* with the concept of the *mercantile bourgeoisie*, but also to reflect the complexity of that dynamic as it unfolds. It is this narrative, constructed on the theoretical and historical discussions which have preceded it, which forms the empirical component of this study. Here, the emphasis has been to move away from rigid factional models which tend to disguise rather than illuminate political development and to concentrate on the underlying determinants: social, political and particularly ideological. The intention has been to show the ideas which inform and motivate political action in contemporary Iran and to emphasize the richness of the philosophical and political debate taking place, so that there can be no doubt of the depth of the movement taking shape around the historically rooted *myth of political emancipation.*

The central thesis of this study argues that a social revolution is taking place which will lead to the institution within Iran of Islamic democracy, in which government will be depersonalized and function in a legal/rational mode akin to that of Western democracies, albeit with an 'oriental' flavour. It is a development with enormous consequences, not only for Iran but for the wider Islamic world. Public opinion will become increasingly important as political consciousness continues to develop. While leaders will remain important to the political process, the nature of elite politics, as it has come to be understood in Iran (and the wider Islamic Middle East), in which a limited oligarchy functions autonomously from society, has been transformed. The relationship is now far more reciprocal, and may even be dictated increasingly by the moods, ambitions and opinions of the social base. Politics, in short, will become more institutionalized and less dependent on personalities, a development which is already evident in the growing acknowledgment that President Khatami is a vehicle for change but not its sole guarantor.

Islam will continue to be important for the vast majority of Iranians, and while it will undoubtedly retain a social function, its overt political role will decline. Religion will provide the social cohesion on which the political base can stand and arguably flourish, in much the same way as suggested in de Tocqueville's analysis of the emergent American democracy. It is a comparison that is as curious as it is real. The determining ideology of this emergent Islamic democracy will be that of 'religious nationalism', in which Islam is wedded to the nation and the nation is seen as the guarantor of the faith. Yet the faith itself will also be subjected to changes, taking on a new dynamic flexibility which is likely to make it more durable and sustainable in a modern environment. The impact of modernization and globalization constitutes a major catalyst for change, with which Iranian politicians are wrestling; resistance has given way to negotiated accommodation and a desire to reintegrate the state, politically and economically, into the international system.

It has also been argued that this process of change is being managed by administrators whose appreciation of Iranian history is acute and for whom the consequences of failure weigh heavily on the mind, frequently encouraging caution when forthright leadership is required. That is not to say that the management of change is always successful, although the reformists have shown a remarkable amount of self-discipline, but simply to argue that considerable thought has gone into this profound process of change – a process which, it is argued, can no longer be easily deflected. Reformists have always accepted that the conservatives will resist, but they remain convinced that ultimately their goal of Islamic democracy will be achieved; and there are, as has been noted, sound material and ideological reasons for holding this conviction.

At the same time, one should not be under any illusion that this process of transformation will be smooth and free from any sort of violence. Yet freedom that is fought for is freedom that is ultimately valued, appreciated and defended. Most societies in which the forces of tradition and modernity have clashed result in the destruction of the former, and there may come a time when the critical mass is reached and a clash occurs. This is unlikely to be a pleasant affair, but it may ultimately speed up a process that could otherwise take several years. It should not be forgotten that this is a *process* and will undoubtedly take time to unfold; accordingly, any interpretation of Iranian development must be dynamic and continuous. History, and an appreciation of the contested nature of Iranian history, remains a vital component of any analysis. Only by properly putting a development in context can one begin accurately to determine its importance for the present and its potential for the future. In truth, much to the undoubted frustration of analysts, Iran remains and will continue to be a complex and dynamic country whose rich social and political tapestry requires time and patience to discern clearly.

The key variable in any assessment of development is not direction but pace, and this will be to a great extent dependent on the competing tendencies' appreciation of their own strengths. The conservatives clearly want to give up as little as possible, while the reformists want to take as much as possible – although it is vital to remember that it is the restriction and containment of the mercantile bourgeoisie that is important, *not* their elimination – such a result would not be desirable even if it were possible. The mercantile bourgeoisie have much to offer the economic life of the country and should be accommodated as a component within a plural socio-economic structure operating within and contributing to society as a whole. The political ambitions of the mercantile bourgeoisie, and indeed the growth of a mercantile bourgeois mentality, have been in part a consequence of perceived political insecurities founded on the persistence of patrimonialism. It follows, therefore, that the gradual transformation of this system of political organization will in time affect the political aspirations of the mercantile bourgeoisie, arguably in a positive manner. Of course, this process of change is already taking place as a new, more cosmopolitan generation replaces its more traditionally-minded fore-fathers and divisions grow among those who are wedded in any degree to conservative authoritarianism and mercantile dogma.

In the immediate future, much will depend on the accommodation or otherwise of Rafsanjani. It is indeed likely that some sort of compromise will be reached and that he will be sympathetic to such a move – in his own day he was, after all, regarded as a reformer.[1] Faced with two contrasting historical legacies, it is unlikely that he will want to be remembered for choosing the wrong side. An accommodation with Rafsanjani will then allow reformists, reinvigorated by increasingly vocal support from senior clerics such as Ayatollah Montazeri, to redirect and reconstitute their energies towards an assault on the activities of the judiciary, whose impartiality has been brought into serious question over the past few years. Imprisonment is increasingly being viewed as a mark of honour and credibility for reformers, and the 'university of Evin' is taking on the symbolic significance of an Iranian 'Bastille', with all the associated implications.

A tendency towards polarization, especially among the more radical student groups, means that a major clash remains a distinct possibility, but it must be emphasized that this is unlikely to lead to the disintegration of the state or a military coup; both trajectories ignore the social cohesion and extent of the reformist movement. Attempts to destabilize the state such as have been alleged against extreme hardliners are unlikely to succeed, both

---

[1] A recent article in the conservative newspaper *Resalat*, for instance, warned Khatami not to stand again for the presidency lest he become another Rafsanjani. There is clearly no love lost between Rafsanjani and the conservative establishment, despite their commonality of interests.

for the same reasons and because the conservative establishment does not regard such destabilization as in its interests. In the words of Abbas Abdi, 'They have realized that Khatami is the last chance of this system and state and they are not particularly prepared to stand up to Mr Khatami strongly.' The option of continued repression and imprisonment is also limited in the long term:

> I do not deny that with the arrests they weaken [the reform movement] but what is the value of it when it has no achievement? The important point is that public opinion will be mobilised against them again. What are they going to achieve by weakening the reform movement? They cannot convince even their children at home. They are facing attrition all the time but this side does not have any attrition at all. This is why if they increase the pressure at most an impasse, blockage and disintegration will be the outcome. But they will not gain anything. They should reconstruct themselves. They should consider what course they should adopt and what has been the problem. They cannot do that. They neither have an economic plan nor a political plan nor a social plan. When we speak to their forces privately we see they do not have self confidence either ... In such conditions they will not succeed by eliminating others. Moreover, how can access to information be prevented in the age of telecommunications? [People] set up sites on the internet and all can write notes. How many people do they want to imprison? ...When they see they are imprisoned for no reason and that unacceptable means are used against them they do not see any reason for passivity and losing their spirit.[2]

The confidence and conviction of the reformists are often difficult to appreciate if the underlying realities on the ground are not recognized. Events following the Majlis elections in 2000 may lead some critics to argue that the reformists are guilty of wishful thinking and at the very least have been premature in their political aspirations. However, the most damning criticism, which persistently emanates from fatalism at home and orientalism abroad, is the view that an Islamic (autocratic) society cannot democratize because of an instinctive social bias towards authoritarianism. This, I have argued, represents the ideological (and to some extent institutional[3]) straitjacket of the analyst, not the reality of change investigated

---

[2] *Bahar*, 3 August 2000, no. 71.

[3] Put simply, there is a dearth of 'Persianists' in key institutions in the West, although as one diplomat told me, there is also the logistical problem that it is far 'easier' to deal with stable autocracies than with fluctuating democracies.

and detailed in this study. In many ways it reveals a *determination* to resist realities on the ground, and to deny them, through fear of the consequences. This is not an exclusively Iranian (or Middle Eastern) trait. Just as there are many Iranian conservatives haunted and shaped by the spectre of the Iran–Iraq War and expatriates re-fighting the trauma of the Islamic Revolution, so too there are many in the West whose views are dictated by the neat and comfortable simplicity of the Cold War. They all represent variables in a conservative vested interest anxious about the consequences of change, not only intellectually and ideologically but also practically. Indeed, the consequences of this development for Iran and the region have yet to be fully appreciated. There is little doubt that some fear the regional consequences of a normalization of ties between a democratizing Iran and the West, and one commentator has privately noted the irony of normalization of ties with the US being the vehicle by which the 'revolution' is truly exported!

One could argue that it has been ideological and cultural resistance which has consistently undermined Iran's democratic development – in other words a prevalent belief that such a development simply cannot happen, and a fear in society of *revolutionizing themselves*. It has been Khatami's (and the reformists') real achievement to make Iranians, and others, begin to appreciate that not only *could* it happen, it *would* happen. It has been the purpose of this study to shed light on this process at work, to highlight the material and ideological determinants of democratization and to show that 'never was any such event stemming from factors so far back in the past so inevitable yet so completely unforeseen'.[4]

---

[4] Alexis de Tocqueville, *The Ancien Régime and the French Revolution*, p. 33.

Select Bibliography

Secondary sources – English

Abrahamian, E. 'The Crowd in Iranian Politics 1905–53', *Past and Present*, no. 41, December 1968, pp. 184–210.

Abrahamian, E. *Khomeinism* (London: I. B. Tauris, 1993).

Afkhami, G. R. *The Iranian Revolution: Thanatos on a National Scale* (Washington, DC: The Middle East Institute, 1985).

Amuzegar, J. 'Adjusting to Sanctions', *Foreign Affairs*, vol. 76, no. 3, May/June 1997, pp. 31–41.

Anderson, L. 'Policy Making and Theory Building: American Political Science and the Islamic Middle East', in H. Sharabi (ed.), *Theory, Politics and the Arab World: Critical Responses* (London: Routledge, 1990).

Arendt, H. *On Revolution* (New York: Penguin, 1965).

Beeman, W. O. 'Double Demons: Cultural Impedance in US–Iranian Understanding', *Iranian Journal of International Affairs*, Summer/Fall 1990, pp. 319–34.

Boroujerdi, M. 'The Encounter of Post-Revolutionary Thought in Iran with Hegel, Heidegger and Popper', in S. Mardin (ed.), *Cultural Transitions in the Middle East* (Leiden: E. J. Brill, 1994).

Boroujerdi, M. *Iranian Intellectuals and the West: The Tormented Triumph of Nativism* (New York: Syracuse University Press, 1996).

Chubin, S. 'Iran's Strategic Predicament', *The Middle East Journal*, vol. 54, no. 1, Winter 2000, pp. 10–24.

Cohen, J. L. and Arato, A. *Civil Society and Political Theory* (Cambridge, MA: MIT Press, 1992).

Collier, R.B. *Paths Towards Democracy* (Cambridge: Cambridge University Press, 1999).

Ehrenberg, J. *Civil Society: The Critical History of an Idea* (New York: New York University Press, 1999).

Ehteshami, A. *After Khomeini: The Iranian Second Republic* (London: Routledge, 1995).

Ehteshami, A. *Political Upheaval and Socio-economic Continuity: The Case of Iran*, RUSEL Working Paper no. 6, Exeter University (undated).

Ehteshami, A. *The Politics of Economic Restructuring in post-Khomeini Iran*, CMEIS Occasional Paper no. 50, Durham, July 1995.

Esposito, J. L. (ed.). *The Iranian Revolution: Its Global Impact* (Miami, FL: Florida International University Press, 1992).

Esposito, J. L. and Voll, J. O. *Islam and Democracy* (Oxford: Oxford University Press, 1996).

Foucault, M. *Politics, Philosophy and Culture: Interviews and Other Writings* (London: Routledge, 1988).

Foucault, M. *Discipline and Punish: The Birth of the Prison* (London: Penguin, 1991).

Furtig, H. 'Universalist Counter-Projections: Iranian Post-Revolutionary Foreign Policy and Globalisation', in K. Fullberg-Stolberg, P. Heidrich and E. Schone (eds). *Disassociation and Appropriation: Responses to Globalisation in Asia and Africa* (Berlin: Zentrum Moderner Orient, 1999), pp. 53–74.

Giddens, A. *Capitalism and Modern Social Theory* (Cambridge: Cambridge University Press, 1971).

Gramsci, A. *Selections from Cultural Writings* (London: Lawrence and Wishart, 1985).

Gramsci, A. *A Gramsci Reader* [ed. D Forgacs] (London: Lawrence and Wishart, 1988).

Habermas, J. *The Structural Transformation of the Public Sphere* (Cambridge: Polity Press, 1989).

Halliday, F. *Iran: Dictatorship and Development* (London: Penguin, 1979).

Halliday, F. *Revolution and World Politics* (London: Macmillan, 1999).

Held, D. (ed.). *Prospects for Democracy* (Stanford, CA: Stanford University Press, 1993).

Herman, E. and Chomsky, N. *Manufacturing Consent: The Political Economy of the Mass Media* (London: Vintage, 1994).

Humphreys, R. S. *Between Memory and Desire: The Middle East in a Troubled Age* (London: University of California Press, 1999).

Hunter, S. 'Iranian Perceptions and the Wider World', *Political Communication and Persuasion,* vol. 2, no. 4, 1985, pp. 393–432.

Hunter, S. *Iran After Khomeini,* The Washington Papers 156, New York, 1992.

Hunter, S. 'Is Iranian Perestroika Possible without Fundamental Change?', *The Washington Quarterly,* vol. 21, no. 4, Autumn 1998, pp. 23–41.

Keddie, N. R. *Iran and the Muslim World: Resistence and Revolution* (London: Macmillan, 1995).

Keddie, N. R. 'Secularism and the State: Towards Clarity and Global Comparison', *New Left Review,* 226, 1997, pp. 21–40.

Kedourie, E. *The Chatham House Version and Other Middle Eastern Studies* (Hanover, NH: Brandeis University Press, University Press of New England, 1984).

Kharrazi, K. Speech by H E Dr Kamal Kharrazi, Minister of Foreign Affairs of the Islamic Republic of Iran, Chatham House, 11 January 2000, unpublished paper.

Kramer, M. 'Islam and Democracy', *Commentary*, January 1993, pp. 35–42.

Kuhn, T. S. *The Structure of Scientific Revolutions* (Chicago, IL: University of Chicago Press, 1962).

Mannheim, K. *Ideology and Utopia* (London: Routledge & Kegan Paul, 1960).

Marx, K. and Engels, F. *The Marx-Engels Reader* [ed. R. C. Tucker] (London: W. W. Norton & Co., 1978).

Milani, M. *The Making of Iran's Islamic Revolution: From Monarchy to Islamic Republic* (London: Westview Special Studies on the Middle East, 1991).

Moore, B. *Social Origins of Dictatorship and Democracy* (London: Allen Lane, 1966).

Mouffe, C. (ed.). *Gramsci and Marxist Theory* (London: Routledge & Kegan Paul, 1979).

Mozaffari, M. 'Revolutionary, Thermidorian and Enigmatic Foreign Policy: President Khatami and the "Fear of the Wave"', *International Relations*, vol. XIV, no. 5, August 1999, pp. 9–28.

Norton, A. R. (ed.) *Civil Society in the Middle East*, 2 vols (Leiden: E. J. Brill, 1996).

Ozdalga, E. and Persson, S. (eds). *Civil Society, Democracy and the Muslim World* (Istanbul: Swedish Research Institute in Istanbul, 1997).

Rajaee, F. A. 'Thermidor of "Islamic Yuppies"? Conflict and Compromise in Iran's Politics', *Middle East Journal*, vol. 53, no. 2, Spring 1999, pp. 217–31.

Resch, R. P. *Althusser and the Renewal of Marxist Social Theory* (Berkeley, CA: University of California Press, 1992).

Rouleau, E. 'The Islamic Republic of Iran: Paradoxes and Contradictions in a Changing Society', *Le Monde Diplomatique*, June 1995.

Roy, O. 'The Crisis of Religious Legitimacy in Iran', *Middle East Journal*, vol. 53, no. 2, Spring 1999, pp. 201–16.

Salame, G. *Democracy Without Democrats* (London: I. B. Tauris, 1994).

Soroush, A. *Reason, Freedom, and Democracy in Islam: Essential Writings of Abdolkarim Soroush* [trans. and ed. M. Sadri and A. Sadri] (Oxford: Oxford University Press, 2000).

de Tocqueville, A. *Democracy in America* (London: Everyman's Library, 1994).

de Tocqueville, A. *The Ancien Régime and the French Revolution* (Manchester: Fontana, 1966).

Tripp, C. 'Islam and the Secular Logic of the State in the Middle East', in A. Ehteshami and A.S. Sidahmed (eds). *Islamic Fundamentalism* (Oxford: Westview Press, 1996), pp. 51–69.

Turner, B. *Weber and Islam* (London: Routledge & Kegan Paul, 1974).

Weber, M. *Economy and Society* (2 vols) (Berkeley, CA: University of California Press, 1978).

Weber, M. *The Protestant Ethic and the Spirit of Capitalism* (London: Routledge, 1992).

Wright, R. 'Iran's New Revolution', *Foreign Affairs*, January/February 2000, vol 79, no. 1, pp. 133–45.

Yoshido, A. *The Texts of the Revolution: Mutaza Mutahhari and Hannah Arendt,* Working Papers Series 3, The Institute of Middle Eastern Studies, International University of Japan, Tokyo, 1985.

Zubaida, A. *Islam, the People and the State: Political Ideas and Movements in the Middle East* (London: I. B. Tauris, 1989).

Magazines and newspapers

BBC Summary of World Broadcasts (SWB)
Financial Times
The Guardian
International Herald Tribune
The Middle East
Middle East Report
The Washington Report on Middle East Affairs

Secondary sources – Persian

'Amniat, shart asly sarmayegozari toleedi' (Security, the first prerequisite of productive investment), *Iran-e Farda*, vol. 8, no. 57, Shahrivar 1378/Aug.–Sept. 1999, pp. 2–4.

'Ba Tasveer (Saeed Emami)' (With picture [Saeed Emami]), *Adineh*, 139, Mordad 1378/August 1999, p. 9.

'Bast, Bast tajrobe-ye Nabavi: goftegu ba baha al din khoramshahi va abdolkarim soroush' (Explain, enlarge upon the experience of Nabavi: an interview with Baha al Din Khoramshahi and Abdolkarim Soroush), *Kiyan*, vol. 9, no. 47, Khordad–Tir 1378/June–July 1999, pp. 4–11.

'Bayaneh elam mavazeh va barnamehaye jame az fa'alan melli-mazhabi baraye entekhabat majlis sheshum' (Manifesto of some of the activists of the religious nationalists for the elections to the sixth majlis), *Iran-e Farda*, vol. 8, no. 64, 24 Azar 1378/14 Dec. 1999, p. 13.

'Baz ham Hoviat?!' (Hoveat again?!), *Iran-e Farda*, no. 26, Tir 1375/ June–July 1996, pp. 2–4.

'Havadess Koye daneshgah tajli cheh bood?' (What do the events of the University dormitory represent?), *Iran-e Farda*, Special Issue, vol. 8, no. 55, Tir 1378/June–July 1999, pp. 2–4.

'Jenayat va mokafat ya jenayat bedoon mokafat?' (Crimes and retribution or crimes without retribution?, *Iran-e Farda*, Special Issue, vol. 8, no. 55, Tir 1378/June–July 1999, p. 7.

'Mafhoom melli-mazhabi be cheh ma'anast?' (What is the meaning of religious-nationalism?), *Iran-e Farda*, vol. 8, no. 64, 24 Azar 1378/14 Dec. 1999, pp. 2–4.

'Melli-Mazhabi, bayan yek gerayesh ya yek nahad?' (Religious nationalism: a trend or a position?), *Iran-e Farda*, vol. 8, no. 64, 24 Azar 1378/ 14 Dec. 1999, p. 16.

'Panj rooz por talatam va rooz shishom (Five days of clashes and day six)', *Payam-e Emrooz*, Mordad, 1378/July–Aug. 1999, pp. 7–27.

'Panj roozi keh Iran ra takan dad' (Five days which shook Iran), *Adineh*, 139, Mordad 1378/August 1999, pp. 10–14.

'Parandeh sar bar balaye koye daneshgah' (Flying over the university dormitory), *Iran-e Farda*, Special Issue, vol. 8, no. 55, Tir 1378/June– July 1999, pp. 5–6.

Rabeteh?! (Relations?!) (Tehran: Salaam, 1378/1999–2000).

'Sokhani dar bare barnameh hoveat' (A discussion on the subject of the Hoveat programme), *Iran-e Farda*, no. 26, Tir 1375/June–July 1996, pp. 4–5.

'Ta Oji degar?' (Till another wave), *Kiyan,* vol. 9, no. 47, Khordad–Tir 1378/June–July 1999, pp. 2–3.

'Tavan' (Penalty), *Payam-e Emrooz*, Mordad 1378/July–Aug. 1999, pp. 4–6.

Various authors, *Beem-ha va Omid-ha (Fears and expectations)* (Tehran: Hamshahri, 1378/1999–2000).

Various authors, *Jame'eh Madani va Iran-e Emrooz (Civil society and today's Iran)* (Tehran: Naqsh and Negar, 1377/1998–9.

Abdi, A. *Ghodrat, Qanun, farhang (Power, law, culture)* (Tehran: Oiyam, 1377/1998–9).

Abedi, M. H. 'Panj sal bad – Abdollah Nuri!' (Five years later – Abdollah Nuri), *Iran-e Javan*, 25 Azar 1378/14 December 1999, pp. 8–11.

Ahmadzadeh, T. 'Moalem modara, azadi va shora' (Teacher of moderation, freedom and consultation), *Iran-e Farda*, vol. 8, no. 57, Shahrivar 1378/Aug.–Sept. 1999, pp. 17–20.

Alamdari, K. 'Raz Napayedari demokrasi' (The secret behind the failure of democracy), *Adineh*, Shahrivar–Mehr 1374/Sept.–Oct. 1995, pp. 51–3.

Alijani, R. 'Nesbat mazhab va melat dar andisheh doktor shariati' (The relationship of religion and nation in the thought of Dr Shariati), *Iran-e Farda*, vol. 8, no. 64, 24 Azar 1378/14 Dec. 1999, pp. 30–33.

Apter, D. 'Sunat-e Roshangari' (The Enlightenment Tradition) [trans. M. M. Shanehchi], *Etela'at Siyasi-Eqtesadi*, vol. 10, nos 105–6, June–July 1996, pp. 73–8.

Ashkori, H. Y. 'Molafhaye Asasi jaryan 'melli-mazhabi' (The foundational works on the issue of religious nationalism), *Iran-e Farda*, vol. 8, no. 64, 24 Azar 1378/14 Dec. 1999, pp. 17–18.

Ashraf, A. 'Nezam Sanafi, Jame'eh Madani va demokrasy dar Iran' (The order of guilds, civil society and democracy in Iran), *Goftegu*, Winter 1375, pp. 17–43.

Bashiriyeh, H. 'Andisheye Michael Oakeshott' (The Thought of Michael Oakeshott), *Etela'at Siyasi-Eqtesadi*, vol. 10, nos 105–6, June–July 1996, pp. 4–10.

Behnood, M. 'Az Azadi Ezhab natarsim' (We should not fear free parties), *Adineh*, Shahrivar–Mehr 1374/Sept.–Oct. 1995, pp. 8–11.

Behnood, M. 'Khoshonat, fa'ejehsaz va doshman eslehat' (Violence, destructive forces and the enemies of reform), *Adineh*, 139, Mordad 1378/August 1999, pp. 15–19.

Behzadi, A. S.'Baharhaye Napayedar-e demokrasi va bahar dovum-e Khordad' (The ephemeral springs of democracy and the spring of the 2nd of Khordad), *Etela'at Siyasi-Eqtesadi*, vol. 13, nos 141–2, June–July 1999, pp. 16–29.

Behzadi, M. 'Vorud-e Hashemi faje'e neest' (The entry of Hashemi is not a disaster), *Iran-e Farda*, vol. 8, no. 64, 24 Azar 1378/14 Dec. 1999, p. 5.

Dad, B. *Sad Rooz ba Khatami (One hundred days with Khatami)* (Tehran: Sahafi, 1377/1998–9).

Dad, B. *Khatami dar Italia (Khatāmi in Italy)* (Tehran: Sahafi, 1378/1999–2000).

Deshiri, M. R. 'Tasir-e Jame Madani bar siyasatgozari-e khareji-ye jomhuri Islami Iran' (The impact of civil society on foreign policy-making in the Islamic Republic of Iran), *Etela'at Siyasi-Eqtesadi*, vol. 14, nos 145–6, Oct.–Nov. 1999, pp. 12–27.

Dorodi, S. 'Mavane Qanuni tashkil hezb dar Iran' (Legal obstacles to the formation of parties in Iran), *Iran-e Farda*, vol. 8 no. 56, Mordad 1378/July–Aug. 1999, pp. 17–18.

Dorodi, S. 'Defa az fard, ya hemayat az andisheh?' (Defence of an individual or freedom of thought?), *Iran-e Farda*, vol. 8, no. 64, 24th Azar 1378/14 Dec. 1999, pp. 7–8.

Farhadpour, M. 'Nokati peeramun sekularism' (Points in search of secularism), *Kiyan*, vol. 5, no. 26, Mordad–Shahrivar 1374/Aug.– Sept. 1995, pp. 14–21.

Ganji, A. *Tarik-khaneh-ye ashbah (The cellar of phantoms)* (Tehran: Tar-e No, 1378/1999–2000).

Ghafouri, M. 'Ainha-ye hezbi va ainha-ye entekhabati' (Party rules and election rules), *Etela'at Siyasi-Eqtesadi,* vol. 14, nos 147–8, Dec. 1999– Jan. 2000, pp. 140–59.

Gharagozloo, M. 'Jame'eh Madani va qanunkerai' (Civil society and the rule of law*), Etela'at Siyasi-Eqtesadi,* vol. 14, nos 145–6, Oct.–Nov. 1999, pp 28–37.

Husseini, M. 'Dar bare-ye yaqin' (On Certainty), *Kiyan,* vol. 9, no. 47, Khordad–Tir 1378/June–July 1999, pp. 28–32.

Jalaipour, H. R. *Pas az dovum khordad (After the 2nd Khordad)* (Tehran: Kavir, 1378/1999–2000).

Kadivar, M. *Baha'ye Azadi: defa'at Mohsen Kadivar (The price of freedom: the defence of Mohsen Kadivar)* (Tehran: Ghazal, 1378/1999–2000).

Kadivar, M. *Hokumat-e Velaye (The government of Guardianship)* (Tehran: Ghazal, 1378/1999–2000).

Kadivar, M. *Nazriyeh-haye dowlat dar fiqheh Shieh (The views of the state on Shia jurisprudence)* (Tehran: Ghazal, 1378/1999–2000).

Kaji, H. *Keesty ma (Who are we?)* (Tehran: Leila, 1378/1999–2000).

Karbaschi, G. *Mohakemeh va Defa (Trial and defence)* (Tehran: Gostar, 1377/1998–9).

Kaviani, H. *Dar jostejoye mohafal jenayatkaran (Investigating the murderous associations)* (Tehran: Negah-ye Emruz,1378/1999–2000).

Kaviani, H. *Ramz peerozi yek rais jumhur (The secrets behind a president's success)* (Tehran: Zekr, 1378/1999–2000).

Khatami, M. *Az donya-ye shahr ta shahr-e donya (From the world of the city to the city of the world)* (Tehran: Ghazal, 1377/1998–9).

Khatami, M. *Hezareh-ye goftegu va tafahom (A thousand discussions and understanding)* (Tehran: Resanash, 1378/1999–2000).

Madani, S. 'Band jenayat aleye "hakemeat" ya "roshanfekran"?' (Is the criminal clique against the establishment or the intellectuals?), *Iran-e Farda*, vol. 8, no. 56, Mordad 1378/July–Aug. 1999, p. 28.

Madani, S. 'Shoresh nojavanan' (The revolt of the young), *Iran-e Farda*, vol. 8, no. 57, Shahrivar 1378/Aug.–Sept. 1999, pp. 7–8.

Mazandi, Y. *Iran: Abar ghodrat-e Gharn?* (Iran: superpower of the century?) (Tehran: Alborz, 1373/1994–5).

Mirzai, H. 'Tarikh sazi baraye melat be-hafeze (History-making for an insecure nation)', *Iran-e Farda*, no 26, Tir 1375/June–July 1996, pp. 57–9.

Mohajerani, A. *Esteziah (Interpellation)* (Tehran: Etela'at, 1378/1999–2000).

Mohammadi, A. 'Radikalism Maghoul, radikalism efrati va masaleh-ye sho'ar' (Prudent radicalism, fanatical radicalism and the issue of slogans), *Iran-e Farda*, Special Issue, vol. 8, no. 55, Tir 1378/June–July 1999, pp. 13–14.

Mohammadi, M. 'Gozar as mohafal be hezb' (Passages from associations to parties), *Iran-e Farda*, vol. 8, no. 56, Mordad 1378/July–Aug. 1999, pp. 19–21.

Montazeri, H. 'Bab moftuh ejtehad: pasokhi be porseshhaye Doktor Abdol-karim Soroush' (The open gate of interpretation: an answer to the questions of Dr Abdolkarim Soroush), *Kiyan,* vol. 9, no. 47, Khordad–Tir 1378/June–July 1999, pp. 12–16.

Mortaji, H. *Jenaha-ye siyasi dar Iran-e Emrooz (Political factions in today's Iran)* (Tehran: Naqsh and Negar, 1378/1999–2000).

Nabavi, I. *Sotoon Panjom (Fifth Column)* (Tehran: Leila, 1378/1999–2000).

Negar, M. B. 'Vijegiha fekri nirohaye melli-mazhabi' (The particular thought of the forces of religious nationalism), *Iran-e Farda*, vol. 8, no. 64, 24 Azar 1378/14 Dec. 1999, pp. 25–9.

Nohi, H. 'Javanan, azadi, roshd' (The young, freedom, growth), *Iran-e Farda*, no. 26, Tir 1375/June–July 1996, pp. 60–65.

Nouri, A. *Shokoran-e Eslah (Hemlock of Reform)* (Tehran: Tar-e No, 1378/1999–2000).

Omrani, M. 'Hesabresi az dowlat moghat ya az hameh?' (Bringing to account the provisional government, or everybody?), *Iran-e Farda*, vol. 8, no. 64, 24 Azar 1378/14 Dec. 1999, pp. 7–8.

Payman, H. '"Amneat" bahaneh peidayesh estebdad' (False 'security', the genesis of despotism), *Iran-e Farda*, vol. 8 no. 56, Mordad 1378/July–Aug. 1999, pp. 35–7.

Payman, H. 'Tabarshenasi rowshanfekran melli-dini Iran' (Understanding the ruin of the religious-nationalist intellectuals of Iran), *Iran-e Farda*, vol. 8, no. 64, 24 Azar 1378/14 Dec. 1999, pp. 19–21.

Popper, K. 'Andishe-i dar bare-ye teory va kar kard-e hokumat mardom salar' (Democratic rule: theory and functions) [trans. K. Zaim], *Etela'at Siyasi-Eqtesadi*, vol. 13, nos 141–2, June–July 1999, pp. 48–57.

Rahimi, M. 'Yek tajrobeh-ye hezbi' (A party experience), *Etela'at Siyasi-Eqtesadi*, vol. 14, nos 149–50, Feb.–March 2000, pp. 104–11.

Saghafi, M. 'Demokrasi va vaghe'at ejtemai' (Democracy and social reality), *Goftegu*, Winter 1375/1996, pp. 7–16.

Sariolghalam, M. 'Sabat-e siyasi va tose-eh ye siyasi' (Political stability and political development), *Etela'at Siyasi-Eqtesadi*, vol. 14, nos 145–6, Oct.–Nov. 1999, pp. 4–11.

Shabestari, M. 'Motun dini va jahan bini-ye naqd-e tarikhi' (Religious foundations and world-view of current history), *Kiyan*, vol. 5, no. 26, Mordad–Shahrivar 1374/Aug.–Sept. 1995, pp. 22–4.

Soroush, A. K. 'Ma'na va mabna-ye sekularism' (The meaning and basis of secularism), *Kiyan*, vol. 5, no. 26, Mordad–Shahrivar 1374/Aug.–Sept. 1995, pp. 4–13.

Soroush, A. K. 'Saghf ma'eshat bar sotun shariat' (The limits of livelihood on the pillars of the Sharia), *Kiyan*, vol. 5, no. 26, Mordad–Shahrivar 1374/Aug.–Sept. 1995, pp. 25–31.

Soroush, A. K. 'Shariati va falsafeh' (Shariati and philosophy), *Iran-e Farda*, no. 26, Tir 1375/ July–Aug. 1996, pp. 16–19.

Soroush, A. K. and Kadivar, M. *Manazere dar bare-ye pluralism dini (A debate on religious pluralism)* (Tehran: Salaam, 1378/1999–2000).

Talebi, A. 'Chahar vaghei dar tarikh jonbesh daneshjui' (Four realities in the history of the student movement), *Iran-e Farda*, Special Issue, vol. 8, no. 55, Tir 1378/June–July 1999, pp. 14–15.

Tehrani, A. 'Majlis ayandeh, rahbord ejad aghaleat maslehat' (The next Majlis – a means to create a dominant minority), *Iran-e Farda*, vol. 8, no. 57, Shahrivar 1378/Aug.–Sept. 1999, p. 11.

Yazdi, I. 'Mobaramtareen masayel konooni jonbesh daneshjooyi' (The most pressing matters of the student movement), *Iran-e Farda*, Special Issue, vol. 8, no. 55, Tir 1378/June–July 1999, p. 12.

Yazdi, I. 'Moshakhasat va resalat melli-mazhabi' (The characteristics and thesis of religious nationalism), *Iran-e Farda*, vol. 8, no. 64, 24 Azar 1378/14 Dec. 1999, pp. 22–4.

Zekryai, M. A. *Hijdahom Tir Mah 78 beh raviat jenahaye siyasi (The 18th Tir 78, from the perspective of political factions)* (Tehran: Kavir, Tehran, 1378/1999–2000).

Zibakalam, S. *Ma chegoneh ma shodeem? Reeshehyabi alal aqab manandegi dar Iran (How we became us? The roots of backwardness in Iran)* (Tehran: Rozneh 1374/1995–6).

Zibakalam, S. *Sunnat va modernism (Tradition and modernism)* (Tehran: Rozneh, 1377/1998–9).

Magazines and newspapers

Magazines

Adineh
Etela'at Siyasi-Eqtesadi
Golagha
Iran-e Farda
Iran-e Javan
Kiyan
Payam-e Emrooz
Vahoman

Newspapers

Aftab-e Emrooz
Arya
Bahar
Fath
Iran
Jame'eh
Jebheh
Keyhan
Khordad
Neshat
Payam-e Azadi
Salaam
Sobh Emrooz
Tous

Index